BEING CHRISTIAN

More from Jim Wilson

Practical Evangelism Series:

Principles of War (Canon Press)

Weapons & Tactics (Canon Press)

Taking Men Alive (Canon Press)

How to Be Free Series:

How to Be Free from Bitterness (Canon Press)

How to be Free from Anger and Fits of Rage (CCM)

How to be Free from Pornography (CCM)

How to be Free from Anxiety (CCM)

How to be Free from Lying (CCM)

How to be Free from Coveting (CCM)

Receiving Bitterness: How to Handle Bitterness toward You (CCM)

Christian Living:

How to Maintain Joy (CCM)

Assurances of Salvation (CCM)

Saturation Love (CCM)

Humility and How to Get There (CCM)

Wayward Children (CCM)

Dead & Alive: The Must & How of Obedience (CCM)

Jim Wilson, *Being Christian: Who We Are and What We Do in Christ*
Second Edition.

Published by Canon Press
P. O. Box 8729, Moscow, ID 83843
800–488–2034 | www.canonpress.com

This second edition published by Canon Press is revised and expanded (2016). The first edition was published in 2001 under the name *On Being a Christian* by Community Christian Ministries (CCM, www.ccmbooks.org).

Cover design by James Engerbretson.
Interior design by Jessica Evans.

Printed in the United States of America.

Library of Congress Cataloging-in-Publication Data is forthcoming.

16 17 18 19 20 10 9 8 7 6 5 4 3 2 1

BEING CHRISTIAN

Who We Are &
What We Do in Christ

JIM WILSON

canonpress
Moscow, Idaho

Dedicated to Roy & Karen Knecht

for being Christian

CONTENTS

PREFACE

This book is the second edition of a collection of devotionals originally published under the title *On Being a Christian: Who We Are and What We Do in Christ*. The essays in this edition were written over a period of thirty-five years. As the title indicates, many of them have to do with "being" and "doing." Some of them have appeared in my blog "Roots by the River" (www.rootsbytheriver.blogspot.com) and in an email circulation of weekly devotionals called "Day and Night." Here they are arranged generally by subject.

This is not a novel or a biography; it has no plot. If you read it straight through, you may miss the message. You may open the book to any page and find something to meditate on and apply in your life.

The first objective of this book is best stated in St. Paul's comment to the Colossians: "that we may present everyone perfect in Christ Jesus" (Col. 1:28).

My second objective is to help you see the Scripture, not my comments. Years ago, our oldest son said something that he meant to be funny. "Dad's idea of teaching is to quote another verse." You will see as you read that he hit the nail on the head. This book is full of strong texts and short teaching. Good Bible teachers cannot take a strong text and make it stronger. They can make it weaker, or they can change it (and make it weaker still). They may not have that intention, but it is like adding water to the soup. It goes farther, but it *is* weaker.

Strong teaching makes strong Christians. And it makes soft-hearted, tender, loving Christians. But soft teaching makes hard, callused Christians. Soft teaching is for people who have itching ears. They do not wish to have their lives interfered with.

Because the teaching in the texts is strong, you may not want to read this book quickly. Take time, meditate, and soak in the Scriptures until your heart and mind agree with them without qualification. Please feel free to disagree with my comments—they may just be water in the soup.

I would like to hear from you if these writings have helped you become more like Jesus. Comments and edits are also welcome (www.canonpress.com/contact-us).

I would like to thank Jan Mahal for typing up many of the older essays; Jen Miller for editing and arranging the newer essays; and Lisa Just for editing this second edition.

All Scripture quotations are from the NIV unless otherwise stated.

In the Lord Jesus Christ,

Jim Wilson
Moscow, Idaho
2016

1

BEING CHRISTIAN

In His death on the cross, Jesus completely provided all the means for our salvation.

> *It is because of him that you are in Christ Jesus, who has become for us wisdom from God—that is, our righteousness, holiness and redemption. (1 Cor. 1:10)*

This is wisdom from God.

Righteousness is the starting point of the Christian life. It is because of Christ's death and our trusting in Him. This righteousness from God happened to us when we were washed, forgiven, at our new birth. Our righteousness:

> *For in the gospel a righteousness from God is revealed, a righteousness that is by faith from first to last, just as it is written: "The righteous will live by faith." (Rom. 1:17)*

But now a righteousness from God, apart from law, has been made known, to which the Law and the Prophets testify. This righteousness from God comes through faith in Jesus Christ to all who believe. There is no difference, for all have sinned and fall short of the glory of God, and are justified freely by his grace through the redemption that came by Christ Jesus. God presented him as a sacrifice of atonement, through faith in his blood. He did this to demonstrate his justice, because in his forbearance he had left the sins committed beforehand unpunished—he did it to demonstrate his justice at the present time, so as to be just and the one who justifies those who have faith in Jesus. (Rom. 3:21–26)

Therefore, since we have been justified through faith, we have peace with God through our Lord Jesus Christ, through whom we have gained access by faith into this grace in which we now stand. (Rom. 5:1–2)

But you were washed, you were sanctified, you were justified in the name of the Lord Jesus Christ and by the Spirit of our God. (1 Cor. 6:11b)

Our righteousness from God is the starting point for our holiness. Holiness is positive obedience. Holiness is not getting dirty. Our holiness:

Since we have these promises, dear friends, let us purify ourselves from everything that contaminates body and spirit, perfecting holiness out of reverence for God. (2 Cor. 7:1)

> *Therefore, prepare your minds for action; be self-controlled; set your hope fully on the grace to be given you when Jesus Christ is revealed. As obedient children, do not conform to the evil desires you had when you lived in ignorance. But just as he who called you is holy, so be holy in all you do; for it is written: "Be holy, because I am holy." (1 Pet. 1:13–16)*

> *And we, who with unveiled faces all reflect the Lord's glory, are being transformed into his likeness with ever-increasing glory, which comes from the Lord, who is the Spirit. (2 Cor. 3:18)*

> *Not that I have already obtained all this, or have already been made perfect, but I press on to take hold of that for which Christ Jesus took hold of me. Brothers, I do not consider myself yet to have taken hold of it. But one thing I do: Forgetting what is behind and straining toward what is ahead, I press on toward the goal to win the prize for which God has called me heavenward in Christ Jesus. (Phil. 3:12–14)*

Both righteousness and holiness are by grace, not by our effort.

> *So then, just as you received Christ Jesus as Lord, continue to live in him. (Col. 2:6)*

> *You foolish Galatians! Who has bewitched you? Before your very eyes Jesus Christ was clearly portrayed as crucified. I would like to learn just one thing from you: Did you receive the Spirit by observing the law, or by believing what you heard? Are you so foolish? After beginning with the Spirit, are you now trying to*

> *attain your goal by human effort? Have you suffered so much for nothing—if it really was for nothing? Does God give you his Spirit and work miracles among you because you observe the law, or because you believe what you heard?* (Gal. 3:1–5)

Our redemption:

> *Dear friends, now we are children of God, and what we will be has not yet been made known. But we know that when he appears, we shall be like him, for we shall see him as he is. Everyone who has this hope in him purifies himself, just as he is pure.* (1 Jn. 3:2–3)

> *Listen, I tell you a mystery: We will not all sleep, but we will all be changed—in a flash, in the twinkling of an eye, at the last trumpet. For the trumpet will sound, the dead will be raised imperishable, and we will be changed. For the perishable must clothe itself with the imperishable, and the mortal with immortality. When the perishable has been clothed with the imperishable, and the mortal with immortality, then the saying that is written will come true: "Death has been swallowed up in victory."* (1 Cor. 15:51–54)

> *But our citizenship is in heaven. And we eagerly await a Savior from there, the Lord Jesus Christ, who, by the power that enables him to bring everything under his control, will transform our lowly bodies so that they will be like his glorious body.* (Phil. 3:20–21)

This redemption is the redemption of our bodies at the Second Coming.

This book is about the righteousness and holiness of the Christian in this present life and in anticipation of the resurrection of the body.

> *For the grace of God that brings salvation has appeared to all men. It teaches us to say "No" to ungodliness and worldly passions, and to live self-controlled, upright and godly lives in this present age, while we wait for the blessed hope—the glorious appearing of our great God and Savior, Jesus Christ, who gave himself for us to redeem us from all wickedness and to purify for himself a people that are his very own, eager to do what is good. (Tit. 2:11–14)*

Zechariah prophesied of Jesus that He came "to rescue us from the hand of our enemies, and to enable us to serve him without fear in holiness and righteousness before him all our days" (Lk. 1:74–75).

When you have finished this book, please consider these two commendations to the Christians at Thessalonica:

> *Finally, brothers, we instructed you how to live in order to please God, as in fact you are living. Now we ask you and urge you in the Lord Jesus to do this more and more. (1 Thess. 4:1)*

> *Now about brotherly love we do not need to write to you, for you yourselves have been taught by God to love each other. And in fact, you do love all the brothers throughout Macedonia. Yet we urge you, brothers, to do so more and more. (1 Thess. 4:9–10)*

After you have done it, do it more and more.

2

UNCOMPROMISING COMMITMENT

Gracious Non-compromisers

> *But Daniel resolved not to defile himself with the royal food and wine, and he asked the chief official for permission not to defile himself this way. (Dan. 1:8)*

> *Daniel spoke to him with wisdom and tact. (Dan. 2:14b)*

Daniel was uncompromising and gracious, and God honored him for it. He was that way as a teenager, and he was still that way as an old man...*because* he was that way as a young man. He started out refusing to compromise on God's word, and he stayed that way. If we start out compromising, it is very difficult to change.

Very often people who refuse to compromise about the truth are also belligerent and ungracious. In fact, there are so many people like this that it might be hard to visualize someone being uncompromising without having a bad attitude about it. The reverse is also true. Many gracious, loving people turn out to be compromisers upon closer inspection.

Refusing to compromise is asking for a confrontation, and confrontation can mean conflict. It may be that the belligerent non-compromisers love *conflict* more than they love the truth. This is why their attitude is what shows most. The gracious compromisers hate conflict more than they love the truth. Again, the attitude shows more than the truth does. Both of these people have their priorities mixed up. Their focus is on the confrontation, not the truth.

So we have two kinds of Christians: gracious compromisers and ungracious non-compromisers. We do not have many *Daniels* people who are very gracious and yet refuse to compromise. These days the vote seems to be going for graciousness rather than ungraciousness. Graciousness is only good *if* it is not afraid of or divorced from the truth.

> *There is no fear in love. But perfect love drives out fear, because fear has to do with punishment. The one who fears is not made perfect in love. (1 Jn. 4:18)*

If the graciousness is God's grace, there will be no fear of conflict. If it is God's grace, it will not be separated from the truth.

> *We have seen his glory, the glory of the One and Only, who came from the Father,* ***full of grace and truth****. (Jn. 1:14)*

We should not make a choice between grace and truth.

Confessing Jesus Christ

> *Isaiah said this because he saw Jesus' glory and spoke about him. Yet at the same time many even among the leaders believed in him. But because of the Pharisees they would not confess their faith for fear they would be put out of the synagogue; for they loved praise from men more than praise from God. (Jn. 12:41–43)*

These leaders had two reasons for being unwilling to confess Jesus Christ—fear and love. They feared men and loved the praise of men instead of fearing God and loving His praise. They put their fear and their love in the wrong place. They feared what might happen in the future (e.g., being put out of the synagogue) and loved what they had already experienced. They knew what it was like to be praised by men, and they enjoyed it. They wanted the pleasant things to continue. They were most concerned about the opinions of the world and, in this particular instance, the part of the world that controlled the church.

Today the problem seems to be the reverse. Pastors value the praise of their congregation more than the praise of God. They fear the criticism of the congregants and the loss of their job. So they preach to please.

Public & Personal

"I think religion is a personal thing."

"It's ok to have religion, as long as you realize it's personal."

These are common thoughts in America today. In the last fifty years or so, evangelical circles have also started using the expression, "Receive Jesus Christ as your personal Savior."

Religion has to be personal—after all, Jesus Christ is a person, and He loves people. That is personal. He saves us as individuals; we go to heaven by ones, not by groups. Yes, Christianity is *personal.* But it doesn't stop there. After it becomes personal, it must also become *public.* Let's look at how Jesus expects this to happen:

> *What I tell you in the dark* [personal], *speak in the daylight* [public]; *what is whispered in your ear* [personal] *proclaim from the roofs* [public]. *(Mt. 10:27)*

If you won't be publicly identified with Jesus Christ and His Word now, He will not identify with you publicly later:

> *If anyone is ashamed of me and my words, the Son of Man will be ashamed of him when he comes in his glory and in the glory of the Father and of the holy angels. (Lk. 9:26)*

Christianity is *personal* in a *public* way. "The isolated Christian is an anomaly."[1] If someone is only private about his faith, he is like a finger removed from the body, trying to exist by itself. He has no source of food, sight, or smell. He cannot continue to exist for long. Even if he does, he will be of no use to the rest of the body.

There is no such thing as a private Christian. All Christians are part of the body of Christ, the Church.

> *From him the whole body, joined and held together by every supporting ligament, grows and builds itself up in love, as each part does its work. (Eph. 4:16)*

1 Howard Guiness, *Total Christian War* (Melbourne, AU: S. John Bacon, 1945).

Christianity is personal *and* public. It is not possible to hide behind the word "personal" and still meet our Lord's qualifications for being a Christian.

Holy Lives

> *Several days later Felix arrived with his wife Drusilla, who was a Jewess. He sent for Paul and listened to him as he spoke about faith in Christ Jesus. As Paul discoursed on righteousness, self-control, and the judgment to come, Felix was afraid and said, "That's enough for now! You may leave. When I find it convenient, I will send for you."* (Acts 24:24–25)

Felix was the governor, and Paul was the prisoner. Yet it was Felix who was afraid. Perhaps it was the subject of their discourse that frightened him: "righteousness, self-control, and the judgment to come."

In the Gospel of John, Jesus spoke of the coming of the Holy Spirit:

> *When he comes, he will convict the world of guilt in regard to sin and righteousness and judgment.* (Jn. 16:8)

You can draw three conclusions from this: 1) Paul was filled with the Holy Spirit. 2) Fear is evidence of guilt and conviction. 3) The Holy Spirit will convict the world through the words and lives of His people.

Are the non-Christians that we know afraid? If they are not, is it because we are not speaking of righteousness, self-control, and the judgment to come, or is it because we are not living righteously?

Self-control

Someone wrote to me once:

> I have a question about "self-control" as a fruit of the Spirit. It doesn't seem right to me that a fruit of the Spirit would have to rely on me...If something is "self" activated, how can it be of the Spirit?

The fruit of the Spirit is "self-activated" by choice, but not by effort. Love is the first fruit of the Spirit, but God also commands us to love. We can obey His commands to love *because* He has given us the fruit of love.

God has also given us the fruit of joy. When He commands us to rejoice always (Phil. 4:4), we are able to rejoice because of that fruit. Read through the list of the fruit of the Spirit (Gal. 5:22). Each of these is also commanded. Self-control is the same. God has given us the fruit, and that is how we obey the command.

To be self-controlled is *not* to grit your teeth, bite your tongue, or count to ten. All obedience should be effortless, as in Colossians 2:

> *So then, just as you received Christ Jesus as Lord, continue to live in him. (Col. 2:6)*

We did not receive Christ by effort. We do not live by effort. It is not possible to try and *trust* at the same time. Through faith we live by grace.

First Things First

During my years in Christian ministry I have seen many different series of teachings sweep through the church. Our ministry has participated in some of these, and some of them we have simply observed. Each time a new teaching swept in, it sounded as if that particular teaching was the final answer. Here are a few of them:

- the indigenous church
- one-on-one evangelism
- the gifts of the Spirit
- sound doctrine
- small-group Bible studies
- city-wide crusades
- the fruit of the Spirit
- authority and submission, shepherds, discipleship
- the church growth movement
- the "user-friendly" church
- Toronto blessing
- networking
- fundraising

My opinions about these are not the issue. The issue is that these teachings are "means," but they are treated as "ends." They are tools to get us to the goal; they are not goals themselves.

In Colossians 1:13–22 Paul speaks of the work Christ did in creation and redemption, "that in everything he might have the supremacy" (v.18). Rather than concentrating on having the perfect methods or gifts or doctrines, we should seek first *our Lord.*

> *Glory in his holy name; let the hearts of those who seek the LORD rejoice.* ***Look to the LORD and his strength; seek his face always.*** *(Ps. 105:3–4)*

> *One thing I ask of the LORD,* ***this is what I seek: that I may dwell in the house of the LORD all the days of my life, to gaze upon the beauty of the LORD and to seek him in his temple.*** *(Ps. 27:4)*

> *My heart says of you, "Seek his face!"* ***Your face, LORD, I will seek.*** *(Ps. 27:8)*

All other things are secondary.

Religion

There are many authoritarian religions today. Whether they are large movements or local ones, each is under the domination of one man. It is never long before such movements stray concerning the person and work of Jesus Christ and become immoral. Let me share a word from the prophet Jeremiah:

> *"I have heard what the prophets say who prophesy lies in my name. They say, 'I had a dream! I had a dream!' How long will this continue in the hearts of these lying prophets, who prophesy the delusions of their own minds? They think the dreams they tell one another will make my people forget my name, just as their fathers forgot my name through Baal worship. Let the prophet who has a dream tell his dream, but let the one who has my word speak it faithfully. For what has straw to do with grain?" declares the LORD. "Is not my word like fire," declares the LORD, "and like a hammer that breaks a rock in pieces? Therefore," declares the LORD, "I am against the prophets who steal from one another words supposedly from me. Yes," declares the LORD, "I am against the prophets who wag their own tongues and yet declare, 'The LORD declares.' Indeed, I am*

against those who prophesy false dreams," declares the LORD. "They tell them and lead my people astray with their reckless lies, yet I did not send or appoint them. They do not benefit these people in the least," declares the LORD. (Jer. 23:25–32)

Gospel

For such men are false apostles, deceitful workmen, masquerading as apostles of Christ. And no wonder, for Satan himself masquerades as an angel of light. It is not surprising, then, if his servants masquerade as servants of righteousness… (2 Cor. 11:13–15)

It is the nature of a lie to sound like the truth. People who are lying do not want you to know they are liars. Jesus said:

Watch out for false prophets. They come to you in sheep's clothing, but inwardly they are ferocious wolves. (Mt. 7:15)

Lies come looking like the truth, wolves come dressed like sheep, the Devil appears like an angel, and his ministers like ministers of righteousness.

There are two sure means of distinguishing those who tell lies from those who tell the truth. One is having a thorough knowledge of the Gospel of God so that you are able to judge every teacher by that knowledge. The other is having first-hand experience with God. These are the criteria the apostle Paul gave to the Galatians.

I am astonished that you are so quickly deserting the one who called you by the grace of Christ and

> *are turning to a different gospel which is really no gospel at all. Evidently some people are throwing you into confusion and are trying to pervert the gospel of Christ. But even if we or an angel from heaven should preach a gospel other than the one we preached to you, let him be eternally condemned! As we have already said, so now I say again: If anybody is preaching to you a gospel other than what you accepted, let him be eternally condemned! (Gal. 1:6–9)*

Saying "a gospel other than the one we preached to you" is judging the content of what is presented. "A gospel other than what you accepted" is a judgment of experience.

Paul defines the true gospel in 1 Corinthians 15:1–4:

> *Now, brothers, I want to remind you of the gospel I preached to you, which you received and on which you have taken your stand. By this gospel you are saved, if you hold firmly to the word I preached to you. Otherwise, you have believed in vain. For what I received I passed on to you as of first importance: that Christ died for our sins according to the Scriptures, that he was buried, that he was raised on the third day according to the Scriptures...*

This is the gospel that was preached and received. This is the gospel that saves.

Truth

There are several words that can honestly be used to describe the word "truth." Here are a few:

- self-evident
- discovered
- proven
- absolute
- experimental
- experiential
- declared
- preached
- established

None of these words causes truth. Truth was always there. Truth is truth whether or not it is taught or believed. Believing the truth does not make it true.

There is a truth called the law of gravity. It existed long before it was formulated as a scientific law. Objects will not stop falling to earth if someone refuses to believe in gravity. Gravity does not care if anyone believes it. It just *is*.

There is one self-evident truth greater than all the others, and that is God:

> *For since the creation of the world God's invisible qualities—his eternal power and divine nature—have been clearly seen, being understood from what has been made, so that men are without excuse. (Rom. 1:20)*

> *The fool says in his heart, "There is no God." They are corrupt, and their ways are vile; there is no one who does good. (Ps. 53:1)*

Believing in God does not make Him God, but not believing in Him has dire consequences.

The Father loves the Son and has placed everything in his hands. Whoever believes in the Son has eternal life, but whoever rejects the Son will not see life, for God's wrath remains on him. (Jn. 3:35–36)

The truth of God's actions is both self-evident and revealed in His Word. There are two great acts of God—the creation and redemption. The God of creation is self-evident to the created. Redemption is a historical act that needs to be proclaimed:

For, "Everyone who calls on the name of the Lord will be saved." How, then, can they call on the one they have not believed in? And how can they believe in the one of whom they have not heard? And how can they hear without someone preaching to them? And how can they preach unless they are sent? As it is written, "How beautiful are the feet of those who bring good news!" (Rom. 10:13–15)

Consequently, faith comes from hearing the message, and the message is heard through the word of Christ. (Rom. 10:17)

Teaching the Truth

Illustrations are an effective way of teaching. They stick in the mind. They also make it difficult to sneak by or ignore a strong command.

On one occasion an expert in the law stood up to test Jesus. "Teacher," he asked, "what must I do to inherit eternal life?" "What is written in the Law?" he replied. "How do you read it?" He answered: "'Love

> *the Lord your God with all your heart and with all your soul and with all your strength and with all your mind'; and, 'Love your neighbor as yourself.'" "You have answered correctly," Jesus replied. "Do this and you will live." But he wanted to justify himself, so he asked Jesus, "And who is my neighbor?" In reply Jesus said: "A man was going down from Jerusalem to Jericho, when he fell into the hands of robbers. They stripped him of his clothes, beat him and went away, leaving him half dead. A priest happened to be going down the same road, and when he saw the man, he passed by on the other side. So too, a Levite, when he came to the place and saw him, passed by on the other side. But a Samaritan, as he traveled, came where the man was; and when he saw him, he took pity on him. He went to him and bandaged his wounds, pouring on oil and wine. Then he put the man on his own donkey, took him to an inn and took care of him. The next day he took out two silver coins and gave them to the innkeeper. 'Look after him,' he said, 'and when I return, I will reimburse you for any extra expense you may have.' Which of these three do you think was a neighbor to the man who fell into the hands of robbers?" The expert in the law replied, "The one who had mercy on him." Jesus told him, "Go and do likewise." (Lk. 10:25–37)*

The expert in the law asked two questions. Jesus asked three.

Expert:

1. "Teacher, what must I do to inherit eternal life?"
2. "Who is my neighbor?"

Jesus:

1. "What is written in the law?"
2. "How do you read it?"
3. "Which of these three do you think was a neighbor to the man who fell into the hands of robbers?"

The expert did not want an answer to either of his questions. He was testing Jesus. Jesus gave him two answers: "Do this and you will live," and "Go and do likewise." The truth of the command to love your neighbor was very clear before the illustration and could not be avoided after it.

Smooth Teaching

> *Go now, write it on a tablet for them, inscribe it on a scroll, that for the days to come it may be an everlasting witness. These are rebellious people, deceitful children, children unwilling to listen to the LORD's instruction. They say to the seers, "See no more visions!" and to the prophets, "Give us no more visions of what is right!* ***Tell us pleasant things, prophesy illusions.*** *Leave this way, get off this path, and stop confronting us with the Holy One of Israel!" Therefore, this is what the Holy One of Israel says: "Because you have rejected this message, relied on oppression and depended on deceit, this sin will become for you like a high wall, cracked and bulging, that collapses suddenly, in an instant. It will break in pieces like pottery, shattered so mercilessly that among its pieces not a fragment will be found for taking coals from a hearth or scooping water out of a cistern." (Is. 30:8–14)*

Notice the unwillingness of the people to listen to the truth even though they *know* it is the truth: "Give us no more visions of what is right! Tell us pleasant things, prophesy illusions" (v. 10). Notice also that their uncorrected iniquity does not result in immediate judgment. But there will be judgment: "This sin will become for you like a high wall, cracked and bulging, that collapses suddenly, in an instant" (v. 13). The judgment is certain and devastating, and the people were given an advance warning of it.

How does this apply to Christians today? We have two temptations. First, we want to hear smooth words. We flock to teachers who speak pleasant things. Paul warned Timothy about this in 2 Timothy 4:3–4:

> *For the time will come when men will not put up with sound doctrine. Instead, to suit their own desires, they will gather around them a great number of teachers to say what their itching ears want to hear. They will turn their ears away from the truth and turn aside to myths.*

The second is a temptation to respond to this demand by becoming the prophet of "smooth things." We cannot escape our responsibility by laying this charge at the feet of liberals. It is a major problem in all denominations.

Evidence of the Spirit

> *And with great power the apostles gave witness to the resurrection of the Lord Jesus. And great grace was upon them all. (Acts 4:33 NKJV)*

Two things strike me as I read this sentence. One is "great power" and the other is "great grace." It is possible to testify to the resurrection of the Lord Jesus without great power, and it is possible to have a body of believers who do not have great grace resting upon them.

Something special preceded that statement of grace in Acts:

> *All the believers were one in heart and mind. No one claimed that any of his possessions was his own, but they shared everything they had. (Acts 4:32)*

People were not attached to their possessions, and they were of one heart. Is this why there was great power and great grace? No. This was *evidence* of that power and grace. Here is the reason for it:

> *After they prayed, the place where they were meeting was shaken. And* ***they were all filled with the Holy Spirit*** *and spoke the word of God boldly. (Acts 4:31)*

The Holy Spirit was the source of the power and grace. The Christians were *all filled* with the Spirit because they *all prayed.*

Are you of one heart with the Christians around you? Are you attached to your possessions? Do you speak the word of God with boldness? Do you give your testimony of the resurrection of the Lord Jesus with great power? Maybe you are not filled with the Holy Spirit.

3

GOD'S CHARACTER

Seeing God

When the Ten Commandments were first given, they were not given in pageantry. They were given in terrifying, first-person reality, three months after the Israelites left Egypt (Exod. 19). Thirty-nine years later, Moses recalled the events surrounding their declaration:

> *Then the LORD spoke to you out of the fire. You heard the sound of words but saw* ***no form****; there was only a voice. (Deut. 4:12)*

> *You saw* ***no form*** *of any kind the day the LORD spoke to you at Horeb out of the fire. Therefore watch yourselves very carefully... (Deut. 4:15)*

> *You were shown these things so that you might know that the LORD is God;* ***besides him there is no other.*** *(Deut. 4:35)*

> *Acknowledge and take to heart this day that the LORD is God in heaven above and on the earth below.* ***There is no other.*** *(Deut. 4:39)*

There are two reasons we are not to make images of God:

1. He is not like any of His physical creation, so no creation can physically be like Him.
2. He is not like any other god, because there is no other God.

God is not like anything or anyone. When the Bible describes Him, it is not in *appearance*, but in *character*:

- *Holy*—as the Ancient of Days in Daniel 7, where His clothing and hair are described gloriously
- *Where He dwells*—"Heaven is my throne." (Is. 66:1)
- *What He does*—"The God of Heaven who made the sea and the land..." (Jon. 1:9); "Sing to the Lord, for He has done glorious things, let this be known to all the world." (Is. 12:5)

> *Brothers and fathers, listen to me.* ***The God of Glory*** *appeared to our father Abraham. (Acts 7:2)*

The Bible depicts God in terms of who He *is* and what He *does*. He is the God of glory; He is the God of hope and the God of peace. Daniel described Him to Nebuchadnezzar this way: "*There is a God in heaven who reveals mysteries*" (Dan. 2:28). Jonah spoke of Him: "*I worship the Lord, the God of heaven, who made the sea and the land*" (Jon. 1:9). God *is*, and God *acts*.

> *Sing to the Lord, for He has done glorious things; let this be known to all the world. (Is. 12:5)*

When we think of God, let us think of Jesus Christ in His glory:

> *So from now on we regard no one from a worldly point of view. Though we once regarded Christ in this way, we do so no longer. (2 Cor. 5:16)*

> *The Son is the radiance of God's glory and the exact representation of his being, sustaining all things by his powerful word. After he had provided purification for sins, he sat down at the right hand of the Majesty in heaven. (Heb. 1:3)*

> *He is the image of the invisible God, the firstborn over all creation. (Col. 1:15)*

> *Jesus answered: "Don't you know me, Philip, even after I have been among you such a long time? Anyone who has seen me has seen the Father. How can you say, 'Show us the Father'?" (Jn. 14:9)*

> *They came to Philip, who was from Bethsaida in Galilee, with a request. "Sir," they said, "we would like to see Jesus."...Jesus replied, "The hour has come for the Son of Man to be glorified." (Jn. 12:21, 23)*

Glorified—this is how God wants to be "seen."

> *And now, Father, glorify me in your presence with the glory I had with you before the world began. (Jn. 17:5)*

Knowing the Father

You have probably heard this saying:

> *Do not be misled: "Bad company corrupts good character." (1 Cor. 15:33)*

Perhaps you also know the truth taught in Romans 1:18–32, which is basically, "Bad *theology* corrupts good character." Even though we know both of these truths, we can still wonder when some Christians end up in immoral situations. The wonder is increased when the Christian involved has emphasized "good company" (nearly to the point of legalism) and "sound doctrine" (to the point of arguing with all who differ).

I spend a good portion of my time with Christians who have fallen into major sin. Some of them turned out not to be Christians; that is a topic for another time. However, some of them were Christians. I have spent many hours listening to them. As they recounted the details of the sins they fell into, I could see that they had not kept bad company and that their theology appeared to be sound. Yet how could I account for their sin? After more questioning, I saw that the basic cause really was bad theology, although not in any area that they might have suspected. What was the explanation?

Most bad theology is the result of false teaching—that is, untrue teaching about God, His being, His character, or His work. We see it in cults, heresies, other world religions, and liberalism. If we know our Bibles, such false teaching is easy to recognize.

But there is another kind of bad theology that is taught by Christians who offer incomplete teaching or overemphasize a particular aspect of theology. Important truth is left out, not because it is not believed, but because it is not part of the current Christian cultural pattern.

Here are a few expressions I hear (and say myself) regularly:

- "Do you know the Savior?"
- "Jesus loves you."
- "Would you like to come to Jesus?"
- "Would you like to come to Christ?"

These can easily fit into good theology. Here are a few expressions I do not hear:

- "Do you know the Father?"
- "The Father loves you."

"I am not saying I will ask the Father on your behalf. No, the Father himself loves you..." (Jn. 16:26b–27a)

- "Would you like to come to the Father?"

"I am the way and the truth and the life. No one comes to the Father except through me." (Jn. 14:6)

These expressions do not fit with the current Christian culture, so they are not used. Then in the vacuum of teaching about the Father, Christians make up their own theology that often comes straight from the enemy of our souls. It is a caricature of the Father. Thus, bad theology is the first result of failing to teach basic truths about God; bad morality is the second.

Since we do not teach that the Father loves us, the resulting bad theology is that the Father does *not* love us. This is not a conclusion I reached only from logical deduction. It is borne out by many Christians' answers to the question, "Would you describe God the Father to me?" In almost every answer, they describe Him as not loving. Those who include love in the answer do so in a way that shows that they do not believe it, e.g., "He is supposed to be loving." As I listen to this bad theology, I see why the person in front of me also has bad morality.

People generally give two types of answers to this question: 1) confirmation class answers (correct answers), and 2) the answers they really believe. By asking similar questions about Jesus and the Holy Spirit, I find that Jesus invariably has a "better" character than the Father. Although I ask these questions of Christians who believe in the Trinity, it is impossible to make their descriptions fit into one Deity. Their answers are polytheistic.

Here are three assignments to help you with your theology of the Father:

1. Read the Gospel of John with a marker in your hand. Highlight every mention of the Father and notice His characteristics and difference from or likeness to Jesus.
2. Go through the New Testament looking for prayers and teaching on prayer. To whom are the prayers addressed?
3. Read the salutations of the letters in the New Testament. What do they say about the Father?

When your theology about the Father becomes truly biblical, it always affects the way you live.

If God has revealed anything to me that I have not obeyed, I will go down when the crisis comes no matter how I may cry to Him.

—Oswald Chambers

As God Sees Things

While Paul was waiting for them in Athens, he was greatly distressed to see that the city was full of idols. (Acts 17:16)

When Paul arrived in Athens, his reaction was not awe at the beauty of the Parthenon; it was distress over the people's idolatry.

You may have been to parts of the world where there are magnificent minarets, Shinto gates and shrines, and beautifully carved statues housed in ornate temples. Do we think like the Apostle Paul when we see these things? If not, is it because he saw them as God sees them and we see them like the rest of mankind? May God help us to be distressed over the worship of false gods.

In vain with lavish kindness
the gifts of God are strown
The heathen in his blindness
bows down to wood and stone.

—Reginald Heber, 1783–1826

Judgment

They are a feared and dreaded people; they are a law to themselves and promote their own honor. (Hab. 1:7)

This is speaking of the Babylonians. In the previous verse, God said that He was "raising up the Babylonians." This was in answer to Habakkuk's complaint that God did not listen and tolerated wrong (vv. 2–3). God was going to punish evil nations with an evil nation. Habakkuk further complains:

Your eyes are too pure to look on evil; you cannot tolerate wrong. Why then do you tolerate the treacherous? Why are you silent while the wicked swallow up those more righteous than themselves? (Hab. 1:13)

God gave several answers to these questions in Habakkuk 2:2–12, but in verse 13 He gives a comprehensive answer:

Has not the LORD Almighty determined that the people's labor is only fuel for the fire, that the nations exhaust themselves for nothing? ***For the earth will be filled with the knowledge of the glory of the LORD, as the waters cover the sea.*** *(Hab. 2:13–14)*

God takes the long view. No one will get away with anything. Psalms 37 and 73 give answers to some of the same questions as Habakkuk raises. I would encourage you to read and meditate on these Scriptures.

Who Is Like You, O Lord?

> *The LORD saw how great man's wickedness on the earth had become, and that every inclination of the thoughts of his heart was only evil all the time. (Gen. 6:5)*

This is God's declaration of the sinfulness of man. God can speak about man's state because His judgment is absolutely right. However, whether I can speak about God's holiness is another thing. Even though I am redeemed and looking forward to the completion of that redemption, I do not yet see Him as He really is.

> *But we know that when he appears, we shall be like him, for we shall see him as he is. (1 Jn. 3:2b)*

Until that time, we know Him as He has revealed Himself in the Scriptures.

The Song of Moses

Moses and the Israelites sang about God's holiness after Israel passed safely through the sea and the Egyptians were drowned:

> *Who among the gods is like you, O LORD? Who is like you—**majestic in holiness, awesome in glory,** working wonders? (Exod. 15:11)*

This song describes God in transcendent terms, not physical ones. *Holiness* and *glory* are not descriptive in a limited way like the words *tall* or *blue* or *sophisticated*. When we add *majestic* and *awesome*, we begin to understand Moses' rhetorical question, "Who is like you?" The obvious answer is that there is no one like Him.

A Song of David

David composed a song when he brought the ark of God to Jerusalem. It was sung to the accompaniment of an orchestra. We do not have the music, but we still have the words—inspired words:

> ***Splendor and majesty*** *are before him;* ***strength and joy*** *in his dwelling place. Ascribe to the LORD, O families of nations, ascribe to the LORD glory and strength, ascribe to the LORD the glory due his name. Bring an offering and come before him; worship the LORD in* ***the splendor of his holiness.*** *Tremble before him, all the earth! The world is firmly established; it cannot be moved. (1 Chr. 16:27–30)*

Splendor and *majesty, strength* and *joy*. These words do not describe God; they describe the things in His presence, as if He is more than the words can encompass and this is what is required just to be in His presence.

The Splendor of His Holiness

Great events inspire great songs. In 2 Chronicles 20, the armies of three nations marched against Judah. Judah's king, Jehoshaphat, led the people in prayer:

> *All the men of Judah, with their wives and children and little ones, stood there before the LORD. (2 Chr. 20:13)*

The Spirit of the Lord answered them through a prophet with a promise of deliverance. Then...

> *Jehoshaphat bowed with his face to the ground, and all the people of Judah and Jerusalem fell down in worship before the LORD. (2 Chr. 20:18)*

The next morning, the army of Judah set out toward the enemies with the choir singing in advance of them. According to the command God had given them through the prophet,

> *...Jehoshaphat appointed men to sing to the LORD and to praise him for the splendor of his holiness... (2 Chr. 20:21)*

They were wonderfully delivered from the enemy.

Songs in His Presence

In Isaiah's vision of the Lord on His throne, the seraphs were calling to one another:

> *...Holy, holy, holy is the LORD Almighty; the whole earth is full of His glory. (Is. 6:3)*

In John's revelation of the throne eight centuries later, the winged creatures were saying,

> *...Holy, holy, holy is the Lord God Almighty, who was, and is, and is to come. (Rev. 4:8)*

There was another song sung by a sea of glass and fire. It was accompanied by harps played by those who had overcome the beast:

> *Great and marvelous are your deeds, Lord God Almighty. Just and true are your ways, King of the ages. Who will not fear you, O Lord, and bring glory*

to your name? For you alone are holy. All nations will come and worship before you, for your righteous acts have been revealed. (Rev. 15:3–4)

His People

My eyes will watch over them for their good, and I will bring them back to this land. I will build them up and not tear them down; I will plant them and not uproot them. I will give them a heart to know me, that I am the LORD. They will be my people, and I will be their God, for they will return to me with all their heart. (Jer. 24:6–7)

This was written of the exiles of Judah in Babylon, so it does not apply directly to us. However, since God does not change, we can learn something about Him from it.

1. He watches over His people for *their* good.
2. He will build them up.
3. He will not tear them down.
4. He will plant them.
5. He will not uproot them.
6. He will give them a heart to know Him.
7. He will have them for His people.
8. He will be their God because they will return to Him with all their heart.

We are His people, too. God is good.

God's Grace

> *But because of his great love for us, God, who is rich in mercy, made us alive with Christ even when we were dead in transgressions—it is by grace you have been saved. And God raised us up with Christ and seated us with him in the heavenly realms in Christ Jesus, in order that in the coming ages he might show the incomparable riches of his grace, expressed in his kindness to us in Christ Jesus. For it is by grace you have been saved, through faith—and this not from yourselves, it is the gift of God—not by works, so that no one can boast. For we are God's workmanship, created in Christ Jesus to do good works, which God prepared in advance for us to do. (Eph. 2:4–9)*

God has great love for us, is rich in mercy, and saves us by His grace. And grace is a gift, not earned.

> *And if by grace, then it is no longer by works; if it were, grace would no longer be grace. (Rom. 11:6)*

As God's love is great and He is rich in mercy, so His grace also comes in great quantities.

His love has no limit;
His grace has no measure;
His power no boundary known unto man.
For out of His infinite riches in Jesus,
He giveth and giveth and giveth again.

—Annie Johnson Flint

> ***How much more did God's grace*** *and the gift that came by the grace of the one man, Jesus Christ,* ***overflow*** *to the many! (Rom. 5:15)*

> *...grace* ***increased*** *all the more... (Rom. 5:20)*

> *God's* ***abundant*** *provision of grace... (Rom. 5:17)*

> *Grace and peace be yours* ***in abundance.*** *(1 Pet. 1:2b)*

> *But he gives us* ***more grace...*** *(Jas. 4:6)*

> *From the* ***fullness*** *of his grace we have all received* ***one blessing after another.*** *(Jn. 1:16)*

> *...and* ***much grace*** *was upon them all. (Acts 4:33)*

> *...because of the* ***surpassing grace*** *God has given you. (2 Cor. 9:14)*

> *...in accordance with* ***the riches of God's grace that he lavished on us...*** *(Eph. 1:7–8)*

God is not stingy with grace. We who know Him know by experience that He is wealthy in grace.

4

PRAYER

Proclaiming & Praying

When I came to you, brothers, I did not come with eloquence or superior wisdom as I proclaimed to you the testimony about God. For I resolved to know nothing while I was with you except Jesus Christ and him crucified...My message and my preaching were not with wise and persuasive words, but with a demonstration of the Spirit's power, so that your faith might not rest on men's wisdom, but on God's power. (1 Cor. 2:1–2, 4–5)

I urge, then, first of all, that requests, prayers, intercession and thanksgiving be made for everyone—for kings and all those in authority, that we may live

> *peaceful and quiet lives in all godliness and holiness. This is good, and pleases God our Savior, who wants all men to be saved and to come to a knowledge of the truth. (1 Tim. 2:1–4)*

These two texts bring us back to first priorities: preaching the cross and praying for kings. Both of these passages relate to the salvation of men. God, in His wisdom, decided that proclaiming the gospel and praying was our part in the salvation of men. It is easy to get side-tracked with pushing for constitutional amendments, a balanced budget, or a Christian government. Paul did not have that luxury, and neither does most of the world today. Let's get our focus back on the real solution to our nation's problems: the gospel of Jesus Christ. Let's change the nation by proclaiming and praying.

Church Growth

> *They seized Peter and John, and because it was evening, they put them in jail until the next day. But many who heard the message believed, and the number of men grew to about five thousand. (Acts 4:3–4)*

> *Then the church throughout Judea, Galilee and Samaria enjoyed a time of peace. It was strengthened; and encouraged by the Holy Spirit, it grew in numbers, living in the fear of the Lord. (Acts 9:31)*

In the first passage, the church was persecuted. In the second, it enjoyed a time of peace. In both cases, the church grew. What did these times have in common? *Preaching the gospel in power.* Church growth is not directly related to persecution or peace. The church can die under persecution, but it does not have to. It can die in times of peace, but it does not have to. The church died in the Middle East, North Africa, and Turkey because of persecution. In the last century, the church in Northern Europe died without it. The birthplace of first-century Christians and the birthplace of the Reformation are now needy mission fields.

God designed His church to flourish under any form of government or religion. There are very prohibitive ones today: communism, dictatorships, Islam, Buddhism, Hinduism, Roman Catholicism, Eastern Orthodoxy, Judaism, and animistic cultures. All of these are strongly opposed to evangelical Christianity.

> *In fact, everyone who wants to live a godly life in Christ Jesus will be persecuted. (2 Tim. 3:12)*

> *You know, brothers, that our visit to you was not a failure. We had previously suffered and been insulted in Philippi, as you know, but with the help of our God we dared to tell you his gospel* ***in spite of strong opposition.*** *(1 Thess. 2:1–2)*

Asking people who do not believe to stop persecuting believers is not God's way. It is asking the devil to play fair.

What is God's way?

> ***Devote yourselves to prayer, being watchful and thankful. And pray for us,*** *too, that God may open a door for our message, so* ***that we may proclaim the mystery of Christ,*** *for which I am in chains. Pray that I may* ***proclaim it clearly, as I should.*** *(Col. 4:2–4)*

> ***And pray in the Spirit on all occasions with all kinds of prayers and requests.*** *With this in mind, be alert and* ***always keep on praying for all the saints. Pray also for me,*** *that whenever I open my mouth, words may be given me so* ***that I will fearlessly make known the mystery of the gospel.*** *(Eph. 6:18–19)*

> *"Now, Lord, consider their threats and enable your servants to speak your word with great boldness..."* ***After they prayed,*** *the place where they were meeting was shaken. And* ***they were all filled with the Holy Spirit and spoke the word of God boldly.*** *(Acts 4:29, 31)*

Prayer for Revival

How should we pray for revival?

1. *With confession.* Since the last revival, the world has acted according to its nature. The Church has not acted according to its nature and needs to take responsibility for the results this has had in the world.
2. *In submission.* The Holy Spirit is sovereign in revival and cannot be manipulated by prayer meetings, fasting, etc. We cannot *produce* revival—it must be given.
3. *With optimism.* If we want to ask for revival in a godly way, we should plead the promises of God in Scripture. In order to do this, we *must* have an optimistic eschatology.
4. *Knowledgeably.* In order to pray for revival intelligently, we need to know what we are asking for. Read histories of previous revivals. The last revival in America was in the mid-nineteenth century.

5. *With focus.* We should pray for the *Church*, not the world. Pray for the preachers and teachers in the Church. If the Church is revived, the world will be affected. As Charles Spurgeon once said, "If the church catches fire, the world will show up to watch it burn."
6. *With sound doctrine.* Pray biblically. Our prayers need to be based on a good grasp of biblical concepts—sin, salvation, the cross and resurrection, etc.
7. *In self-control.* Because of our great revival drought, there will be a strong temptation to emotionalism and sensationalism if revival comes. Pray for self-control with self-control.

Confident Prayer

> *This is the* ***confidence*** *we have in approaching God: that* ***if we ask anything according to his will, he hears us.*** *(1 Jn. 5:14)*

Often our prayers are wishful, hopeful, anxious, or desperate. The following texts give God's conditions for answered prayer:

> ***Do not be anxious*** *about anything, but in everything, with prayer and petition,* ***with thanksgiving, present your requests*** *to God. And the peace of God, which transcends all understanding, will guard your hearts and your minds in Christ Jesus. (Phil. 4:6–7)*

> *Until now you have not asked for anything* ***in my name.*** *Ask and you will receive, and your joy will be complete. (Jn. 16:24)*

You did not choose me, but I chose you and appointed you to go and bear fruit—fruit that will last. Then the Father will give you whatever you ***ask in my name.*** *This is my command: love each other. (Jn. 15:16–17)*

But when he asks, ***he must believe and not doubt,*** *because he who doubts is like a wave of the sea, blown and tossed by the wind. That man should not think he will receive anything from the Lord... (Jas. 1:6–7)*

When you ask, you do not receive, because ***you ask with wrong motives,*** *that you may spend what you get on your pleasures. (Jas. 4:3)*

If I had cherished sin in my heart, the Lord would not have listened; *but God has surely listened and heard my voice in prayer. Praise be to God, who has not rejected my prayer or withheld his love from me! (Ps. 66:18–20)*

Doubting, anxiety, wrong motives, sin in our hearts. These are explanations for unanswered prayer. Here are the conditions for answered prayer: confidence, praying in the will of God, giving thanks, believing, and praying in Jesus' name.

You have probably experienced answered prayer even when you violated all of the conditions except the last one, "in Jesus' name." If God is *that* faithful to us, we can lean on His faithfulness. That is the meaning of faith. Faith is trusting in *the faithfulness of God.*

The preparation for believing prayer is 1) having a clean heart and 2) being saturated with Scripture.

Faith comes from hearing the message, and the message is heard through the word of Christ. (Rom. 10:17)

If we are prepared this way, answered prayer will not be a surprise to us as it was to the believers in Acts 12:

So Peter was kept in prison, but the church was earnestly praying to God for him... Suddenly an angel of the Lord appeared and a light shone in the cell. He struck Peter on the side and woke him up. "Quick, get up!" he said, and the chains fell off Peter's wrists... He went to the house of Mary the mother of Jn., also called Mark, where many people had gathered and were praying. Peter knocked at the outer entrance, and a servant named Rhoda came to answer the door. When she recognized Peter's voice, she was so overjoyed she ran back without opening it and exclaimed, "Peter is at the door!" "You're out of your mind," they told her. When she kept insisting that it was so, they said, "It must be his angel." But Peter kept on knocking, and when they opened the door and saw him, they were astonished. (Acts 12: 5, 7, 12–16)

Persevering in Prayer

Then Jesus told his disciples a parable to show them that they should always pray and not give up. He said: "In a certain town there was a judge who neither feared God nor cared about men. And there was a widow in that town who kept coming to him with the plea, 'Grant me justice against my adversary.' For some time he refused. But finally he said to himself,

> *'Even though I don't fear God or care about men, yet because this widow keeps bothering me, I will see that she gets justice, so that she won't eventually wear me out with her coming!'" And the Lord said, "Listen to what the unjust judge says. And will not God bring about justice for his chosen ones, who cry out to him day and night? Will he keep putting them off? I tell you, he will see that they get justice, and quickly. However, when the Son of Man comes, will he find faith on the earth?" (Lk. 18:1–8)*

What annoys the unjust judge does not annoy God. Jesus tells us to keep it up. We cannot irritate God this way. We can not ask Him too often or for too much.

> *Now to him who is able to do immeasurably more than all we ask or imagine, according to his power that is at work within us, to him be glory in the church and in Christ Jesus throughout all generations, for ever and ever! Amen. (Eph. 3:20–21)*

> *He will not let your foot slip—he who watches over you will not slumber; indeed, he who watches over Israel will neither slumber nor sleep. (Ps. 121:3–4)*

ANXIETY

> *Do not be anxious about anything, but in everything, by prayer and petition, with thanksgiving, present your requests to God. And the peace of God, which transcends all understanding, will guard your hearts and your minds in Christ Jesus. (Phil. 4:6–7)*

Anxiety is sin. It is fear. Like all fear, it anticipates something that is going to happen or that might happen in the future. Like all sin, it is based upon a lie from the Enemy. To quote Mark Twain, "I have had many troubles in my life, most of which never happened."

Faith and hope are also feelings about the future. They anticipate good things. This is why Philippians says to forsake anxiety and present everything to God with thanksgiving. What will happen? The peace of God! What kind of peace? The kind that baffles our comprehension.

How do we start? Go back to verse 4:

Rejoice in the Lord always. I will say it again: Rejoice!

It is difficult to be anxious when we are busy rejoicing in the Lord and thanking Him. How do we rejoice? Read Philippians and 2 Corinthians.

Paul's Prayers

Paul's prayers are gradually making an impression on me. I have been conscious of them for sixty-three of my sixty-eight years as a Christian. Notice some of the phrases from his prayers in Ephesians 1:15–19, 3:14–18, Philippians 1:9–11, and Colossians 1:9–12:

- "His incomparably great power to us who believe"
- "that you may be filled to the measure of all the fullness of God"
- "that your love may abound more and more in knowledge and depth and insight"
- "that you may be pure and blameless until the day of Christ"

- "that you may please Him in every way, bearing fruit in every good work"
- "that the eyes of your heart may be enlightened"
- "the hope of His calling"
- "the riches of His glorious inheritance in the saints"
- "to know this love that surpasses knowledge"
- "that He may strengthen you with power through His Spirit in your inner being"
- "to fill you with the knowledge of His will through all spiritual wisdom and understanding"
- "that you may live a life worthy of the Lord"
- "that you may please Him in every way"
- "that you would bear fruit in every good work"

When Paul prayed for the saints, he prayed in superlatives. It seems too much to us to pray that way. God inspired these prayers. If that is true, then God would answer them, and if answered, the Colossian saints were indeed "filled with the knowledge of His will through all spiritual wisdom and understanding."

None of the things in these phrases are commands or suggestions. No one can *obey* them. The only way for them to happen is for *God* to do them, in answer to our prayers.

Pray for Fathers

Recently I was struck by the spiritual needs of three fathers in the New Testament and how Jesus Christ met their needs. The first was a nobleman whose son was at the point of death (Jn. 4). The second was the Philippian jailer who was about to take his own life because his jail had fallen apart (Acts 16). The third was Cornelius, a Roman army officer who was searching for God (Acts 10). All of their needs were urgent—

so urgent that each man sought help and got the help he wanted, and more, in a wonderful way.

Here is something extra that blessed me in reading these passages:

> *Then the father realized that this was the exact time at which Jesus had said to him, "Your son will live."* ***So he and all his household believed.*** *(Jn. 4:53)*

> *The jailer brought them into his house and set a meal before them;* ***he was filled with joy*** *because he had come to believe in God—**he and his whole family.** (Acts 16:34)*

> *He and all his family were devout and God-fearing; he gave generously to those in need and prayed to God regularly...The next day Peter started out with them, and some of the brothers from Joppa went along. The following day he arrived in Caesarea. Cornelius was expecting them and had* ***called together his relatives and close friends...*** *While Peter was still speaking these words,* ***the Holy Spirit came on all who heard the message.*** *(Acts 10:2, 24, 44)*

When the father found the answer, the whole family found the answer. If a wife and children are not doing well, it is very likely because the father is not urgently seeking God about his needs. Let us pray for fathers.

Pray for Workers

> *When he saw the crowds, he had compassion on them, because they were harassed and helpless,*

> *like sheep without a shepherd. Then he said to his disciples, "The harvest is plentiful but the workers are few. Ask the Lord of the harvest, therefore, to send out workers into his harvest field."* (Mt. 9:36–38)

A few words stand out to me:

- crowds
- compassion
- harassed and helpless
- plentiful harvest
- few workers
- ask the Lord

Some of us have seen the crowds, but with anger. Others have seen the crowds with compassion, but haven't seen the harvest. We see how few the workers are and despair. Let us ask the Lord for the workers. He will send them.

5

EVANGELISM

Then I preached Christ, and when she heard the story,—
Oh! is such triumph possible to men?
Hardly, my King, had I beheld Thy glory,
Hardly had known Thine excellence till then.

Then with a rush the intolerable craving
Shivers throughout me like a trumpet call,
Oh! to save these; to perish for their saving,
Die for their life; be offered for them all.

—F. W.H. Meyer [2]

But you, dear friends, build yourselves up in your most holy faith and pray in the Holy Spirit. Keep

2 From his poem "St. Paul"

> *yourselves in God's love as you wait for the mercy of our Lord Jesus Christ to bring you to eternal life. Be merciful to those who doubt; snatch others from the fire and save them; to others show mercy, mixed with fear hating even the clothing stained by corrupted flesh. (Jude 20–23)*

This book is a compilation of short teachings on the Christian life which apply to all Christians. This chapter on evangelism is also for *all* Christians.

The Commands

> *Then Jesus came to them and said, "All authority in heaven and on earth has been given to me. Therefore go and make disciples of all nations, baptizing them in the name of the Father and of the Son and of the Holy Spirit, and teaching them to obey everything I have commanded you. And surely I am with you always, to the very end of the age." (Mt. 28:18–20)*

There is a sequence to the commands laid out by Jesus in the Great Commission:

- Make disciples of all nations.
- Baptize them.
- Teach them to obey everything I have commanded you.

The disciples are to *obey everything*, which includes these three commands. They are to obey everything, which includes teaching their own disciples to obey everything. We are *all* converts of that initial command. Every one of us is to make disciples of all nations.

> *As you go, preach this message: "The kingdom of heaven is near." (Mt. 10:7)*

We are to make disciples *as we go*. The word for "as you go" in the Greek text is the same word as the "go" of "go and make disciples." We are to make disciples as we go. We are to preach as we go. It should be a normal part of our daily life. It is not just for pastors and full-time evangelists.

> *On that day a great persecution broke out against the church at Jerusalem, and* ***all except the apostles*** *were scattered throughout Judea and Samaria...Those who had been scattered* ***preached*** *the word wherever they went. (Acts 8:1, 4)*

Everyone *except* the apostles were scattered and preached as they went. This was thousands of people, perhaps tens of thousands.

> *Therefore, if anyone is in Christ, he is a new creation; the old has gone, the new has come! All this is from God, who reconciled us to himself through Christ and* ***gave us the ministry of reconciliation:*** *that God was reconciling the world to himself in Christ, not counting men's sins against them. And* ***he has committed to us the message of reconciliation. We are therefore Christ's ambassadors,*** *as though God were making his appeal through us. We implore you on Christ's behalf: Be reconciled to God. God made him who had no sin to be sin for us, so that in him we might become the righteousness of God. (2 Cor. 5:17–21)*

This passage is about "anyone who is in Christ." What does it say about them?

- They were given the ministry of reconciliation.
- They were given the message of reconciliation.
- They are Christ's ambassadors to speak to people on His behalf that they be reconciled to Him.

Examples

> *But some of them became obstinate; they refused to believe and publicly maligned the Way. So Paul left them. He took the disciples with him and had discussions daily in the lecture hall of Tyrannus. This went on for two years, so that all the Jews and Greeks who lived in the province of Asia heard the word of the Lord. (Acts 19:9–10)*

Paul did not travel through Asia. He taught daily in one place. The other six major churches in Asia were started by Paul's students.

> *You became imitators of us and of the Lord; in spite of severe suffering, you welcomed the message with the joy given by the Holy Spirit. And so you became a model to all the believers in Macedonia and Achaia. The Lord's message rang out from you not only in Macedonia and Achaia—your faith in God has become known everywhere. Therefore we do not need to say anything about it. (1 Thess. 1:6–8)*

Paul had only taught in Thessalonica for three Sabbath days before he was run out of town. All of Macedonia and Achaia got the message.

Every Christian

If we added up all of the apostles, pastors, evangelists, teachers, and missionaries through the centuries, their converts would not come close to the total number of saved people in heaven or on earth. The overwhelming majority of Christians received Christ through some Christian not called to full-time ministry.

The majority of pastors are not engaged in evangelism. They are ministering to Christians, and that is good. However, they are not teaching the Christians in their congregations to evangelize. They are not sending others into the harvest field. Those pastors who preach the gospel tell their congregants to bring sinners to church so that they can be evangelized. As far as the Great Commission is concerned, this is counter-productive. The Church is for the saved people, not the unsaved.

Christians are often intimidated by people who say, "Don't preach to me." Who made *them* the authority on what we should do? It is also easy to be intimidated by those who tell the laity that they are not qualified to preach. Obviously, the scattered thousands were qualified, and they were certainly not all ordained ministers. The gift of evangelism does not save people. It is the gospel that saves, *Jesus* who saves.

The One who has all authority told us to preach. To fulfill the Great Commission, every Christian must be involved. Jesus sent everyone to everyone. Let us encourage one another to do this. When done with the weapon of the fullness of the Holy Spirit, this preaching is effective in the winning of souls.

Opening Eyes

Today an increasing number of people believe that all religions are equally valid, that there is no one "right" source of revelation. This leads them to dismiss anything you tell them from the Bible. How do you approach someone who believes this in a way that will open the door to sharing the Word of God with them?

The unbeliever does not believe the Word of God. This is natural. Why does he not believe it? "Faith comes by hearing, and hearing by the Word of Christ" (Rom. 10:17). The Word is the only source of faith. Before he can believe it, he must hear it.

What the unbeliever wants or does not want to hear should not determine what you say. We get our orders from God, not from non-Christians. However, that does *not* mean we should force the Word on people. Before we give the gospel, their eyes must be opened so they can see its light:

> *I am sending you to them to open their eyes and turn them from darkness to light, and from the power of Satan to God, so that they may receive forgiveness of sins and a place among those who are sanctified by faith in me. (Acts 26:18)*

A method I have found effective is to give people a book that is not a direct declaration of the gospel. They are not likely to read a declaration. Give them one that they will not be able to put down. Here are a few suggestions:

- *Peace Child* by Don Richardson
- *And the Word Came with Power* by Joanne Shetler
- *In Search of the Source* by Neil Anderson

- *Through Gates of Splendor* by Elisabeth Elliot
- *To the Golden Shore* by Courtney Anderson
- *A Prisoner and Yet* by Corrie ten Boom

The unbeliever thinks he knows what Christians are. In reality, he does not know. By reading these books, he may realize that he does not know and may want to find out. Of course, *you* should read the books first.

Spiritually Discerned

> *The man without the Spirit does not accept the things that come from the Spirit of God, for they are foolishness to him, and he cannot understand them, because they are spiritually discerned.* (1 Cor. 2:14)

Not understanding God's Word is one of the clearest means of identifying someone as a non-Christian. We hesitate to make that identification, perhaps because it is not "politically correct" or because we do not want to be told not to judge. Even if we never state it, we should at least recognize that a man who lacks this kind of understanding is not a Christian.

In his preface to *Androcles and the Lion*, George Bernard Shaw admitted that he could not make any sense out of the New Testament unless he used a very select means of interpretation. He did not understand the things of the Spirit of God. Why? He did not have the Spirit of God. He was brilliant, but blind.

> *The God of this age has blinded the minds of unbelievers, so that they cannot see the light of the*

gospel of the glory of Christ, who is the image of God. (2 Cor. 4:4)

The Good News

Who were they who heard and rebelled? Were they not all those Moses led out of Egypt? (Heb. 3:16)

Therefore, since the promise of entering his rest still stands, let us be careful that none of you be found to have fallen short of it. For we also have had the gospel preached to us, just as they did; but the message they heard was of no value to them, because those who heard did not combine it with faith. Now we who have believed enter that rest, just as God has said, "So I declared an oath in my anger, 'They shall never enter my rest.'" And yet his work has been finished since the creation of the world. (Heb. 4:1–3)

For, "Everyone who calls on the name of the Lord will be saved." How, then, can they call on the one they have not believed in? And how can they believe in the one of whom they have not heard? And how can they hear without someone preaching to them? And how can they preach unless they are sent? As it is written, "How beautiful are the feet of those who bring good news!" But not all the Israelites accepted the good news. For Isaiah says, "Lord, who has believed our message?" Consequently, faith comes from hearing the message, and the message is heard through the word of Christ. (Rom. 10:13–17)

Faith is caused by hearing Christ preached. It is not automatic, though. It is possible to hear and learn, hear and rebel, or hear and not combine learning with faith.

There are many who *cannot* believe because they have not heard the gospel. There are some who *can* believe because they have heard the gospel, but they refuse to learn, refuse to combine their hearing with faith, or refuse to repent. The majority of unbelievers are not in this category. The majority of the lost cannot believe because they have not yet heard the good news.

Who Will Enter the Kingdom?

> *When one of those at the table with Him heard this, he said to Jesus, "Blessed is the man who will eat at the feast in the kingdom of God." Jesus replied: "A certain man was preparing a great banquet and invited many guests. At the time of the banquet he sent his servant to tell those who had been invited, 'Come, for everything is now ready.' But they all alike began to make excuses. The first said, 'I have just bought a field, and I must go and see it. Please excuse me.' Another said, 'I have just bought five yoke of oxen, and I'm on my way to try them out. Please excuse me.' Still another said, 'I just got married, so I can't come.' The servant came back and reported this to his master. Then the owner of the house became angry and ordered his servant, 'Go out quickly into the streets and alleys of the town and bring in the poor, the crippled, the blind and the lame.' 'Sir,' the servant said, 'what you ordered has been done, but there is still room.' Then the master told his servant,*

'Go out to the roads and country lanes and make them come in, so that my house will be full. I tell you, not one of those men who were invited will get a taste of my banquet.'" (Lk. 14:15–24)

There are three stages of invitation to the great supper. The first is the formal invitation to people who are used to attending great suppers. They are wealthy. They are not hungry, and they make excuses. The second invitation is to the helpless and to the people in extreme poverty. There is no danger that they will refuse—they are hungry. The third invitation is to everyone else. These people were not invited; they were compelled to come.

The first invitation to the kingdom of God was to people who had other priorities and thought they had no need of this feast. The second group was in need, knew it, and had no other priorities. The third may or may not have known their need, but it made no difference. The important thing was that the house be filled. They were forced to come to the dinner.

I believe this process is going on in every generation in every nation. The first group in Jesus' time was the Jewish people:

He came to that which was His own, but His own did not receive Him. (Jn. 1:11)

For I am not ashamed of the gospel, because it is the power of God for the salvation of everyone who believes: first for the Jew, then for the Gentile. (Rom. 1:16)

Then Paul and Barnabas answered them boldly: "We had to speak the word of God to you first. Since you reject it and do not consider yourselves

> *worthy of eternal life, we now turn to the Gentiles." (Acts 13:46)*

Today the first group might still be the Jews, or it might be those who have grown up in Christian families or Christian churches but who are not saved.

The second group is the Gentiles who are destitute and know it. This group is normally glad to hear the good news. They are the prisoners, the orphans, the widows, the alcoholics, the foreigners in the land, and people outside the normal hearing of the gospel, like tribes in remote parts of the world.

I do not know what to think of the third group. It may be all or some of those not previously invited. How God will coerce them to come in, I do not know. That He will is certain.

How does this pertain to us? We are charged with doing the inviting.

> *In the past God overlooked such ignorance, but* ***now He commands all people everywhere to repent.*** *For He has set a day when He will judge the world with justice by the man He has appointed. He has given proof of this to all men by raising Him from the dead. (Acts 17:30–31)*

> ***We are therefore Christ's ambassadors, as though God were making His appeal through us.*** *We implore you on Christ's behalf: Be reconciled to God. God made Him who had no sin to be sin for us, so that in Him we might become the righteousness of God. (2 Cor. 5:20–21)*

Our Freedom

Part of the freedom man has received from the Lord is having the ability to refuse to listen to Him. Man has exercised this freedom many times.

> ***But they refused to hearken,*** *and pulled away the shoulder, and stopped their ears, that they should not hear. Yea, they made their hearts as an adamant stone, lest they should hear the law, and the words which the LORD of hosts hath sent in his spirit by the former prophets: therefore came a great wrath from the LORD of hosts. (Zech. 7:11–12 KJV)*

But God has the same kind of freedom:

> ***Therefore*** *it is come to pass, [that] as he cried, and they would not hear; so they cried, and* ***I would not hear, saith the LORD of hosts.*** *(Zech. 7:13 KJV)*

This is a dreadful statement. God had also said He would not listen one and two hundred years earlier in Jeremiah 11:11 and Isaiah 1:15. There is something He will listen to, though—a prayer of repentance. But repentance is more than just saying, "I'm sorry." It is a change of heart, mind, and actions. Look at the conditions for repentance in Isaiah 1:16–18:

> *Wash you, make you clean; put away the evil of your doings from before mine eyes; cease to do evil; learn to do well; seek judgment, relieve the oppressed, judge the fatherless, plead for the widow. Come now, and let us reason together, saith the LORD: though your sins be as scarlet, they shall be as white*

as snow; though they be red like crimson, they shall be as wool. (KJV)

Justice or Vengeance?

You have heard that it was said, "Eye for eye, and tooth for tooth." But I tell you, Do not resist an evil person. If someone strikes you on the right cheek, turn to him the other also. And if someone wants to sue you and take your tunic, let him have your cloak as well. If someone forces you to go one mile, go with him two miles. Give to the one who asks you, and do not turn away from the one who wants to borrow from you. (Mt. 5:38–42)

Jesus quoted "Eye for eye and tooth for tooth" as "it was said." It was said as a justification for vengeance and retaliation. Jesus countermanded this saying. But wasn't it a quotation from the Old Testament? Yes it was, but it is not to the Old Testament passage that Jesus was referring. If it were, He would not have said, "You have heard that it was *said*." He would have said, "It is *written*," and He would not have disagreed with the Scripture. Jesus was disavowing the *misquotation* of this Scripture by people who wished to excuse vengeance. Here is the full paragraph from Exodus 21:

If men who are fighting hit a pregnant woman and she gives birth prematurely but there is no serious injury, the offender must be fined whatever the woman's husband demands and the court allows. But if there is serious injury, you are to take life for life, eye for eye, tooth for tooth, hand for hand, foot for foot, burn for burn, wound for wound, bruise for bruise. (Exod. 21:22–25)

This law covers two kinds of premature birth when a pregnant woman is injured during a fight between men. The first kind is where the baby (or the woman) is not seriously injured. In that case, the man who caused the injury is fined by two standards: 1) what the husband demands, and 2) what the court allows. It is a civil suit. The court might or might not allow what the husband demands. It is a *court* decision, not personal vengeance.

This second kind is where serious injury is inflicted on the baby or the woman. This is a criminal offense. The court is to assign specific penalties to the guilty party. What are they? "You are to take life for life, eye or eye, tooth for tooth, hand for hand, foot or foot, burn for burn, wound for wound, bruise for bruise." This was instituted by God through Moses at the same time that He gave the Ten Commandments. This is *just* law. It does not require a "life or a hand" or a "life for a bruise." It requires "life for a life" and a "bruise for a bruise." It does not punish too harshly, nor does it allow for the person who inflicted the injury to go unpunished. It is neither severe nor lenient; it is just.

Jesus was not speaking to this law in Matthew 5. He was speaking to the out-of-context quotation of the law. Three other Scriptures verify that the Bible does not allow vengeance:

1. God provided six cities of refuge for the Israelites to protect people from avengers.
2. Do not repay anyone evil for evil. (Rom. 12:17)
3. Do not take revenge, my friends, but leave room for

> God's wrath, for it is written, "It is mine to avenge; I will repay" says the Lord. (Rom. 12:19)

The teaching from the Sermon on the Mount is not a change of God's mind. The Old Testament passage was a teaching on justice. Here Jesus taught on personal responses to evil directed at you. Your personal response is different from justice.

What Is the Teaching?

The teaching is self-evident, if we do not enter the text with questions like, "Where do we draw the line?" Since that question is not answered in the text, assume there is no line. Jesus did not qualify His teaching.

Let's break the text down. The basic sentence is, "Do not resist an evil person" (v. 39). The examples which follow assume the other person is evil. He intends harm, theft, or mischief, with evil motives—gain to him and harm or loss to you.

1. *"If someone strikes you on the right cheek turn to him the other also" (v. 39).* My father taught me to fight back, and yet he tried to keep me out of fights. In the eighth and ninth grades, I was in five serious fistfights, and another one in the eleventh grade. I did not know Jesus' teaching, but if I had I would not have taken it seriously. My view of honor, pride, courage, and masculinity, and the peer pressure I was under all forbade turning the other cheek. However, Jesus was speaking about an actual evil person really hitting you on the right cheek and you really turning the left cheek to him so he could hit that one, too.

2. *"If someone wants to sue you and take your tunic, let him have your cloak as well" (v. 40).* An evil person wants to sue you. You are to voluntarily settle out of court, give him your shirt, and throw in your coat. This is not "one of your shirts" and "one of your coats." It is your shirt (singular) and your coat (singular). It is probably all the clothing you have.
3. *"If someone forces you to go one mile, go with him two miles" (v. 41).* This force is at sword, spear, or gunpoint. The man is evil. The second mile is a free gift to him. The first cheek, the first article of clothing, and the first mile are all taken by force. The second cheek, the second piece of clothing, and the second mile are gifts to the evil person.
4. *"Give to the one who asks you" (v. 42).*
5. *"Do not turn away from the one who wants to borrow from you" (v. 42).*

Over the years I have listened to many "what ifs" regarding these last two. Most of them are based upon the notion that the other person might not return the money. Of course he won't! That is a given. The person is *evil.* People who want to draw a line on this teaching draw it where nothing gets obeyed.

Why the Teaching?

Why does Jesus teach this? The passage gives no hint as to why. If you want a reason before you will be willing to obey, 1 Corinthians gives a clue:

> *Though I am free and belong to no man, I make myself a slave to everyone, to win as many as possible. (1 Cor. 9:19)*

There is no force involved here. Paul is absolutely free. So what does he do? He uses his freedom to lose his freedom. He puts himself under voluntary servitude. Why? To win as many as possible. It was Paul's method of evangelism. I believe Paul (and Peter) learned this from Jesus:

> *To this you were called, because Christ suffered for you, leaving you an example, that you should follow in his steps. "He committed no sin, and no deceit was found in his mouth." When they hurled their insults at him, he did not retaliate; when he suffered, he made no threats. Instead, he entrusted himself to him who judges justly. He himself bore our sins in his body on the tree, so that we might die to sins and live for righteousness; by his wounds you have been healed. (1 Pet. 2:21–24)*

This comes immediately after Peter's teaching on how Christian slaves should behave and immediately before his teaching to wives on how to win their husbands. The Cross is the way of salvation. Jesus' death on the cross was forced by others, but was also *voluntary*. We should not proclaim the cross in a different manner than the one Jesus had when He went to the cross. "*To this you were called, because Christ suffered for you, that you should follow in his steps*" (1 Pet. 2:21).

Paul was imitating Jesus. In 1 Cor. 10:32–11:1 he says to us,

> *Do not cause anyone to stumble, whether Jews, Greeks or the church of God— even as I try to please everybody in every way. For I am not seeking my own good but the good of many, so that they may be saved.*

> *Follow my example, as I follow the example of Christ.*

One reason for Jesus' teaching to not resist an evil person is to *win* him to Christ. Kindness leads people to repentance (Rom. 2:4).

Our experience may not make us sure that this works, because not many Christians obey this command. However, we have many examples of people not obeying it, and we know experientially that resisting evil people does not win them for Christ. We should base our decision to obey on Jesus' command and on His example and Paul's example.

Love & Peace

> *But the fruit of the Spirit is love, joy, peace... (Gal. 5:22a)*

Love and peace are words which indicate things of indescribable value and quality. Today these words are used as synonyms for temporal, physical events such as sexual relationships and the absence of war.

I can think of two other words which are not as unlimited in meaning but where there has been no attempt to change the meaning. They are largely ignored. This is a time of violent expression and polarization of peoples, nations, and opinions. Even Christians find themselves choosing up sides and thereby refusing to use these words and to practice what they stand for.

The words are "gentle" and "kind." Ephesians 4:31–32 says,

> *Let all bitterness and wrath and anger, and clamor and evil speaking be put away from you with all malice: And be ye kind one to another, tenderhearted, forgiving one another, even as God for Christ's sake*

hath forgiven you.

Wrath, anger, clamor, and evil speaking are motivated by malice and bitterness. This is a perfect description of a great part of the world today. The forgiveness in verse 32 is motivated by and expressed with kindness and tenderheartedness. This is the kind of forgiveness we have received in Christ. Much of what people call "forgiveness" today is shallow and unreal.

As the opposition to the gospel becomes more violent, the temptation is to "fight fire with fire." In our desire to witness for Jesus Christ we may sound harsh and we may argue with heat. Such behavior contradicts 2 Timothy 2:23:

> *But stay away from foolish and ignorant arguments; you know that they end up in quarrels. The Lord's servant must not quarrel. He must be* ***kind*** *toward all, a good and patient teacher, who is* ***gentle*** *as he corrects his opponents.*

In times like this, recognize the temptation for what it is—a temptation. Do not quarrel. Be kind and gentle. When the disciples were not received by a village in Samaria and James and John wanted to call down fire from heaven to consume them, Jesus rebuked them with these words: "*Ye know not what manner of Spirit ye are of*" (Lk. 9:54). Isn't this a good reminder to us today? Are we Christians as easily recognized by our *manner* as by our message? This is a day of confrontation, and we must recognize that violence, evil speaking (which includes sarcasm), and putting down our opponents are not becoming to Christians.

How do we sound at business meetings? The grocery store? Neighborhood discussions? The family dinner table?

Do we *sound* like Christians? James wrote in his letter,

> *But if ye have bitter envying and strife in your hearts, glory not and lie not against the truth. This wisdom descendeth not from above, but is earthly, sensual, devilish. For where envying and strife is, there is confusion and every evil work. But the wisdom that is from above is first pure, then peaceable, gentle and easy to be entreated, full of mercy and good fruits, without partiality and without hypocrisy. (Jas. 3:14–17 KJV)*

Paul made this the basis of his entreaty to the church at Corinth when he wrote, "*I, Paul, myself entreat you, by the meekness and gentleness of Christ*" (2 Cor. 10:1). To the believers at Thessalonica he could say that his actions were "*gentle among you, like a nurse taking care of her children*" (1 Thess. 2:7).

May we remind ourselves that this gentleness and kindness comes from one Source alone:

> *Come to me, all who labor and are heavy laden, and I will give you rest. Take my yoke upon you, and learn from Me; for I am gentle and lowly in heart, and you will find rest for your souls. For my yoke is easy, and my burden is light. (Mt. 11:28–30)*

Revival

The Christian Church has been blessed with several revivals in recent history:

1. The East African Revival of the 1930s, '40s, and '50s. See Roy Hession's *The Calvary Road*, Norman

Grubb's *Continuous Revival*, and Festo Kivengere's *Revolutionary Love*.

2. The Welsh Revival very early in the 20th century, where tens of thousands were converted in a few weeks. See Jessie Penn-Lewis' *The Awakening in Wales*.
3. The Korean Revival and the North China Revival, also early in the 20th century. See *When the Spirit's Fire Swept Korea* by Jonathan Goforth.
4. The Great Awakening in the middle of the 18th century and the Second Great Awakening in the middle of the 19th century. These two hit England, Scotland, Wales, the Colonies, and the United States.

The United States did not experience anything in the 20th century that could remotely be called revival. We had two World Wars and the ascendancy of liberalism in the Church, but Europe took most of the damage in both.

The nations that did have revivals also experienced other things by the middle of the century: genocide (e.g., in Rwanda), communism in China and North Korea, and a very dead secular community in Wales.

Each century has four or five generations in it, and each one of us knows a portion of the two generations before us and the two after us.

> *But as for me, I will always have hope; I will praise you more and more. My mouth will tell of your righteousness, of your salvation all day long, though I know not its measure. I will come and proclaim your mighty acts, O Sovereign Lord; I will proclaim your righteousness, yours alone. Since my youth, O God, you have taught me, and to this day I declare*

> *your marvelous deeds. Even when I am old and gray, do not forsake me, O God, till I declare your power to the next generation, your might to all who are to come. (Ps. 71:14–18)*

This is next-generation evangelism.

> *You shall not make for yourself an idol in the form of anything in heaven above or on the earth beneath or in the waters below. You shall not bow down to them or worship them; for I, the Lord your God, am a jealous God, punishing the children for the sins of the fathers to the third and fourth generation of those who hate me, but* ***showing love to a thousand generations*** *of those who love me and keep my commandments. (Deut. 5:8)*

Loving and obeying God is good for a thousand generations. Loving God, obeying Him, and proclaiming His righteousness are the primary means of having continuous revival. Christians confessing sin is the secondary means.

The enemy always counter-attacks after successful evangelism. In the book of Acts there were violent reactions in Jerusalem (Acts 7–9), Damascus (Acts 9), Antioch (Acts 13), Iconium (Acts 14), Lystra (Acts 14), Philippi (Acts 16), and Thessalonica (Acts 17).

The Spring of Living Water

> *My people have committed two sins: They have forsaken me, the spring of living water, and have dug their own cisterns, broken cisterns that cannot hold water. (Jer. 2:13)*

Do you see the difference between these two sins? The first is forsaking an artesian well, a flowing spring of life-giving water. There is no end to the supply. God is this life-giving spring. To forsake Him is both evil and foolish.

The second sin has to do with recognizing the need for water, but trying to get it from a cistern. The sin is digging the cistern. It is salvation by effort. Digging a cistern does not provide water to fill it. Even if water came, it would be stagnant. There is another problem, too: it is a leaky cistern. Soon there will be no water, not even stagnant water. Digging this cistern is a foolish attempt at creating your own salvation. It does not provide life.

> *Jesus answered, "Everyone who drinks this water will be thirsty again, but whoever drinks the water I give him will never thirst. Indeed, the water I give him will become in him a spring of water welling up to eternal life." (Jn. 4:13–14)*

6

LITERATURE EVANGELISM

Our Primary Source

Of making many books there is no end. (Ecclesiastes 12:12)

A recent article in a secular business journal reported that the Christian literature industry is booming. The market has grown so much that leading secular publishing houses are now printing Christian books, and those books are even finding their way onto the supermarket racks.

We should rejoice that Christian literature is being so widely circulated, yet at the same time we ought to pray that biblical standards be maintained in the expanding market.

A serious temptation accompanies the widespread availability of Christian books, and those of us involved in literature ministry are particularly susceptible. Because so many books have been written about a multitude of subjects, it is far too easy to turn to a Christian book before opening the Bible. Books written by Christians are profitable only when they are approached as a *supplementary* source of guidance. True godliness is cultivated in those who labor in the Scriptures, for there we find the Lord's counsel (2 Tim. 2:15, 3:15–17).

Luke commended the saints in Berea who measured the teaching of Paul and Silas against the Word of God:

> *Now the Bereans were of more noble character than the Thessalonians, for they received the message with great eagerness and examined the Scriptures every day to see if what Paul said was true. (Acts 17:11)*

The Bereans are a good example to all of us who desire to pattern our lives according to God's will.

Book Flow

Books are inanimate. However, they are written by living people. They are also read by people, published by people, sold by people, loaned by people, given by people, and most of them are about people. When they are being read, books are very much alive. They are like the telephone wires in a phone conversation—not living, but carrying life. Books on shelves, whether in homes, stores, or libraries, are dead things. The communication is there, but no one is listening.

There are ways to bring these dead books to life.

1. *Read them.* There are many good books that I have refused to read because of prejudice or have delayed reading because I was not in the mood, and then

eventually read. In each instance I remember I was greatly blessed and sorry that I had not read them sooner.

2. *Recommend them to many other people.*
3. *Give books to others.* If a book is good and there are several people you really want to read it, you may need to purchase copies for them yourself.
4. *Loan someone your copy.* If you want it back, keep a record of the person and the title you loaned. Do not count on their character or competence of memory to get it back to you. I do not keep a record of the books I loan, but I don't know where they are, either. Most books I just give away.
5. *Sell the books.* Find a used-book seller or have a yard sale.

Money moves in a healthy economy. Books move in a healthy book economy. The first is called cash flow, so let's call the second book flow. Cash flow means that many people use the same dollar over and over again. Book flow means that many people use the same book over and over again. Money in the bank may be relatively stagnant, but it does collect interest while it's there. Books on the shelf only collect dust.

Recently I finished reading a biography of a man who died in India in 1857. It was a wonderful account. The book was published in 1869, and I bought it at a secondhand bookstore. Many of the pages were still attached to each other because it had never been read. It had remained dead for more than 130 years.

How is your book flow? Here is a suggestion: go through your books and pick out the ones that have helped you but that you are sure you will not read again. Keep at least one in your car at all times to give to your doctor, barber, hairdresser, neighbor, or friend. Watch what happens.

Biography

The most effective teaching is by example and imitation. That is how we learned our native language. It is how we learned to do good things and bad things. Example and imitation are also God's means of conforming us to the image of his Son:

> *To this you were called, because Christ suffered for you, leaving you an* ***example****, that you should follow in his steps. (1 Pet. 2:21)*

> ***Be imitators of God****, therefore, as dearly loved children. (Eph. 5:1)*

> ***Follow my example****, as I follow the* ***example*** *of Christ. (1 Cor. 11:1)*

> *Remember your leaders, who spoke the word of God to you. Consider the outcome of their way of life and* ***imitate their faith****. (Heb. 13:7)*

Find a person who follows the example of Christ and then follow his example. You have considered the outcome of his way of life, and now you can imitate his faith.

There are not that many good examples, and you may not be near enough to imitate the ones there are. This was Paul's solution for the Corinthians who had the same problem:

> *Even though you have ten thousand guardians in Christ, you do not have many fathers, for in Christ Jesus I became your father through the gospel.*

> *Therefore I urge you to* ***imitate me.*** *For this reason I am sending to you* ***Timothy,*** *my son whom I love, who is faithful in the Lord. He* ***will remind you of my way of life*** *in Christ Jesus, which agrees with what I teach everywhere in every church. (1 Cor. 4:15–17)*

Paul followed the example of Christ. Timothy followed Paul's example. The Corinthians followed Timothy.

We can do like the Corinthians and follow examples of examples, or we can follow people who are already in Heaven. That is why Hebrews 11 was written.

My life has been greatly influenced by other people. Some of them I could not have known because they lived in another age. Some of them were my ancestors, but some were not related to me at all. Their influence came to me through books. God must have thought that biography was a good way of communicating truth, because He uses it abundantly in the Bible: the lives of Abraham, Noah, Moses, David, Jesus, and Paul are just of few. These biographies are abbreviated, but they are loaded with truth. I remember Bill Pape (author of *The Lordship of Jesus Christ*) saying years ago that God crammed the Creation, the Fall, the Flood, and hundreds of years of history into just eleven chapters, as if he were in a hurry to tell us about Abraham. Then He spent thirty-nine chapters telling us about Abraham, Isaac, Jacob, and Joseph.

Biography is important. It takes truth out of the abstract and puts it into a practical, observable form. Then we can see that the truth can be lived and *how* it has been lived by people not a lot different from ourselves.

Some of the best biographies were not authored by good writers, so they are not great literature. But they are about men and women who loved and obeyed God. With such books, the *person* holds my attention, not the author or the writing itself. A few of the people who have influenced my life are George Müller, James Fraser, Amy Carmichael, William Carey, Hudson Taylor, Jim Elliot, Henry Martyn, Adoniram Judson, William Tyndale, and Corrie ten Boom.

What do these people have in common? They were all more interested in pleasing God than they were in conforming to the evangelical church (including the more dedicated evangelicals). They were all "cross-cultural" missionaries. They were all people of prayer, the Word, and obedience. Fraser, Martyn, Carey, Tyndale, and Judson all translated the New Testament into other languages. Tyndale and Elliot were killed for their faith; Martyn and Judson suffered much.

I would encourage you to read biographies of people who obeyed God. If you are interested in ones I have mentioned, here are a few of the books about them:

- Books written by Corrie ten Boom about her life: *A Prisoner and Yet* (Christian Literature Crusade), *Amazing Love* (CLC), *Not Good if Detached* (CLC), *The Hiding Place* (Spire), and *Tramp for the Lord* (Revell).
- Books about Jim Elliot by his wife Elisabeth: *Journals of Jim Elliot* (Revell), *Shadow of the Almighty* (Harper & Row), and *Through Gates of Splendor* (Tyndale).
- James Fraser: *Behind the Ranges* by Geraldine Taylor (Moody Press), *Mountain Rain* by Eileen Crossman (Overseas Missionary Fellowship), and *Prayer of Faith* by James Fraser (OMF).
- Hudson Taylor: *Hudson Taylor's Spiritual Secret* by Howard Taylor (Moody Press) and *Hudson Taylor*

by J.H. Hudson (Bethany).

- George Müller: *George Müller of Bristol* by A.T. Pierson (Revell) and *George Müller, Delighted in God* by Roger Steer (Harold Shaw Press).
- William Tyndale: *God's Outlaw—The Story of William Tyndale* by B. Edwards (Presbyterian & Reformed Publishing Company).
- Adoniram Judson: *To the Golden Shore* by Courtney Anderson (Judson Press).

This is only a brief list. There are many more worthy biographies available.

As you read about the lives of famous Christians, consider these things:

- An autobiography will be closest to the truth, but may leave out embarrassing things or major failures.
- Autobiographies that are co-authored will not be as close to the truth, because the co-author may embroider to make the book more readable.
- Biographies written by another person after the subject has died may be biased to make the person too much of a hero.

Biographies are not inspired, but they can be useful in helping us make right decisions that we otherwise might avoid.

Book Publishing

The Bible speaks of the sins of whole nations in many places. Here is one of them:

This is what the Lord says: For three sins of Israel, even for four, I will not turn back my wrath... (Amos 2:6)

Scripture also speaks of the sins of cities (e.g., Amos 1:3, 6). Jesus spoke of judgment on Chorazin and Bethsaida in Matthew 11:21 and of possible judgment on five of the seven churches in Asia in Revelation 2 and 3. The collective sins of the people brought about these judgments. The people of the Church today are not known for confessing their sins. We are even less known for confessing the sins of the whole church or city or nation as Daniel did in Daniel 9. As far as we know, Daniel was not personally guilty of the sins he confessed.

In our ministry we read books, and we also distribute them by loaning, giving, and selling. However, our object is not to distribute books. The distribution is only a means to an end. Here is the end we have in mind:

We proclaim him, admonishing and teaching everyone with all wisdom, so that we may present everyone perfect in Christ. To this end I labor, struggling with all his energy, which so powerfully works in me. (Col. 1:28–29)

Our goal is to present everyone perfect in Christ. To achieve this end, we should distribute books that

1. Proclaim Him
2. Admonish everyone with all wisdom
3. Teach everyone with all wisdom

This kind of book is increasingly difficult to find. When I began working in the literature ministry in 1958, there were about six thousand Christian books in print in English. Now there are about six million.[3] Thirty years ago, the covers of the books were terrible and the content was good. Today the covers are beautiful and the content is terrible.

Why is the percentage of good books far less than it was thirty years ago? I suggest seven reasons:

1. We publish what sells. We publish what Christians *want*, not what they need. Paul writes in 2 Timothy 4:3:

   For the time will come when men will not put up with sound doctrine. Instead, to suit their own desires, they will gather around them a great number of teachers to say what their itching ears want to hear.

   This is an example of supply and demand at work in the church. Readers demand teachers who give them what they want, and the demand is met. A great number of publishers are willing to "gather around them" and print what their itching ears want to hear. The Christian literature industry is following consumer fads instead of offering solid biblical content.

   We are tossed back and forth by the waves, and blown here and there by every wind of teaching and by the cunning and craftiness of men in their deceitful scheming. (Eph. 4:14)

   The quality of the books that follow each surge of demand is often inversely proportional to the quantity published.

3 Statistic obtained from the Center for the Study of Global Christianity, Gordon-Conwell Theological Seminary (2006).

These books sell until there is a new demand. People eat them up, but the church does not increase in godliness with this kind of consumption.

There is not such a demand for biblical teaching on the gospel, on holiness, prayer, obedience, or evangelism. Because there is little demand, there is little supply. However, the need is there.

Then Jesus came to them and said, "All authority in heaven and on earth has been given to me. Therefore go and make disciples of all nations, baptizing them in the name of the Father and of the Son and of the Holy Spirit, and teaching them to obey everything I have commanded you." (Mt. 28:18-20a)

God has commanded us to preach Christ and teach obedience to His commands. We should supply and distribute according to what is *needed* and what is *commanded*, not according to what sells best.

Writers, publishers, booksellers, and readers all respond to reader fads. The books that start these fads may not be bad. They might simply hit a chord in the reading public, and books in that line will sell until the public is tired of them. The first book I remember this happening with was *Through Gates of Splendor* by Elisabeth Elliot. It was followed by many good missionary biographies. After this short period came years where it was like pulling teeth to get Christians to read a missionary book. Hal Lindsey's *The Late Great Planet Earth* was followed by truckloads of exciting eschatology. *The Christian Family* started a trend that saturated Christian bookstores with volumes on the Christian family.

With one or two exception of the missionary biographies and one or two others, all of the books in the fads I mentioned have one common denominator: they are *exciting*. Even the self-help books have examples of awful situations that keep the reader hooked. Another common trait is that these books may not be solidly backed by Scripture, even though they include enough references to keep the reader assured that each book is acceptably evangelical..[4]

2. Our books reflect the culture they come from. They are written *in* an evangelical culture *to* an evangelical culture. What is the problem with this? The evangelical culture is copying the world's culture, although it is five or ten years behind. We copy the world's psychology, its language (by downplaying sin with words like "gay," "affair," and "lifestyle"), its music, and its tolerance. We are supposed to set an example for the world, not reflect it.

   You are the salt of the earth. But if the salt loses its saltiness, how can it be made salty again? It is no longer good for anything, except to be thrown out and trampled underfoot. You are the light of the world. A town built on a hill cannot be hidden. Neither do people light a lamp and put it under a bowl. Instead they put it on its stand, and it gives light to everyone

4 I recognize that these comments do not apply across the board, but I could make my case with the majority of them.

in the house. In the same way, let your light shine before others, that they may see your good deeds and glorify your Father in heaven. (Mt. 5:13–16)

We are meant to be prophetic voices to the church and the world. Instead, we write worldly, cultural books, not biblical books.

3. Many authors are not qualified to teach, and their readers are not people of the Book. They have not saturated themselves with Scripture. They do not think in Scriptures. Christian readers do not know the Bible well enough to know what the authors are writing about. Several best-selling Christian authors have committed adultery, and/or been divorced and remarried. This is not a judgment on the people involved; it is a judgment on *us* for looking the other way.

4. Our object has not been to change the world; it has been to make a living or a name for ourselves. Is it legitimate to make a living? Yes, but we cannot have two primary objectives. If our primary objective is to change the world with the gospel, making a living will be secondary. If making money is primary, changing the world will be secondary. We should always seek first the kingdom of God.

5. We are not willing to give a book to someone who needs it, much less give away millions of books.

6. We are afraid that strong teaching on basic subjects like sin, death, hell, judgment, faith, grace, Scripture, salvation,

and holiness will turn people off. We ignore these truths or find "gentle" synonyms for them.

7. Generally speaking, Christian publishers lack integrity. My wife and I commented to a famous Christian once that a certain biography written with a co-author was not the same as the original autobiography. Facts had been changed. Did this Christian know it? Yes, he knew, but he believed that the changes were alright because they would bring glory to God.

   On another occasion, I wrote to a publisher regarding thirteen factual errors in two magazine articles. I received a very kind reply saying that they were very seldom sent such gracious letters of correction. They agreed with my recognition that the articles were written for the glory of God and thus concluded that corrections were unnecessary. Lying does not bring glory to God, even if the lies are "nice" ones.

   In the music industry, promoters play up the artist with floor displays, life-size posters, etc. Fans want the posters and other advertising material along with the product. Just like the world, the Christian public is always looking someone to adulate, and publishers know this. Authors are set up as examples for us whether they are biblically qualified or not.

Please pray for a change in writing, publishing, distributing, and reading books.

The Cultured and the Ignorant

> *I have a duty to both the Greek and the Barbarian, to both the cultured and the ignorant. And so, for my part, I am ready to tell the Good News to you also who are in Rome. For I am not ashamed of the Good News; it is the power of God which brings Salvation to everyone who believes in Christ, to the Jew first, but also to the Greek. For in it there is a revelation of the Divine Righteousness resulting from faith and leading on to faith; as Scripture says—"Through faith the righteous man shall find Life." (Rom. 1:14–17 20th Century NT)*

We may not think in terms of Greeks and barbarians today, but we can think in terms of the cultured and the ignorant. They are our mission field. We have three locations in university towns where the culture is relatively high, but our ministry is to both the cultured and the ignorant. Our stores are places of love and understanding. Because of this, they draw people who need to be loved. This includes people who are slow in learning and people who can't or don't read, as well as those who are highly educated.

This may surprise you, but many university students do not read. The have grown up on televisions, computers, and iPods. The distraction of technology now replaces time for reading. Recently I was talking to a married woman with grown children who is a first-year law student with a very high GPA. She had never heard of *Pilgrim's Progress* or its author, John Bunyan. I gave her a copy.

We need to love all kinds of people and teach them to read, motivate them to read, read to them, and provide books for them.

7

OBEDIENCE

God's Grace & Our Faith

God's grace is wonderful. The Bible calls it "lavish," "overflowing," and "abundant." It saves and forgives and gives us strength, power, and boldness to obey. God gives it in great quantities for our needs, whatever they are, and it is always sufficient for those needs.

If you look for the word "grace" in the Bible, you will find expressions like these:

> *Now Stephen, a man* ***full of God's grace*** *and power, did great wonders and miraculous signs among the people. (Acts 6:8)*

> *When the congregation was dismissed, many of the Jews and devout converts to Judaism followed Paul*

> *and Barnabas, who talked with them and urged them to* ***continue in the grace of God.*** *(Acts 13:43)*

> ***Grace and peace*** *to you from God our Father and the Lord Jesus Christ. (1 Cor. 1:3)*

Grace belongs to God, and He gives it to us.

Now do the same search with the word "faith."

> *For this reason, ever since I heard about your* ***faith in the Lord Jesus*** *and your love for all the saints... (Eph. 1:15)*

> *I have declared to both Jews and Greeks that they must turn to God in repentance and have* ***faith in our Lord Jesus.*** *(Acts 20:21)*

> *So keep up your courage, men, for I have* ***faith in God*** *that it will happen just as he told me. (Acts 27:25)*

Faith belongs to man. It is also a gift from God, and it is to be placed in Him.

Here are two verses to meditate on:

> *Therefore, since we have been* ***justified through faith,*** *we have peace with God through our Lord Jesus Christ, through whom we have gained* ***access by faith into this grace*** *in which we now stand. (Rom. 5:1-2a)*

> *When Apollos wanted to go to Achaia, the brothers encouraged him and wrote to the disciples there to welcome him. On arriving, he was a great help to* ***those who by grace had believed.*** *(Acts 18:27)*

GRACE & FAITH 1

Unlike grace, we do not need faith in quantity. Jesus used quantitative terms when speaking of faith, but notice how He used them:

> *Immediately Jesus reached out his hand and caught him. "You of* ***little faith,*** *he said, "why did you doubt?" (Mt. 14:31)*

Jesus equates "little faith" to doubt:

> *But when he asks, he must believe and not doubt, because he who* ***doubts*** *is like a wave of the sea, blown and tossed by the wind. (Jas. 1:6)*

> *But the man who has* ***doubts*** *is condemned if he eats, because his eating is not from* ***faith****; and everything that does not come from faith is sin. (Rom. 14:23)*

Jesus also used the word "small" to describe faith:

> *Then the disciples came to Jesus in private and asked, "Why couldn't we drive it out?" He replied, "Because you have so* ***little*** *faith. I tell you the truth, if you have faith as* ***small*** *as a mustard seed, you can say to this mountain, 'Move from here to there' and it will move. Nothing will be impossible for you." (Mt. 17:19–20)*

With *little* faith nothing happens. With *small* faith, great things happen.

Jesus had another word for the faith of the Canaanite woman whose daughter was demon-possessed:

> *Then Jesus answered, "Woman, you have* ***great faith!*** *Your request is granted." And her daughter was healed from that very hour. (Mt. 15:28)*

"Great" was an expression of the reality and strength of her faith, not the quantity of it.

> *The apostles said to the Lord, "Increase our faith!" He replied, "If you have* ***faith as small as a mustard seed,*** *you can say to this mulberry tree, 'Be uprooted and planted in the sea,' and it will obey you." (Lk. 17:5–6)*

Why should Jesus increase your faith? You do not need much if the faith you have is real. Look at the story Jesus told immediately after this:

> *Suppose one of you had a servant plowing or looking after the sheep. Would he say to the servant when he comes in from the field, "Come along now and sit down to eat"? Would he not rather say, "Prepare my supper, get yourself ready and wait on me while I eat and drink; after that you may eat and drink"? Would he thank the servant because he did what he was told to do?* ***So you also, when you have done everything you were told to do, should say, "we are unworthy servants; we have only done our duty."*** *(Lk. 17:7–10)*

The last sentence is Jesus' answer to their request for increased faith. The way to increase your faith is to obey God.

Grace & Faith 2

Saving faith is a gift from God. Faith in spirits, idols, and false gods is not. Faith from God can be recognized by 1) its object—God, 2) its unwavering quality, and 3) its saving results. God causes this kind of faith in a particular way:

> *Consequently, faith comes from hearing the message, and the message is heard through the word of Christ. (Rom. 10:17)*

Faith is caused by hearing the Word preached. It should not surprise us when someone says, "Don't use the Bible," or, "Don't preach to me, I don't believe that stuff." Of course he does not believe—he hasn't heard it.

> *For there is no difference between Jew and Gentile—the same Lord is Lord of all and richly blesses all who call on him, for, "Everyone who calls on the name of the Lord will be saved." How, then, can they call on the one they have not believed in? And how can they believe in the one of whom they have not heard? And how can they hear without someone preaching to them? And how can they preach unless they are sent? As it is written, "How beautiful are the feet of those who bring good news!" (Rom. 10:12–15)*

The miracle in Acts 2:1–13 did not get saving results. It got an audience. It was the *preaching* in Acts 2:22–41 that resulted in three thousand converts. The same thing happened with the miracles and preaching in Acts 3 and Acts 14.

Faith & Obedience

In evangelical circles, the word "faith" has a good reputation. Every Christian knows that he entered the kingdom of God by it. Unfortunately, that is often the last time we had firsthand experience with the word. We admire faith in others, especially if they are dead and famous, like George Müller, Corrie ten Boom, Amy Carmichael, Hudson Taylor, or James Fraser. Reading their biographies can encourage our faith, or it can be a means of trying to have a vicarious faith.

The word "obedience" does not have such a high reputation. Many Christians have the idea that obedience is an exercise in *effort*, and therefore a work. They associate obedience with reluctance, trial and failure, and works righteousness.

It is my intention to show from the Scriptures that obedience is *not* opposed to grace and faith and, consequently, it is not the near synonym of works righteousness that people think it is. Obedience is made possible by God's grace and is a near synonym of *faith*.

Romans, the great book on justification by faith, opens and closes with verses which closely connect belief and obedience:

> *Through him and for his name's sake, we received grace and apostleship to call people from among all the Gentiles to* ***the obedience that comes from faith.*** *(Rom. 1:5)*

> *Now to him who is able to establish you by my gospel and the proclamation of Jesus Christ, according to the revelation of the mystery hidden for long ages past, but now revealed and made known through the prophetic writings by the command of the eternal*

> *God, so **that all nations might believe and obey him...** (Rom. 16:25–26)*

The great faith chapter, Hebrews 11, represents obedience as a result of faith: *"By faith Abraham...obeyed"* (v. 8). Earlier in Hebrews, there is this great salvation text:

> *Although he was a son, he learned obedience from what he suffered and, once made perfect, **he became the source of eternal salvation for all who obey him.** (Heb. 5:8–9)*

"Obey Him" shows up in all English translations of this passage. Salvation is not by works, but somehow people are saved by *obeying* Jesus Christ.

> *He will punish those who do not know God and do not **obey the gospel** of our Lord Jesus. (2 Thess. 1:8)*

Hebrews tells us that we are saved by obeying Jesus Christ. Thessalonians tells us that God will punish those who do not know Him and who do not obey the gospel of our Lord Jesus. Jesus Christ and the gospel are both to be obeyed.

How can you obey the gospel? Well, obedience is always a response to a command. What is the command of the gospel?

> *In the past God overlooked such ignorance, but now **he commands all people everywhere to repent.** For he has set a day when he will judge the world with justice by the man he has appointed. He has given proof of this to all men by raising him from the dead. (Acts 17:30–31)*

Repentance is obedience to the gospel.

There is a teaching today that repentance is a false requirement for salvation because it is telling people to clean up their act and then come to Jesus. If repentance were that, it would be a false requirement, because we could never clean up our act. *God* is the only one who can do that.

Let's look at a few more passages on repentance:

> *In those days John the Baptist came, preaching in the Desert of Judea and saying, "**Repent**, for the kingdom of heaven is near." (Mt. 3:1–2)*

> *From that time on Jesus began to preach, "**Repent**, for the kingdom of heaven is near." (Mt. 4:17)*

> *Peter replied, "**Repent** and be baptized, every one of you, in the name of Jesus Christ **for the forgiveness of your sins**. And you will receive the gift of the Holy Spirit." (Acts 2:38)*

> ***Repent**, then, and **turn to God, so that your sins may be wiped out**, that times of refreshing may come from the Lord...When God raised up his servant, he sent him first to you to bless you **by turning each of you from your wicked ways**. (Acts 3:19, 26)*

> *I have declared to both Jews and Greeks that they must **turn to God in repentance** and have faith in our Lord Jesus. (Acts 20:21)*

> *I will rescue you from your own people and from the Gentiles. I am sending you to them to open their eyes and turn them from darkness to light, and from*

> *the power of Satan to God, so that they may receive forgiveness of sins and a place among those who are sanctified by faith in me. First to those in Damascus, then to those in Jerusalem and in all Judea, and to the Gentiles also, I preached that they should* ***repent and turn to God and prove their repentance by their deeds.*** *(Acts 26:17–18)*

> *Those who oppose him he must gently instruct, in the hope that* **God will grant them repentance** *leading them to a knowledge of the truth, and that they will come to their senses and escape from the trap of the devil, who has taken them captive to do his will. (2 Tim. 2:25–26)*

In the first two passages, John the Baptist and Jesus urgently command the people to repent. In the next four, Peter and Paul command repentance, and in the last passage, we discover that God gives repentance.

The gospel is obeyed through repentance. Peter ended his first two recorded sermons with commands to repent, and the result was five thousand new believers. Everyone has been commanded to repent, and everyone who is truly a Christian repented (that is, obeyed the gospel) when he came to Christ.

Notice that in Acts 20:21, God required repentance *and* "faith in our Lord Jesus." Repentance is not the same thing as faith, but it comes at the same time. Repentance is:

- *God's activity:* "He sent him first to you to bless you by turning each of you from your wicked ways" (Acts 3:26); "God will grant them repentance..." (2 Tim. 2:25).

- *A command:* "He commands..." (Acts 17:30).
- *For everyone:* "All people everywhere..." (Acts 17:30); "both Jews and Greeks..." (Acts 20:21).
- *Resulting in salvation:* "Repent and be baptized, every one of you, in the name of Jesus Christ so that your sins may be forgiven. And you will receive the gift of the Holy Spirit" (Acts 2:38).

By faith we believe the gospel and act on it. Belief without the action of obeying through repentance is a hollow belief: *"Otherwise, you have believed in vain"* (1 Cor. 15:2).

All true faith results in obedience. It is possible to obey without believing, but it is *not* possible to believe without obeying. Such belief is not biblical faith.

Love & Obedience

The Bible speaks of the Church as the Bride of Christ. In this relationship, the Church is feminine, and Christ is masculine. A man's love for a woman is originating love. A bride's love for her husband is *responsive* love. She loves because he loved her first. The more he loves her, the more she loves him.

We love Him, because He first loved us. (1 Jn. 4:19 KJV)

God's love for us is sacrificial. Our responsive love towards Him is obedience. Make a study from the Bible on how much God loves, and how much He loves *us.* Keep this study going. You will find your love for Him growing. You will find your obedience growing, too.

What Are We To Obey?

As Christians, are we to obey all the commands in the Bible, including keeping the Torah and the Sabbath? If not, where do we draw the line?

The New Testament has specific statements about the laws found in the Torah (the first five books of the Old Testament). I hope you are willing to look them up, as there are too many to print out:

- *Health Law:* Mark 7:1–23. The key phrase is in verse 19: "In saying this, Jesus declared all foods clean."
- *Civil Law:* Romans 13:1–7. Since we are no longer in a theocracy, God has transferred this authority to the civil government.
- *Sacrificial Law:* Hebrews 9:26–28 and 10:10–14. These sacrifices were fulfilled in Christ. It would be sin to practice them now because it would deny the sufficiency of Christ's sacrifice for our sins.
- *The Sabbath Law:* Romans 14:5–8, Luke 6:1–10, Mark 7:27. We can learn several things from these passages:
    - God allows and receives those who consider every day alike.
    - We are allowed to do good on the Sabbath.
    - The Sabbath was made for man. It is a gift of rest for us.

- *Moral Law*—Romans 3:20, 5:20, 7:7–8, 8:3–4, and 1 Timothy 1:8–11. The law cannot save; it is meant to lead us to Christ. After we are saved, it is possible to obey this law.

With these Scriptures as a preamble, read 2 Timothy 3:16–17 and 1 Corinthians 10:6–11:

> *All Scripture is God-breathed and is useful for teaching, rebuking, correcting and training in righteousness, so that the servant of God may be thoroughly equipped for every good work. (2 Tim. 3:16–17)*

> *Now these things occurred as examples to keep us from setting our hearts on evil things as they did. Do not be idolaters, as some of them were; as it is written: "The people sat down to eat and drink and got up to indulge in revelry." We should not commit sexual immorality, as some of them did—and in one day twenty-three thousand of them died. We should not test Christ, as some of them did—and were killed by snakes. And do not grumble, as some of them did—and were killed by the destroying angel. These things happened to them as examples and were written down as warnings for us, on whom the culmination of the ages has come. (1 Cor. 10:6–11)*

It is good to wash our hands before we eat, but it does not save us or make us holy. It is right to obey civil laws, as long as they do not cross God's laws. It is right to obey the moral law because God's standards of morality do not change.

Faith obedience makes the impossible possible, by God's grace. God's requirements have not changed, but our ability to perform them has. The commands in Matthew 5–7, Colossians 3, and Ephesians 5 go far beyond the Torah. They cover obedience in the heart, not just the obedience of refraining from committing acts of sin. Matthew 22:37–40:

> *Jesus replied: "Love the Lord your God with all your heart and with all your soul and with all your mind." This is the first and greatest commandment. And the second is like it: "Love your neighbor as yourself."* ***All the Law and the Prophets hang on these two commandments.***

Relaxing the Law

> *Think not that I have come to abolish the law and the prophets. I have come not to abolish them but to fulfill them. For truly, I say to you, till heaven and earth pass away, not an iota, not a dot, will pass from the law until all is accomplished. Whoever then relaxes one of the least of these commandments and teaches men so, shall be called least in the kingdom of heaven but he who does them and teaches them shall be called great in the kingdom of heaven. For I tell you, unless your righteousness exceeds that of the scribes and Pharisees, you will never enter the kingdom of heaven. (Mt. 5:17–20 RSV)*

Jesus taught that there are three eternal destinies:

- Least in the kingdom
- Great in the kingdom
- Never in the kingdom

In the rest of Matthew 5 Jesus taught how He fulfilled the law by going back to the motives of the heart—hatred, lust, and love. This has to do with the *spirit* of the law, not just the letter of the law. The spirit of the law is never less than the letter—it is always more. The Pharisees were living only the letter and would not make it into the kingdom. Others who relaxed the letter of the law would be least in the kingdom.

Christians today think that there are only two choices: keeping the letter and relaxing it. The United States abounds with legalists. It also abounds with *relaxed* doers and teachers. The choice between "not in the kingdom" and "least in the kingdom" seems a poor one to me.

There is a third option: "whoever keeps them and teaches others to do so."

> *You have heard that it was said: "You shall not commit adultery." I, however, say to you that anyone who looks at a woman with an impure intention has already committed adultery with her* ***in his heart.*** *(Mt. 5:27–28, RSV)*

Being great in the kingdom means following the fulfilled law seriously, from the heart.

It is very easy to become a "relaxer" of the law. The majority of Christians do it. First we look at the letter of the law (e.g., "You shall not commit adultery.") and say, "To observe that would be Old Testament legalism." Then we look at the fulfilled law ("Anyone who looks at a woman with an impure intention has already committed adultery with her in his heart.") and say, "That is nice, but it is idealism. If I tried to obey that I would be riddled with guilt constantly." By relaxing both the letter of God's law and the heart motive behind it, we leave the door wide open for violating the law in both thought and action. This is why an increasing number of Christians find themselves in serious sexual sin. The person who has been redeemed by the

Lord Jesus should have no difficulty believing His teaching and getting power from Him to obey that teaching.

The Word

> *All Scripture is God-breathed and is useful for teaching, rebuking, correcting and training in righteousness... (2 Tim. 3:16*

Evangelicals stand on the full inspiration of the Word of God. Sadly, we are not as firm when it comes to *applying* the Word. We believe the Bible from cover to cover in debate, but when we look inside the covers on our own, we have problems. The texts can be history, prophecy, promises, commands, or statements of fact. Our problems are not problems of understanding; they are problems of unbelief. Our solutions are:

- Stay ignorant.
- Run lightly over the text.
- Do much explaining of what the text "really" means.

A few examples of statement-of-fact passages are Colossians 3:9, Romans 1:6, Galatians 2:20, Romans 8:9. The chapters these verses are in make the truths much clearer.

Here are some clear commands Christians are hesitant to obey:

1. Church discipline: 1 Corinthians 5, especially verses 9–13.

> *I wrote to you in my letter not to associate with sexually immoral people—not at all meaning the*

people of this world who are immoral, or the greedy and swindlers, or idolaters. In that case you would have to leave this world. But now I am writing to you that ***you must not associate with anyone who claims to be a brother or sister but is sexually immoral or greedy, an idolater or slanderer, a drunkard or swindler.*** *Do not even eat with such people. What business is it of mine to judge those outside the church? Are you not to judge those inside? God will judge those outside. "Expel the wicked person from among you."*

2. Relationships with evil people and enemies: Matthew 5:39–45.

   But I tell you, do not resist an evil person. If anyone slaps you on the right cheek, turn to them the other cheek also. And if anyone wants to sue you and take your shirt, hand over your coat as well. If anyone forces you to go one mile, go with them two miles. Give to the one who asks you, and do not turn away from the one who wants to borrow from you. You have heard that it was said, "Love your neighbor and hate your enemy." But I tell you, love your enemies and pray for those who persecute you, that you may be children of your Father in heaven. He causes his sun to rise on the evil and the good, and sends rain on the righteous and the unrighteous.

3. Qualifications for elders and deacons: 1 Timothy 3:1–13, Titus 1:6–9, and 1 Peter 5:1–4.

Here is a trustworthy saying: Whoever aspires to be an overseer desires a noble task. Now the overseer is to be above reproach, faithful to his wife, temperate, self-controlled, respectable, hospitable, able to teach, not given to drunkenness, not violent but gentle, not quarrelsome, not a lover of money. He must manage his own family well and see that his children obey him, and he must do so in a manner worthy of full respect. (If anyone does not know how to manage his own family, how can he take care of God's church?) He must not be a recent convert, or he may become conceited and fall under the same judgment as the devil. He must also have a good reputation with outsiders, so that he will not fall into disgrace and into the devil's trap. In the same way, deacons are to be worthy of respect, sincere, not indulging in much wine, and not pursuing dishonest gain. They must keep hold of the deep truths of the faith with a clear conscience. They must first be tested; and then if there is nothing against them, let them serve as deacons. In the same way, the women are to be worthy of respect, not malicious talkers but temperate and trustworthy in everything. A deacon must be faithful to his wife and must manage his children and his household well. Those who have served well gain an excellent standing and great assurance in their faith in Christ Jesus. (1 Tim. 3:1–13)

An elder must be blameless, faithful to his wife, a man whose children believe and are not open to the charge of being wild and disobedient. Since an overseer manages God's household, he must be blameless—not overbearing, not quick-tempered, not given to drunkenness, not violent, not pursuing dishonest gain. Rather, he must be hospitable, one who loves what is good, who is self-controlled, upright, holy and disciplined. He must hold firmly to the trustworthy message as it has been taught, so that he can encourage others by sound doctrine and refute those who oppose it. (Tit. 1:6–9)

To the elders among you, I appeal as a fellow elder and a witness of Christ's sufferings who also will share in the glory to be revealed: Be shepherds of God's flock that is under your care, watching over them—not because you must, but because you are willing, as God wants you to be; not pursuing dishonest gain, but eager to serve; not lording it over those entrusted to you, but being examples to the flock. And when the Chief Shepherd appears, you will receive the crown of glory that will never fade away. (1 Pet. 5:1–4)

4. Complaining and arguing: Philippians 2:14.

   Do everything without grumbling or arguing.

5. Being thankful: 1 Thessalonians 5:16–18.

   Rejoice always, pray continually, give thanks in all circumstances; for this is God's will for you in Christ Jesus.

6. Hospitality: Luke 14:12–14.

> *Then Jesus said to his host, "When you give a luncheon or dinner, do not invite your friends, your brothers or sisters, your relatives, or your rich neighbors; if you do, they may invite you back and so you will be repaid. But when you give a banquet, invite the poor, the crippled, the lame, the blind, and you will be blessed. Although they cannot repay you, you will be repaid at the resurrection of the righteous."*

We have many excuses for why we do not obey texts like these. One option we do not often take is confessing our disobedience and unbelief and obeying them.

You might wonder how I am doing in these areas. It is a good question. At one time I tried to obey by willpower and effort. I was not successful. In recent years, I have learned to obey by grace. When I do not obey, I acknowledge it as sin and get forgiven by grace. I put in more time being an example of obedience than I do teaching it. It is a more effective way of instructing.

> *For this reason I am sending to you Timothy, my son whom I love, who is faithful in the Lord. He will remind you of my way of life in Christ Jesus, which agrees with what I teach everywhere in every church. (1 Cor. 4:17)*

You Died with Christ

> *Since you died with Christ... (Col. 2:20)*

> *Since then you have been raised with Christ... (Col. 3:1)*

For you died... (Col. 3:3)

Although these things were written to the church at Colossae, I believe that if they are true, they apply to all Christians. Each of the verses ends in an instruction or a command based on the truths:

> *Since you died with Christ to the basic principles of this world, why, as though you still belonged to it, do you submit to its rules: "Do not handle! Do not taste! Do not touch!"? These are all destined to perish with use, because they are based on human commands and teachings. (Col. 2:20–22)*

> *Since, then, you have been raised with Christ, set your hearts on things above, where Christ is seated at the right hand of God. Set your minds on things above, not on earthly things. For you died, and your life is now hidden with Christ in God. When Christ, who is your life, appears, then you also will appear with him in glory. Put to death, therefore, whatever belongs to your earthly nature: sexual immorality, impurity, lust, evil desires and greed, which is idolatry. (Col. 3:1–5)*

If Christians have trouble obeying God's commands, it may be because they have trouble believing that they have died with Christ. Or perhaps they have not died with Christ (in other words, they are not Christians). Our obedience is based upon the completed work that Christ has already done in us. Read Romans 6 a few times.

Dead

As for you, you were dead in your transgressions and sins. (Eph. 2:1)

What shall we say, then? Shall we go on sinning so that grace may increase? By no means! We died to sin; how can we live in it any longer? (Rom. 6:1–2)

When it comes to sin, we are all dead. We are either "dead in" sin or "dead to" it. When we were dead *in* sins, we lived in them. Once we are dead *to* sin, living in it is neither normal nor possible. A Christian may sin, but he cannot make it his way of life:

No one who lives in him keeps on sinning. No one who continues to sin has either seen him or known him... No one who is born of God will continue to sin, because God's seed remains in him; he cannot go on sinning, because he has been born of God. (1 Jn. 3:6, 9)

Obeying the Commands

And he said to them: "You have a fine way of setting aside the commands of God in order to observe your own traditions!" (Mk. 7:9)

J.B. Phillips translates this, "It is wonderful to see how..." The Pharisees and the teachers of the law made a sophisticated effort to disobey.

Just before Jesus said this, He quoted the prophet Isaiah:

> *These people come near to me with their mouth and honor me with their lips, but their hearts are far from me. Their worship of me is based on merely human rules they have been taught. (Is. 29:13)*

Nonreligious people do not need elaborate reasons to disobey. They do it deliberately, are ignorant of the commandments, or simply do not care about obeying. Religious people come up with complicated rationalizations to make their wrongs look right. On top of this, they teach their disobedience to others. I have used the word "religious" here, but Christians are also guilty of this.

Read through the New Testament, keeping an eye out for the commandments. There are many (those in Colossians 3 and 1 Thessalonians 5, for example). Write down your expositions of them.

Do you have involved explanations for why you do not have to obey?

Repentance

> *"What do you think? There was a man who had two sons. He went to the first and said, 'Son, go and work today in the vineyard.' 'I will not,' he answered, but later he changed his mind and went. Then the father went to the other son and said the same thing. He answered, 'I will, sir,' but he did not go. Which of the two did what his father wanted?" "The first," they answered. Jesus said to them, "I tell you the truth, the tax collectors and the prostitutes are entering the kingdom of God ahead of you. For John came to you to show you*

> *the way of righteousness, and you did not believe him, but the tax collectors and the prostitutes did. And even after you saw this, you did not repent and believe him." (Mt. 21:28–32)*

Jesus is not teaching the merits of delayed obedience in this passage. He is teaching repentance for both the person who initially refused and for the one who promised to obey and did not.

The Pharisees were like the second son who said he would work and did not. The Pharisees knew the law, but they thought that being able to quote it was the same as obeying it. The prostitutes and tax collectors were the first son. They had no intention of obeying and said so. John the Baptist came preaching repentance to Pharisees, tax collectors, and prostitutes. The latter two repented. The Pharisees did not think that they needed to repent.

When my wife Bessie was in Japan over sixty years ago, a young man named Kai came to see her. Their conversation went something like this:

"Miss Dodds, I want to become a Christian."

Bessie began to explain sin to him.

"Oh, Miss Dodds, you have it all wrong. You see, I am not a sinner. I am not like other boys. I am good, and I want to become a Christian."

Bessie replied, "Kai, I cannot help you. Neither can Jesus. Come back when you are a sinner." She took him to the door. She did not think she would see him again. A few weeks later he came back, admitted he was a sinner, repented of his sins, and put his faith in the Lord Jesus.

Obedience Is Easy

Why is obedience so hard?

- Obedience is an infringement on our freedom. Since we are free in Christ, we conclude that obedience must not be good. Yet we know it *is* good. Thus, we become confused.
- Obedience means works. We have been justified by grace through faith and are opposed to works, so we are also opposed to obedience.
- We have tried to obey and failed—frequently. Therefore, the only solution must be to disobey and confess.
- We confuse obedience to men with obedience to God.

Each of these statements is a misconception. Here are the corrections:

- Obedience is freedom, not an infringement of it. It is a voluntary act, which means it can only take place if the will is *free*.

Then you will know the truth, and the truth will set you free. (Jn. 8:32)

- Obedience is not related to works. It is related to faith.

By faith *Noah, when warned about things not yet seen, in holy fear built an ark to save his family. By his* ***faith*** *he condemned the world and became heir of the righteousness that comes by faith.* ***By faith Abraham,*** *when called to go to a place he would later receive as*

> *his inheritance, **obeyed** and went, even though he did not know where he was going. (Heb. 11:7–8)*

Obedience does not earn us salvation; that has been paid for already. When we obey, we are acting by faith.

- Trying to obey is the opposite of trusting to obey. When we try, we are being self-centered, not God-centered. When we trust God, He provides the strength for us to obey.
- Although obedience to God and obedience to man can be the same thing (see Rom. 13, 1 Pet. 2 and 3, Ephesians 5 and 6, Col. 3, and Tit. 2), sometimes they are not (Col. 2:20–23, Mk. 7, 1 Tim. 4:1–5, and Acts 4:19–20). We can avoid confusion if we know the Scriptures well enough to differentiate between the commands of men and the commands of God.

When you set out to obey God, remember these things:

- God provides a way out of sin in every situation (1 Cor. 10:13).
- We are indwelt with the Holy Spirit. Obedience is the natural way of life for those who live by the Spirit of God (see Gal. 5:22–23).
- Jesus died that we might be dead to sin (Rom. 6, 1 Pet. 2:24).
- God gave us the Scriptures to prevent sin (1 Jn. 2:1).

God wants us to obey Him, and He knows that we cannot do it on our own. He wonderfully provides for our obedience by His death and resurrection and His gifts of faith, grace, the indwelling Holy Spirit, and a new and glorious nature.

Sin is based on two things: a lie and a rebellion. Many of us, like Eve, have believed a lie. Once we buy the lies, rebellion is the consequence.

> *But I fear, lest by any means, as the serpent beguiled Eve through his* ***subtlety****, so your minds should be corrupted from the* ***simplicity*** *that is in Christ. (2 Cor. 11:3 KJV)*

Obeying Immoderate Commands

> *Now may the Lord of peace himself give you peace at all times and in every way. The Lord be with all of you. (2 Thess. 3:16)*

> ***May the God of peace****, who through the blood of the eternal covenant brought back from the dead our Lord Jesus, that great Shepherd of the sheep,* ***equip you with everything good for doing his will****, and may he work in us what is pleasing to him, through Jesus Christ, to whom be glory for ever and ever. Amen. (Heb. 13:20–21)*

Please look at every phrase in these benedictions, for I will not comment on all of them. Notice that God gives us peace "*at all times* and *in every way*" and equips us with "*everything good* for doing His will." The God of peace does a thorough work in us.

If you are familiar with the Bible, you may have noticed that it has very few moderate commands. You may also have noticed how many Christians moderate the commands. We think it is alright to bring them down to our size because they are so extreme. This is neither honest nor necessary.

The Bible also contains many great promises like the ones I have just quoted. In the immoderate promises God gives us what we need to obey the immoderate commands.

Be Holy

But just as he who called you is holy, so be holy in all you do; for it is written: "Be holy, because I am holy." (1 Pet. 1:15–16)

Be perfect, therefore, as your heavenly Father is perfect. (Mt. 5:48)

These are commands, not suggestions. They are also "be" commands, not "do" commands—they relate to what you *are*, not just what you do. Since we live by God's grace, it is safe to assume that He will not command us to be something that He does not provide the means for us to be. Therefore, we should not think that these commands are impossible to obey. If we do, we are not believing God. We are following the suggestions of the Enemy.

Thank God that He has made holiness possible for you. Start obeying by *believing* that it is possible and by *wanting* to be holy.

Being Self-controlled & Alert

Be self-controlled and alert. Your enemy the devil prowls around like a roaring lion looking for someone to devour. (1 Pet. 5:8)

Of all the reasons Christians sin, this one is the most disheartening. It happens to very strong Christians who are not alert.

When I was midshipman over sixty years ago, there was a framed picture in the Department of Seamanship and Navigation at the Naval Academy. It was a photograph of seven destroyers grounded on the beach in the Santa Barbara Channel in California. There are eight destroyers in a squadron. The captain of the eighth destroyer decided not to follow the leader. Underneath the picture was this caption: "The price of good navigation is constant vigilance."

> *The great dragon was hurled down—that ancient serpent called the devil, or Satan, who leads the whole world astray. He was hurled to the earth, and his angels with him. Then I heard a loud voice in heaven say: "Now have come the salvation and the power and the kingdom of our God, and the authority of his Christ. For the accuser of our brothers, who accuses them before our God day and night, has been hurled down." (Rev. 12:9–10)*

The name of the ancient serpent is the Accuser. I am aware of churches whose elders are accusing or being accused. Some of the accusation is within a church, and some of it is between churches. The saints in these churches may have believed a lie that a fellow believer is the enemy. The fellow believer may have believed a lie and passed it on as truth. That puts him in the wrong camp. It makes him an accuser and a gossiper, but he is never the enemy, even if he is in great sin.

There seems to be a misreading or misapplication of Ephesians 5:8-14a:

> *For you were once darkness, but now you are light in the Lord. Live as children of light (for the fruit of the light consists in all goodness, righteousness and truth) and find out what pleases the Lord. Have nothing to do with the fruitless deeds of darkness, but rather expose them. For it is shameful even to mention what the disobedient do in secret. But everything exposed by the light becomes visible, for it is light that makes everything visible.*

- What we are: "*Light in the Lord*"
- What we are commanded: "*Live as children of light.*"
- What light is: "*All goodness, righteousness and truth.*"
- Additional comment: "*Find out what pleases the Lord.*"
- Negative comment: "*Have nothing to do with the fruitless deeds of darkness.*"
- Positive comment: "*Expose them.*"
- How not to expose them: "*For it is shameful even to mention what the disobedient do in secret.*"
- How to expose them: "*Light exposes.*"

The misapplication is that people think that the way to expose the fruitless deeds of darkness is to talk about them. When we expose deeds of darkness this way, we mention "what the disobedient do in secret." But this passage says that is shameful. It is our *life of light* that should expose things, not our talk of darkness. The accuser should confess the accusations he has made. The accused should not defend against the accuser or accusations, but if he has sinned, he should confess it to the Lord.

Pleasing God

Do you want to please God?

> *Without faith it is impossible to please God... (Heb. 11:6)*

> *This is the victory that has overcome the world, even our faith. Who is it that overcomes the world? Only he who believes that Jesus is the Son of God. (1 John 5:4–5)*

How crowded our lives get! How unnecessary are the things that clutter them up in comparison to having this kind of faith! Salvation from sin is ours by faith. Day-by-day protection from sin is ours by faith.

> *And without faith it is impossible to please God, because anyone who comes to him must believe that he exists and that he rewards those who earnestly seek him. (Heb. 11:6)*

God diligently rewards those who seek Him.

A Purpose of Heart

> *But Daniel* ***purposed in his heart*** *that he would not defile himself with the portion of the king's delicacies, nor with the wine which he drank; therefore he requested of the chief of the eunuchs that he might not defile himself. (Dan. 1:8 NKJV)*

> *When he [Barnabas] came and had seen the grace of God, he was glad, and encouraged them all that with*

purpose of heart they should continue with the Lord. *(Acts 11:23 NKJV)*

Daniel's decision and Barnabas' exhortation had one thing in common: a purpose of heart. Daniel made a single decision that affected every day of his next three years. He did this on principle. The principle was that "he would not defile himself." He did not wait until breakfast to make the decision not to eat when there was food in front of him and he was hungry. Why? He would have compromised. Daniel "purposed in his heart" once to obey God for a long time. He did not know how he was going to carry out his purpose. He trusted that if he acted on principle, God would provide the means for him to live it out.

Barnabas exhorted the saints "that with purpose of heart they should continue with the Lord." He did not tell them how to continue with the Lord. He assumed that if they had purposed in their hearts to do it, the Lord would uphold them.

There are practical ways to not defile yourself and practical ways to continue with the Lord, but they are of little value unless you have a purpose of heart first. If we let our decision wait until the event is upon us, we will almost surely compromise.

Partial Obedience

But Samuel replied: "Does the LORD delight in burnt offerings and sacrifices as much as in obeying the voice of the LORD? To obey is better than sacrifice, and to heed is better than the fat of rams. For rebellion is like the sin of divination, and arrogance like the evil of idolatry. Because you have rejected the word of the LORD, he has rejected you as king." (1 Sam. 15:22–23)

Open your Bible right now and read 1 Samuel 15.

Have you read it? Notice *why* Saul spared the animals (vv. 21,24). Instead of repenting when confronted with his sin, Saul backtracked and tried to claim that he had obeyed the Lord while all around him was the evidence of his *disobedience*: bleating sheep and lowing cattle.

Saul called his "partial obedience" obedience. God had another name for it: disobedience. He called that disobedience rebellion, and rebellion He likened to witchcraft. God also compared Saul's arrogance to idolatry.

Unless we have God's view of our actions, we will stumble along with excuses like "But we love each other," "The government wastes money anyway," "But I found it," "Everyone does it..." To the Samuels of this world, our excuses sound like bleating sheep, and to God they look like idolatry and witchcraft.

Aspects of Obedience

Christian obedience has three primary aspects. The first is *refraining from disobedience*; the second is *walking in the light*; and the third is *an active, positive obedience.*

Refraining from Disobedience

Disobedience is doing, thinking, or saying what we are told not to do or think or say. It is also *not* doing, not thinking, or not saying what we are commanded to do and think and say.

Jesus replied: "'Love the Lord your God with all your heart and with all your soul and with all your mind.' This is the first and greatest commandment." (Mt. 22:37–38)

It is easier to measure disobedience by what we do than by what we do not do. However, this does not mean that our neglect is not sin. Not loving the Lord in this way is a violation of the first and greatest commandment.

The first way to refrain from disobedience is to *know the commandments*. Ignorance is no excuse. God gave us instructions in the Bible, and it is our responsibility to be familiar with them. Here is what Leviticus has to say about unintentional sin:

If a member of the community sins unintentionally and does what is forbidden in any of the LORD's commands, he is guilty. (Lev. 4:27)

If a person sins and does what is forbidden in any of the LORD's commands, even though he does not know it, he is guilty and will be held responsible. (Lev. 5:17)

The second means of refraining from disobedience is to *know God's character*. If you know Him, you will be able to recognize anything that does not have His characteristics and know that it is from the Enemy.

He was a murderer from the beginning, not holding to the truth, for there is no truth in him. When he lies, he speaks his native language, for he is a liar and the father of lies. (Jn. 8:44b)

Both the liar and the truth-teller say, "I am telling the truth." You need to know the truth-teller well enough to recognize the liars by their character. In *The Lion, the Witch, and the Wardrobe* by C.S. Lewis, both Lucy and Edmund had visited the parallel world of Narnia. When Lucy told her siblings Peter and Susan about the wonders in Narnia, she expected Edmund to back her up. Instead, Edmund said that Lucy was playing make-believe. Both children *said* they were telling the truth. What Lucy said sounded unbelievable, and Edmund's lie made sense. Peter and Susan went to see Professor Kirk for advice. After hearing their story, the Professor replied, "Does your experience lead you to regard your brother or your sister as the more reliable? I mean, which is more truthful?" Peter said, "Up till now, I'd have said Lucy every time." Then the professor asked Susan the same question. "Well, in general, I'd say the same as Peter." The Professor replied, "You know she doesn't tell lies, and it is obvious that she is not mad. For the moment then, and unless any further evidence turns up, we must assume that she is telling the truth." Do you know God's character as Peter and Susan knew Lucy's?

The third way to refrain from sin is to *avoid temptation.* You cannot blame all your temptations on the enemy:

> *But each one is tempted when,* ***by his own evil desire,*** *he is dragged away and enticed. (Jas. 1:14)*

How do you avoid temptation? First, choose not to feed your evil desires. Second, ask God to keep the evil one from tempting you. God will answer the prayer He taught us to pray:

> *And lead us not into temptation, but deliver us from the evil one. (Mt. 6:13)*

The fourth means of refraining from sin is to *not be overly confident.*

> *So if you think you are standing firm, be careful that you don't fall! (1 Cor. 10:12a)*

Sin is like falling off a cliff. Christians do not want to fall, but they *do* want to admire the view. So they get as close to the edge as they can, thinking they will not fall because they don't intend to. Do not be overconfident or careless, and *do not admire the view*. Stay away from the edge!

Sometimes we need to get close to the edge to help someone who has fallen or who is about to fall. The New Testament has two strong texts to guide us in doing this:

> *Brothers, if someone is caught in a sin, you who are spiritual should restore him gently. But watch yourself, or you also may be tempted. (Gal. 6:1)*

> *Be merciful to those who doubt; snatch others from the fire and save them; to others show mercy, mixed with fear—hating even the clothing stained by corrupted flesh. (Jude 22–23)*

Only spiritual people should do the restoring, and they need to watch out, not to keep from sinning, but to keep from even being *tempted*. You must abhor sin if you are going to be in the rescuing business.

Having a good, stout fence at the edge of a cliff is much more valuable than keeping an ambulance parked in the valley below. Fences are made of the Word, prayer, and fellowship with other Christians. If you are going to be a rescuer, having a group of Christians praying for you is like a safety line around your waist. Do not be overconfident!

> *No temptation has seized you except what is common to man. And God is faithful; he will not let you be tempted beyond what you can bear. But when you are tempted, he will also provide a way out so that you can stand up under it. (1 Cor. 10:13)*

God is faithful to us *during* temptation. This does not mean He will physically or spiritually pull us out of it. It means that He limits temptations by their nature ("common to man"), by their strength ("not beyond what you can bear"), and by providing a way out. It still requires a decision on your part.

The fifth and sixth means of keeping from sin go together. They are: *make a stand against the devil*, and *run away from him*:

> *Submit yourselves, then, to God. Resist the devil, and he will flee from you. (Jas. 4:7)*

> *But you, man of God, flee from all this, and pursue righteousness, godliness, faith, love, endurance and gentleness. (1 Tim. 6:11)*

> *Flee the evil desires of youth, and pursue righteousness, faith, love and peace, along with those who call on the Lord out of a pure heart. (2 Tim. 2:22)*

Either the devil flees or you flee. One of you must run. Resisting is by far the best way. Make the devil do the running. That is the way Jesus handled temptation. The devil attacked, and Jesus counter-attacked with the Word of God.

There are prerequisites for resistance:

> *But he gives us more grace. That is why Scripture says: "God opposes the proud but gives grace to the humble." Submit yourselves, then, to God. Resist the devil, and he will flee from you. (Jas. 4:6–7)*

Before you can resist the devil, you must submit to God in humility, whereby you receive grace for resistance. Ephesians gives two more conditions:

> *Finally, **be strong in the Lord** and in his mighty power. **Put on the full armor** of God so that you can take your stand against the devil's schemes. (Eph. 6:10–11)*

Standing against the devil is only effective when we have God's armor and God's power. It was the same for Jesus:

> *Then Jesus was **led by the Spirit** into the desert to be tempted by the devil. (Mt. 4:1)*

If you cannot meet these conditions, then you need to run. In fact, there are certain temptations you must always flee from, such as the desire to get rich, the love of money, and eagerness for money.

> *But you, man of God, flee from all this, and pursue righteousness, godliness, faith, love, endurance and gentleness. (1 Tim. 6:11)*

Flee the one and pursue the other.

Walking in the Light

But if we walk in the light,
As he is in the light,
We have fellowship with one another,
And the blood of Jesus, His Son,
Purifies us from all sin.
(1 Jn. 1:7)

This verse presents such wonderful truth that I have set it in poetic form. It is based on the truth of 1 John 1:5:

> *God is light; in him there is no darkness at all. (1 Jn. 1:5b)*

Although I am seated in a well-lit room, there is darkness in it. How do I know? Because if I look outside I can see the brightness of the sunshine on the lawn, and this room is not that bright. However, there is also darkness outside where the trees, houses, and cars cast shadows. There is always a place of more light, except in the presence of God. "*In Him there is no darkness at all.*" God is the very essence of light, the source of all other lights.

What does this mean for us? "*If we walk in the light, as He is in the light...*" The kind of light we are to walk in is pure and absolute. It is not the light of a candle or a lantern. Those lights draw attention to the darkness with their flickering and casting of shadows. If you and I walk in the "no darkness at all" kind of light, two things happen: the blood of Jesus purifies us from all sin, and we have real fellowship with one another.

> *We proclaim to you what we have seen and heard, so that you also may have fellowship with us. And our*

> *fellowship is with the Father and with his Son, Jesus Christ. (1 Jn. 1:3)*

When we walk in the light, we have fellowship with each other, with the Father and the Son, and with all others who are walking in the light. Walking in the light also means being continually purified from sin. God does not say we *cannot* sin if we are walking in the light, but rather that when sin occurs there is no place to hide. Sin is immediately shown for what it is so that we can confess and be cleansed by the blood of Jesus.

1 John 1 lays out two paths we can take. Here is the first option:

> *If we claim to have fellowship with him yet walk in the darkness, we lie and do not live by the truth...If we claim to be without sin, we deceive ourselves and the truth is not in us...If we claim we have not sinned, we make him out to be a liar and his word has no place in our lives. (1 Jn. 1:6, 8, 10)*

Each of these verses begins with "If we claim." All of the claims are dishonest. However, the people who make these claims generally believe them. Many people who are not walking in the light at all are convinced that they *are* walking in it.

The second path is in verses 5, 7, and 9:

> *This is the message we have heard from him and declare to you: God is light; in him there is no darkness at all... But if we walk in the light, as he is in the light, we have fellowship with one another, and the blood of Jesus, his Son, purifies us from all sin...If we confess our sins, he is faithful and just and will forgive us our sins and purify us from all unrighteousness. (1 Jn. 1:5, 7, 9)*

These verses begin with God and move to our relationship with Him and the good consequences which flow from it as a result of His actions and His faithfulness. The consequences are fellowship, purification from all unrighteousness, and forgiveness of sins. This is the atmosphere which God provides for us in order that we may live an obedient life.

Positive Obedience

Once we have learned to refrain from disobedience and to walk in the light, we are ready for active, positive obedience.

Start out by learning to recognize the positive commands in Scripture. They are almost always expressed in superlatives. For example:

> *Rejoice in the Lord always. I will say it again: Rejoice! (Phil. 4:4)*

Because the positive commands are so all-encompassing, it is easy for us to think of them as ideals rather than realistic requirements. So the next thing to do is accept them as they are. The Bible does not qualify them, and we do not have the freedom to qualify them either.

God provides several wonderful means of obeying these commands. The first is the death of Christ. We all know that Jesus died so we could be forgiven. Few of us realize that He died so we could be *obedient*. See Romans 6 for an explanation of the efficacy of the Cross in accomplishing obedience.

The second means of obedience is the fruit of the Spirit which God gives us when we receive Christ (Gal. 5:22–23). The fruit of the Spirit is also *commanded* in these passages:

- Love: Matthew 5:44
- Joy: Philippians 4:4
- Peace: Colossians 3:15
- Patience: 1 Timothy 6:11
- Kindness: Ephesians 4:32
- Goodness: Psalm 34:14
- Faithfulness: 1 Corinthians 4:2
- Gentleness: 2 Timothy 2:25
- Self-control: 1 Corinthians 9:24–25

The third means of obedience is the prayers of others for us. Colossians 1:9–10, Philippians 1:9, and Ephesians 3:14 are all examples of praying in the will of God for believers' obedience. Wouldn't you like to wake up in the morning *"filled with the knowledge of God's will through all spiritual wisdom and understanding, pleasing God in every way and bearing fruit in every good work"* (Col. 1:9–10), all because someone prayed this for you?

The fourth means of obedience is using our will, but not willpower. It is as effortless as the first three.

> *To this end I labor, struggling with all his energy, which so powerfully works in me. (Col. 1:29)*

Although Paul labors and struggles, he does it with *God's* energy. Paul also says,

> *So then, just as you received Christ Jesus as Lord, continue to live in him, rooted and built up in him, strengthened in the faith as you were taught, and overflowing with thankfulness. (Col. 2:6–7)*

The three important words in this passage are *as*, *received*, and *continue*. *As* you received Christ Jesus as Lord. How did we receive Him? By grace through faith, not by our own goodness or by trying hard to receive Him. If we are to continue just like we started, then we are to live by faith, not by trying. The obedient life is like being born again continually. Grace and faith alone are the way we live in the kingdom.

The book of Galatians was written to people who were trying to be good after they had trusted Christ for salvation. Paul called them foolish. Trusting and trying are opposites. We cannot do them both at the same time. One of the common expressions I hear from Christians after they have fallen is, "But I tried." That is the reason they fell. *They tried.*

The positive, obedient, Christian life is based on 1) the death of Christ, 2) the fruit of the Spirit, 3) the prayers of others, and 4) choosing to obey by trusting, not by trying. God's standards are high, but His provision is just as high. His work takes the effort out of obedience.

Types of Sinners

Have mercy on me, O God,
According to your unfailing love;
According to your great compassion
Blot out my transgressions.
Wash away all my iniquity
And cleanse me from my sin.
For I know my transgressions,
And my sin is always before me.
Against you, you only, have I sinned
And done what is evil in your sight,

So that you are proved right when you speak
And justified when you judge.
(Ps. 51:1–4)

The Bible speaks of several types of sinners. The types are not based on what they have done, but on their attitudes towards God and towards their sin. Here are four examples:

1. *Jerusalem staggers, Judah is falling; their words and deeds are against the LORD, defying his glorious presence. The look on their faces testifies against them; they parade their sin like Sodom; they do not hide it. Woe to them! They have brought disaster upon themselves. (Is. 3:8–9)*

2. *Woe to those who call evil good and good evil, who put darkness for light and light for darkness, who put bitter for sweet and sweet for bitter. Woe to those who are wise in their own eyes and clever in their own sight. Woe to those who are heroes at drinking wine and champions at mixing drinks, who acquit the guilty for a bribe, but deny justice to the innocent. Therefore, as tongues of fire lick up straw and as dry grass sinks down in the flames, so their roots will decay and their flowers blow away like dust; for they have rejected the law of the LORD Almighty and spurned the word of the Holy One of Israel. (Is. 5:20–24)*

3. *The LORD saw how great man's wickedness on the earth had become, and that every inclination of the thoughts of his heart was only evil all the time. (Gen. 6:5)*

4. *The wrath of God is being revealed from heaven against all the godlessness and wickedness of men who suppress the truth by their wickedness, since what may be known about God is plain to them, because God has made it plain to them. For since the creation of the world God's invisible qualities–his eternal power and divine nature–have been clearly seen, being understood from what has been made, so that men are without excuse. For although they knew God, they neither glorified him as God nor gave thanks to him, but their thinking became futile and their foolish hearts were darkened. Although they claimed to be wise, they became fools and exchanged the glory of the immortal God for images made to look like mortal man and birds and animals and reptiles. (Rom. 1:18–23)*

Do you see the difference between these people and David? David had a great view of God, His mercy, His love, His compassion, and His Holiness. He also had a right view of his own sin; he realized that it was a terrible violation of God's holiness. Sin is not a social impropriety. The world has deified man, humanized God, and minimized sin. Consequently, there is no repentance and no forgiveness.

Forgiveness & Consequences

Then David said to Nathan, "I have sinned against the Lord." Nathan replied, "The Lord has taken away your sin. You are not going to die. But because by doing this you have made the enemies of the Lord show utter contempt, the son born to you will die." (2 Samuel 12:13–14)

You can read the complete story of David's awful sins in 2 Samuel 11–12. David violated these commands: "You shall not covet your neighbor's wife," "You shall not commit adultery," "You shall not murder." To hide his adultery, David called Uriah home from battle so Bathsheba's pregnancy would be attributed to him. The lie did not work—Uriah was too honorable. He returned to Jerusalem, but refused to go home while his men remained on the battlefield. The next day David gave a dinner for Uriah and made him drunk. He still did not go home, so David had him killed and took his wife for himself.

David did not confess these sins. He was still hiding them (or thought he was) when he was confronted by Nathan the prophet. Before David confessed, Nathan prophesied awful consequences. After David confessed, he prophesied another consequence. David was forgiven, but the consequences still came. The baby son died. One of his other sons raped one of his daughters. Another son killed the son who raped the daughter. That son was exiled. He returned from exile, conspired against David, and openly committed adultery with his father's concubines; then he was killed. These were the consequences of David's sin.

How do we know that David was forgiven?

> *Then I acknowledged my sin to you and did not cover up my iniquity. I said, "I will confess my transgressions to the Lord"—and you forgave the guilt of my sin. (Ps. 32:5)*

> *Against you, you only, have I sinned and done what is evil in your sight, so that you are proved right when you speak and justified when you judge...Cleanse me*

> *with hyssop, and I will be clean; wash me, and I will be whiter than snow. Let me hear joy and gladness; let the bones you have crushed rejoice. Hide your face from my sins and blot out all my iniquity. Create in me a pure heart, O God, and renew a steadfast spirit within me. Do not cast me from your presence or take your Holy Spirit from me. Restore to me the joy of your salvation and grant me a willing spirit, to sustain me...Save me from bloodguilt, O God, the God who saves me, and my tongue will sing of your righteousness...You do not delight in sacrifice, or I would bring it; you do not take pleasure in burnt offerings. The sacrifices of God are a broken spirit; a broken and contrite heart, O God, you will not despise. (Pss. 51:4, 7–12, 14, 16–17)*

The difference between the two kings was in their responses. David did not minimize his sins like Saul had minimized his (1 Sam. 15). He confessed and counted on God's great mercy, love, and compassion. David knew that he had forfeited his kingdom just as Saul had done:

> *Now the Spirit of the LORD had departed from Saul... (1 Sam. 16:14)*

> *Cast me not away from thy presence; and take not thy holy spirit from me. (Ps. 51:11 KJV)*

When the prophet Samuel confronted Saul, Saul responded by making excuses and trying to shift the blame. When David was confronted, he made no excuses. He repented and confessed, and the Lord forgave him. He was allowed to keep his kingdom. David still had other consequences to face, but he had the joy of forgiven sins.

Revenge

There are two sayings I know well because of hearing them many times. The first was said by children, in anger: "I'll get even." The second was said by adults, not in anger: "I don't get mad, I get even."

If there is any relative merit in these sayings, the badge goes to the first. A child's anger does not last long, so the plan for revenge is soon forgotten. For the adult who meditates on revenge, the sin is bad and long-lasting.

There are two examples of the second case in fiction. The books are *The Count of Monte Cristo* and *Ben Hur*. In both, the "hero" seems to have an unlimited amount of time and an unlimited amount of money to exercise his revenge. There is another book which says something different:

> *Do not repay anyone evil for evil. Be careful to do what is right in the eyes of everybody. If it is possible, as far as it depends on you, live at peace with everyone. Do not take revenge, my friends, but leave room for God's wrath, for it is written: "It is mine to avenge; I will repay," says the Lord. On the contrary: "If your enemy is hungry, feed him; if he is thirsty, give him something to drink. In doing this, you will heap burning coals on his head." Do not be overcome by evil, but overcome evil with good. (Rom. 12:17–21)*

Big & Little Sins

Have you ever wondered how men who have been Christians a long time fall into sexual immorality, divorce their wives, or are dishonest or unethical? Christians tell me these leaders are special targets of the Enemy because they are so greatly used. Although that is a possibility, I have difficulty with it because the Bible gives several passages of advice which, if heeded, would prevent these sins. The first is 1 Corinthians 10:12–13, which says:

> *So if you think you are standing firm, be careful that you don't fall! No temptation has seized you except what is common to man. And God is faithful; he will not let you be tempted beyond what you can bear. But when you are tempted, he will also provide a way out so that you can stand up under it.*

If a man sins, it is not caused by the greatness of temptation, or by God's unfaithfulness. Man thinks he is strong, so he is not careful. He is caught off guard and sins. As in everything, the little precedes the big. In C.S. Lewis' *The Lion, the Witch, and the Wardrobe*, Peter and Susan sought out the wise professor's help when they were trying to figure out why Lucy was telling such "whoppers." The professor's conclusion was that since Lucy did not lie about little things, she would not be telling big lies. It was more likely that their brother Edmund was telling the big lie because he was accustomed to telling little ones. The professor's answer points us to Luke 16:10:

> *Whoever can be trusted with very little can also be trusted with much, and whoever is dishonest with very little will also be dishonest with much.*

The test for trust or dishonesty in big things is trust or dishonesty in little things.

The second passage of advice is in Psalm 19.

> *Keep your servant also from willful sins; may they not rule over me. Then will I be blameless, innocent of great transgression. (Ps. 19:13)*

Why do gross sins seem to just pop up in evangelical churches? The answer is very simple: they don't. They have always been festering a long time. They were preceded by many "invisible" sins. Willful sins are endemic. When they are allowed to run rampant in churches, there is no way to stop *great transgressions*. Ask God to keep you from willful sins, so that they will not rule over you, and you will not have to watch out for the big temptations.

The third passage of advice is 1 John 2:1–2:

> *My dear children, I write this to you so that you will not sin. But if anybody does sin, we have one who speaks to the Father in our defense—Jesus Christ, the Righteous One. He is the atoning sacrifice for our sins, and not only for ours but also for the sins of the whole world.*

Read all of 1 John. It tells us the means of not sinning and the means of being forgiven if we do sin.

The fourth passage is the action churches are to take on great transgressions:

> *When you are assembled in the name of our Lord Jesus and I am with you in spirit, and the power of our Lord Jesus is present, hand this man over to Satan, so that the sinful nature may be destroyed and his spirit saved on the day of the Lord. Your boasting is not good. Don't you know that a little yeast works through the whole batch of dough? Get rid of the old*

> *yeast that you may be a new batch without yeast—as you really are. For Christ, our Passover lamb, has been sacrificed. Therefore let us keep the Festival, not with the old yeast, the yeast of malice and wickedness, but with bread without yeast, the bread of sincerity and truth. I have written you in my letter not to associate with sexually immoral people—not at all meaning the people of this world who are immoral, or the greedy and swindlers, or idolaters. In that case you would have to leave this world. But now I am writing you that you must not associate with anyone who calls himself a brother but is sexually immoral or greedy, an idolater or a slanderer, a drunkard or a swindler. With such a man do not even eat. What business is it of mine to judge those outside the church? Are you not to judge those inside? God will judge those outside. "Expel the wicked man from among you." (1 Cor. 5:4–13)*

These four teachings are clear. If great sins keep "popping up," it is because these commands are being ignored.

Good Things

There are many things that it is legitimate for us to desire. They are more than our desires; God promises them to us. Isaiah 58:11 has a beautiful description of them. This text hangs on our living room wall in English and Japanese:

> *And the Lord will guide you continually, and satisfy your desire with good things, and make your bones strong; and you shall be like a watered garden, like a spring of water, whose waters fail not. (KJV)*

Here is the condition to God's promise of continued guidance and spiritual refreshment:

> *If you take away the yoke from your midst, the pointing of the finger, and speaking wickedness, if you extend your soul to the hungry and satisfy the afflicted soul, then your light shall dawn in the darkness, and your darkness shall be as the noonday. (Is. 58:9b-10 NKJV)*

Earlier in Isaiah 58, we learn that God will answer when we call, that our righteousness will go before us and His glory will come behind us, and that "*your light [will] break forth like the dawn, and your healing shall spring up speedily*" (v. 8). How could we ask for more? This is a promise of exuberant life, light that "breaks," and health that "springs"! What are the conditions?

> *Is not this the kind of fasting I have chosen: to loose the chains of injustice and untie the cords of the yoke, to set the oppressed free and break every yoke? Is it not to share your food with the hungry and to provide the poor wanderer with shelter—when you see the naked, to clothe him, and not to turn away from your own flesh and blood? (Is. 58:6–7)*

- Setting men free from evil
- Removing their burdens
- Delivering men from oppression
- Feeding the hungry from your own supply
- Bringing the poor and afflicted to your own house

- Clothing the naked
- Taking care of your family

Doing

For Ezra had devoted himself to the study and observance of the Law of the Lord, and to teaching its decrees and laws in Israel. (Ezra 7:10)

Ezra devoted himself to three things: studying the law, observing the law, and teaching the law. We can study to acquire information. We can teach to impart information. But the strongest of the three is *doing*. Doing validates the studying and the teaching.

Biblical teaching is not just imparting information. The most neglected phrase in the Great Commission is the one on teaching:

...teaching them to obey everything I have commanded you. (Mt. 28:20)

We are to teach *obedience* to God's commands. We are not to teach information only. If we follow Ezra's example, we will study, obey, and teach obedience.

I know several churches that seek to teach obedience to the saints. Amazingly, they have picked up a reputation for being legalistic, works-righteousness churches. But they are only fulfilling Christ's command to *teach obedience*.

A Well of Living Water

On the last and greatest day of the Feast, Jesus stood and said in a loud voice, "If anyone is thirsty, let him come to me and drink." (Jn. 7:37)

> *Jesus answered her, "If you knew the gift of God and who it is that asks you for a drink, you would have asked him and he would have given you living water."... Jesus answered, "Everyone who drinks this water will be thirsty again, but whoever drinks the water I give him will never thirst. Indeed, the water I give him will become in him a spring of water welling up to eternal life." (Jn. 4:10, 13–14)*

This spring provides living water in such abundance that streams of it flow from the Christian. Notice that the person who has this well does not drink from it. He only has the well in himself *after* he drinks. "*Indeed, the water I give him* ***will become*** *in him a spring...*" "*If anyone is thirsty, let him come to* ***Me*** *and drink.*"

The well of the Holy Spirit is not for our benefit only. Once we have drunk the living water Jesus gives us, we become a source of living water for others.

Are you a flowing well of living water?

8

THE WORD OF GOD

The Word of Authority

To what or whom does the Christian look as his ultimate authority? First, authority always resides in some*one*, not some*thing*. The highest law of our land is the Constitution of the United States. We mistakenly speak of it as the final authority, but it is actually only an expression of the authority of the *people*. Similarly, God, not the Bible, is the final authority for Christians. The Bible is the primary expression of God's authority, but it is not the only expression.

> *In the past God spoke to our forefathers through the prophets at many times and in various ways, but in these last days he has spoken to us by his Son, whom he appointed heir of all things, and through whom he made the universe. (Heb. 1:1–2)*

Jesus Christ is the other main way God expresses His authority to us. However, since Jesus is a person, He is more than just an expression of God's authority—He possesses that authority Himself. How do we know this? He made the worlds, and they are sustained by Him alone (Jn. 1:1–5; Col. 1:15–20).

Unlike the Constitution, the Bible does not need amendments. God is not imperfect like people, and He does not change like people. His revelation does not need correction.

Because God is not static, impersonal, or limited, there is nothing to prevent Him from expressing His authority to us in the future. If He does, we can be confident of several things:

- The new expression will not contradict or change God's previous revelation.
- It will not be pointless or futile.
- It will not need to be corrected later.

Even in recent history, books have surfaced which purport to be revelations from God. The *Book of Mormon* is a good example. This book contradicts the Bible and has been modified many times since its first appearance in the early 1800s. This contradiction and change demonstrate that the *Book of Mormon* is not a revelation authorized by God. The teaching in other books like *God Calling* and *Angels on Assignment* is also proved false by this same test.

As Christians, we believe that the Bible is an inerrant expression of God's authority. We must never transfer our faith in His revelation to the writings of mere men. God is our final authority. Thus far He has chosen to communicate His perfect revelation in only two expressions: His Word, the Bible, and His Word, the Son.

The Errancy of Man

But among you there must not be even a hint of sexual immorality, or of any kind of impurity, or of greed, because these are improper for God's holy people. Nor should there be obscenity, foolish talk or coarse joking, which are out of place, but rather thanksgiving. (Eph. 5:3–4)

About forty years ago I copied these verses on a poster and hung it on the wall of the stairwell leading to the school mailboxes at a Christian college. The entire student body came down those steps at least once a day.

The effect on some of the students surprised me. Until that time, they had thought that using the Lord's name in vain was the only form of profanity. They carefully avoided it while participating in other kinds of dirty talk. This told me that they did not read the Bible completely, carefully, or often, nor did they read it with the anticipation of finding some undiscovered truth to obey. If this text catches you like it caught them, perhaps you need some help in your Scripture reading. The next sections will give you that help.

Reading the Scriptures

All Scripture is God-breathed and is useful for teaching, rebuking, correcting and training in righteousness, so that the man of God may be thoroughly equipped for every good work. (2 Tim. 3:16–17)

In the presence of God and of Christ Jesus, who will judge the living and the dead, and in view of his

> *appearing and his kingdom, I give you this charge: Preach the Word; be prepared in season and out of season; correct, rebuke and encourage—with great patience and careful instruction. (2 Tim. 4:1–2)*
>
> *Until I come, devote yourself to the public reading of Scripture, to preaching and to teaching. (1 Tim. 4:13)*

There was a time when there were very few Bibles, even in cultured lands. There were no printing presses, and most of the people were illiterate. If they received the Word it was through the public reading of the Scriptures. Today we can read, and most of us own at least one Bible.

A few years ago at one of our schools of practical Christianity, we asked the students three questions: "How long have you been a Christian? How many times have you read the entire New Testament? How many times have you read the entire Old Testament?" We found that the average reading of the New Testament was once every 2.5 years and the average reading of the Old Testament was once every 7 years.

Recently I asked the same three questions at a men's conference. The total number of years of Christianity was 514.5. The total number of times through the New Testament was 36, and the number of times through the Old Testament was 18. That means that, on average, they had read the New Testament once every 14 years and the Old Testament once every 28 years. That amounts to spending *less than 30 seconds a day* in the Bible. That is not very encouraging.

READ THE NEW TESTAMENT IN 67 DAYS

Many Christians read the Scriptures sporadically in both time and place. In other words, they read them "now and then" and "here and there." They gravitate to their favorite chapters. Some of them have never even read the whole New Testament through. The body of Christ is appallingly ignorant of God's Word, and there is a corresponding lack of obedience.

There is no substitute for reading the Word of God. Listening to the best Bible teachers in the world will not make up for personal ignorance of Scripture or replace the benefits of spending time with the Lord in His Word.

Here are some helps for you to consider when reading the Word. First, the genealogies in the New Testament take up less than two chapters. If they are a problem to you, skip them for now go back over them separately; it will only take five minutes. They would not be there if they were not important. However, they are not intended to stop you from reading the rest of the New Testament.

Second, do not stop for hard-to-understand passages; keep reading. They will make more sense when you do that, and they will make even more sense the second time through.

Third, if you think the Bible is dull reading, start with the exciting parts like Luke and Acts.

Fourth, if you are a slow reader (e.g., 150 words a minute), you can still read the whole Bible in eighty hours. The reason it takes so long to get through is the days, weeks, or months that you do not read it at all. If you are a listener instead of a reader, you can get an audio recording and listen to the whole Bible being read aloud. I keep an edition in my car and enjoy it very much.

Fifth, try a schedule. If you read four chapters each day, it will only take you a week to read Matthew and a week to read Acts. The other twenty-five books of the New Testament will take less than a week each, and seventeen of those have six chapters or fewer, so they can be read in a maximum of one and a half days each.

The object is not to get through the Bible so you can say, "I finished." The object is to know God better and obey Him more and more. You cannot say that you know what God wants from you without knowing all His revelation and His revelational will.

Here is a plan for reading the New Testament in 67 days:

Name of Book	No. of Chapters	No. of Days
Matthew	28	7
Mark	16	4
Luke	24	6
John	21	5
Acts	28	7
Romans	16	4
1 Corinthians	16	4
2 Corinthians	13	3
Galatians	6	1.5
Ephesians	6	1.5
Philippians	4	1
Colossians	4	1
1 Thessalonians	5	1
2 Thessalonians	3	1
1 Timothy	6	1.5
2 Timothy	4	1
Titus	3	1
Philemon	1	1
Hebrews	13	3
James	5	1
1 Peter	5	1
2 Peter	3	1
1 John	5	1
2 John	1	1
3 John	1	1
Jude	1	1
Revelation	22	5.5

Scripture—True or False?

Here are a few thoughts for looking at Scripture, especially the verses that sound great but seem hard to live. When confronted with such verses, ask yourself this question: Is it true or false? Make yourself answer the question. That way you cannot slide over it.

Having answered, "True," thank God for it. From now on, you cannot ignore it. You have just given thanks for it.

Here is an example:

> *Be joyful always; pray continually; give thanks in all circumstances, for this is God's will for you in Christ Jesus. (1 Thess. 5:16–18)*

True or false? True! Thank God. Now it is just a question of how to pray continually and give thanks in everything, not a question of whether we can. We have thanked God for this command, and we are now *willing* to obey.

Here are three more verses to practice your true-and-false test on:

> *His divine power has given us everything we need for life and godliness through our knowledge of him who called us by his own glory and goodness. (2 Pet. 1:3)*

> *And God is able to make all grace abound to you, so that in all things at all times, having all that you need, you will abound in every good work. (2 Cor. 9:8)*

> *Now to him who is able to do immeasurably more than all we ask or imagine, according to his power that is at work within us, to him be glory in the church*

and in Christ Jesus throughout all generations, for ever and ever! Amen. (Eph. 3:20–21)

We say "True" the first time because we are Christians, and we are supposed to say "True" to Scripture. After you answer, "True," and thank God for each truth, read the verses again. Answer, "Very true," and thank Him again. Continue doing this until the truth of your answer begins to seep into you, so that you are overwhelmed with wonder because of the magnitude of these words. Now we can believe and obey God from our hearts as well as our heads.

"No"

The Bible has several clear texts that describe the way the world does things with an attached command that says "no" to that kind of conduct:

So I tell you this, and insist on it in the Lord, that you must no longer live as the Gentiles do, in the futility of their thinking. They are darkened in their understanding and separated from the life of God because of the ignorance that is in them due to the hardening of their hearts. Having lost all sensitivity, they have given themselves over to sensuality so as to indulge in every kind of impurity, with a continual lust for more. (Eph. 4:17–19)

Do not lie to each other, since you have taken off your old self with its practices and have put on the new self, which is being renewed in knowledge in the image of its Creator. (Col. 3:9–10)

What then? Shall we sin because we are not under law but under grace? By no means! Don't you know

> *that when you offer yourselves to someone to obey him as slaves, you are slaves to the one whom you obey—whether you are slaves to sin, which leads to death, or to obedience, which leads to righteousness? But thanks be to God that, though you used to be slaves to sin, you wholeheartedly obeyed the form of teaching to which you were entrusted. You have been set free from sin and have become slaves to righteousness. (Rom. 6:15–18)*

> *If any of you has a dispute with another, dare he take it before the ungodly for judgment instead of before the saints? Do you not know that the saints will judge the world? And if you are to judge the world, are you not competent to judge trivial cases? Do you not know that we will judge angels? How much more the things of this life! Therefore, if you have disputes about such matters, appoint as judges even men of little account in the church! I say this to shame you. Is it possible that there is nobody among you wise enough to judge a dispute between believers? But instead, one brother goes to law against another—and this in front of unbelievers! The very fact that you have lawsuits among you means you have been completely defeated already. Why not rather be wronged? Why not rather be cheated? Instead, you yourselves cheat and do wrong, and you do this to your brothers. (1 Cor. 6:1–8)*

Are these texts true? Has God given us provision to obey them? Do you desire to obey them?

MEDITATION

I have hidden your word in my heart, that I might not sin against you. (Ps. 119:11)

There are many kinds of Bible study: reading, synthetic Bible studies, group Bible studies, Old Testament references in context, subject studies, and more. There is a kind of Bible study that goes beyond these. It is meditation. Meditation is more mystical and more practical than these other types of Bible study.

In order to explain this, let me tell you first what meditation is *not*. It is not looking for a deeper, hidden meaning in the passage. It is not numerology or looking for a codified arrangement of the text. It is not saying that the plain meaning of the text is not the right meaning. Meditation does not have to do with our understanding of the text, but rather *where* we understand it.

Studying generally results in head knowledge. If we memorized Matthew 5:38–48, we might come up with all the right answers on a written exam about it. Would we do as well if we were put into a laboratory with evil people who sued us, hit us, forced us to carry their belongings, asked us for money, and persecuted us?

In order to pass the lab test, I need have my head knowledge transferred to my heart. Having Scripture knowledge in my heart makes it *practical*. My actions—planned and unplanned—come from there. That is where I should store all this good stuff so that when I overflow, good comes out. Here are three teachings from the gospels that describe how what we store up inside affects our actions:

> *You brood of vipers, how can you who are evil say anything good? For out of the overflow of the heart the mouth speaks. The good man brings good things out of the good stored up in him, and the evil man brings evil things out of the evil stored up in him. (Mt. 12:34–35)*

> *He went on: "What comes out of a man is what makes him 'unclean.' For from within, out of men's hearts, come evil thoughts, sexual immorality, theft, murder, adultery, greed, malice, deceit, lewdness, envy, slander, arrogance and folly. All these evils come from inside and make a man 'unclean.'" (Mk. 7:20–23)*

> *The good man brings good things out of the good stored up in his heart, and the evil man brings evil things out of the evil stored up in his heart. For out of the overflow of his heart his mouth speaks. (Lk. 6:45)*

Early in my Christian life I memorized hundreds of Scripture verses. I knew them word-for-word, with their references. I could call them up at anytime. It did not occur to me, or to others, that I was not living them out. It was probably three years before I began to grow suspicious. I realized that it was one thing for my brain to spout Scripture, and it was another thing entirely for my heart to overflow. I thought that memorizing Scripture was hiding God's word in my heart. It was not; it was hiding His word in my *head*. I might have been able to pass a written test on the Bible, but it was a sure thing that I would *not* pass the lab test.

I thank God that neither test is given, since we have been saved by grace. After we are saved, we are to be careful to do good works:

> *For we are God's workmanship, created in Christ Jesus to do good works, which God prepared in advance for us to do. (Eph. 2:10)*

Whether our good works are the fruit of the Spirit or words and actions, they come from our *hearts*. Let's look at a few examples from the Bible:

> *Then Jesus said to his host, "When you give a luncheon or dinner, do not invite your friends, your brothers or relatives, or your rich neighbors; if you do, they may invite you back and so you will be repaid. But when you give a banquet, invite the poor, the crippled, the lame, the blind, and you will be blessed. Although they cannot repay you, you will be repaid at the resurrection of the righteous." (Lk. 14:12–14)*

> *Do everything without complaining or arguing, so that you may become blameless and pure, children of God without fault in a crooked and depraved generation, in which you shine like stars in the universe as you hold out the word of life—in order that I may boast on the day of Christ that I did not run or labor for nothing. (Phil. 2:14–16)*

> *But I tell you, Do not resist an evil person. If someone strikes you on the right cheek, turn to him the other also. And if someone wants to sue you and take your tunic, let him have your cloak as well. If someone*

> *forces you to go one mile, go with him two miles. Give to the one who asks you, and do not turn away from the one who wants to borrow from you.* (Mt. 5:39–42)

Each of these passages contains imperatives. Look at them again. What do they say? Do you understand them? You may have questions about them. If you have questions like, "Where do you draw the line?" "You mean I cannot invite my parents?" "How rich?" "Suppose he is wrong!" "Suppose he is evil!" then you probably understand in your head and *not with your heart.*

To understand with your heart, ask this question: "Is the command clear?" Then ask yourself: "True or false?" After you say, "True," praise God for the command *with thanksgiving.* When you do this, you have begun to hide the Word in your heart. Continue to hide it in your heart by soaking in the Scriptures, musing and meditating on them. Pray for the lame and the blind, your enemies, and evil people. Confess anything that is hindering willing obedience. Then begin to long for and pray for opportunities to obey the commands unconditionally.

If you are a Christian and you do not understand what I am saying, something is very wrong. You might be hesitating because you would be out of step with your friends if you suddenly started obeying these commands from the heart. In other words, you do not want to be godly if it means being different from the rest of the saints.

Meditation does not take study. It takes prayerful, willing submission to the text. That is why it can be done all of the time.

> *Do not let this Book of the Law depart from your mouth; meditate on it day and night, so that you may*

be careful to do everything written in it. Then you will be prosperous and successful. (Josh. 1:8)

Blessed is the man who does not walk in the counsel of the wicked or stand in the way of sinners or sit in the seat of mockers. But his delight is in the law of the LORD, and on his law he meditates day and night. He is like a tree planted by streams of water, which yields its fruit in season and whose leaf does not wither. Whatever he does prospers. (Ps. 1:1–3)

Is the Bible just in your *head*, or is it in your *heart*? We are in the lab all of the time.

9

EVERYDAY HOLINESS

God's direction

> *"Woe to the rebellious children," says the Lord, "who carry out a plan, but not mine, who make a league, but not of my Spirit that they may add sin to sin who set out to go down to Egypt without asking for my counsel." (Is. 30:1–2)*

This text applies to nations, the world, and individuals. They make plans and implement them. They draw up treaties, agreements, and contracts. The plans are not God's. They do not ask the Lord for advice. Many Christians also follow this pattern. God says, "Woe to the rebellious children."

In the early stages of the conquest of Canaan, the Gibeonites deceived Joshua into making a treaty with them under oath:

The men of Israel sampled their provisions but did not inquire of the LORD. Then Joshua made a treaty of peace with them to let them live, and the leaders of the assembly ratified it by oath. (Josh. 9:14–15)

There is a way to follow God's plans that is not good, but is still better than following your own way:

Be not like a horse or a mule, without understanding, which must be curbed with a bit and bridle, else it will not keep with you. (Ps. 32:9)

It is not pleasant to have a bit in your mouth, a bridle on your head, and no understanding of where you are going. If we do not seek God's will on our own, God, in His faithfulness, will jerk us around with a bit and bridle to ensure that we do not miss it.

God has a better way, His perfect way:

I will instruct you and teach you the way you should go: I will guide you with mine eye. (Ps. 32:8)

This personal guidance from God is based on a relationship with Him which presupposes the forgiveness David prayed for earlier in the psalm.

In all thy ways acknowledge him, and he shall direct thy paths. (Prov. 3:6 KJV)

"All our ways" includes business dealings, purchases, vacation plans, friendships, recreation, and every other area of our lives. If we are honest with ourselves, we will acknowledge that we seldom if ever share these with our heavenly Father.

Perhaps if we started to share the details of our lives with Him, the joy and relief from strain would equip us for the big decisions that come our way.

The Will of God

What is the meaning of God's will? What do we have to do in order to do God's will? How can we know God's will?

There are two expressions of God's ultimate will in the Scriptures. The first is our salvation:

> *This is good, and pleases God our Savior, who wants all men to be saved and to come to a knowledge of the truth. (1 Tim. 2:3–4)*

The second is our sanctification:

> *It is God's will that you should be sanctified. (1 Thess. 4:3a)*

Both of these were accomplished by Jesus Christ:

> *It is because of him that you are in Christ Jesus, who has become for us wisdom from God—that is, our righteousness, holiness and redemption. (1 Cor. 1:30)*

The will of God for us is our salvation, which includes our justification (conversion), holiness (sanctification), and the redemption of our bodies at the Second Coming. Since we have already experienced justification, our concern now is our holiness (sanctification). Remember, it is already provided for:

> *His divine power has given us everything we need for life and godliness through our knowledge of him who called us by his own glory and goodness. (2 Pet. 1:3)*

But the fruit of the Spirit is love, joy, peace, patience, kindness, goodness, faithfulness, gentleness and self-control. Against such things there is no law. Those who belong to Christ Jesus have crucified the sinful nature with its passions and desires. (Gal. 5:22–24)

Knowing the details of God's will for the decisions we need to make in our lives is not difficult if we are walking in the light. If we are not walking in it, the will of God could be written on the wall and we would not be able to read it.

Knowing the Will of God

The important thing in any major decision is to seek to know the will of God. Here are a few principles from the Bible which you can use as a start to help you determine God's will:

1. *Want* to know the will of God.

   If anyone chooses to do God's will, he will find out whether my teaching comes from God or whether I speak on my own. (Jn. 7:17)

   If I want to be in the will of God, and God wants me to be in His will, there is no way I will miss it.

2. The desires of your heart.

   Delight yourself in the LORD and he will give you the desires of your heart. (Ps. 37:4)

   Your desires are not necessarily wrong. If you delight in the Lord, He will give you your desires.

3. The witness and leading of the Spirit.

   Because those who are led by the Spirit of God are sons of God. (Rom. 8:14)

   But if you are led by the Spirit, you are not under law. (Gal. 5:18)

   Whether you turn to the right or to the left, your ears will hear a voice behind you, saying, "This is the way; walk in it." (Is. 30:21)

4. The Word of God, both in general principles and specifics. Here is Jesus' specific statement to the rich young ruler:

   Jesus looked at him and loved him. "One thing you lack," he said. "Go, sell everything you have and give to the poor, and you will have treasure in heaven. Then come, follow me." (Mk. 10:21)

   This is not general. If it were, everyone would have to do it. An example of the Word of God in general is:

   Do not be yoked together with unbelievers. For what do righteousness and wickedness have in common? Or what fellowship can light have with darkness? What harmony is there between Christ and Belial? What does a believer have in common with an unbeliever? What agreement is there between the temple of God and idols? For we are the temple of the living God. As God has said: "I will live with them and walk among them, and I will be their God, and they will be my people." (2 Cor. 6:14–16)

This text applies to all believers all of the time. We do not need to seek guidance about marrying an unbeliever. We already have the direction in the Word.

Here is another general statement that applies to all Christians:

Then Jesus came to them and said, "All authority in heaven and on earth has been given to me. Therefore go and make disciples of all nations, baptizing them in the name of the Father and of the Son and of the Holy Spirit, and teaching them to obey everything I have commanded you. And surely I am with you always, to the very end of the age." (Mt. 28:18–20)

5. Circumstances over which you have no control.

   And we know that in all things God works for the good of those who love him, who have been called according to his purpose. (Rom. 8:28)

6. The counsel and opinions of your father.

7. The counsel and opinions of mature Christians. Do not seek the counsel of close friends. They are too likely to agree with you.

8. Get underway in a certain direction and watch God open or close doors.

Next, make a list of the pros and cons for each of your options. This will help you think in a straight line.

Lastly, here are a few questions to consider:

- Have you been effective in evangelism?
- Would you rather build up believers or evangelize the lost?
- Do you want to be holy?
- What is your present profession?
- Do you care what the world thinks?
- Do you care what the saints think?
- What are your spiritual gifts?
- What are your natural gifts and training?

Life & Doctrine

For this reason I am sending to you Timothy, my son whom I love, who is faithful in the Lord. He will remind you of my way of life in Christ Jesus, which agrees with what I teach everywhere in every church. (1 Cor. 4:17)

I hope in the Lord Jesus to send Timothy to you soon, that I also may be cheered when I receive news about you. I have no one else like him, who takes a genuine interest in your welfare. For everyone looks out for his own interests, not those of Jesus Christ. (Phil. 2:19–21)

Timothy was known for his godliness. Paul later wrote these instructions to him:

Be diligent in these matters; give yourself wholly to them, so that everyone may see your progress. ***Watch***

> ***your life and doctrine closely.*** *Persevere in them, because* ***if you do, you will save yourself and your hearers.*** *(1 Tim. 4:16)*

Your holy life and your clear teaching of the gospel is the effective salvation message. What is the life?

> *Don't let anyone look down on you because you are young, but set an example for the believers in speech, in life, in love, in faith and in purity. (1 Tim. 4:12)*

What is the teaching?

> *Until I come, devote yourself to the public reading of Scripture, to preaching and to teaching. (1 Tim. 4:13)*

Life and doctrine include what you are and what you teach, what you do and what you say. There really isn't anything else. If your doctrine does not make you more like Jesus, then it is either not sound doctrine or it is doctrine that is only in your head, not in your heart.

Paul's instructions are simple and complete: watch these two areas closely. The result is salvation for yourself and those you teach.

Recently I was talking with a young woman who had gone to a Christian high school and graduated from a well-known Christian college. Her parents were in Christian work. When I asked her when was the last time she had read through the New Testament, she replied that she had never read the whole thing. And of course she had read the Old Testament even less. This is now a standard question I ask, and it is almost a standard answer. Christians are not watching their life and doctrine closely. So I pass the same instruction on to you—"Watch your life and doctrine closely."

Sound Doctrine

False teaching or false doctrine come up several places in the New Testament (e.g., 1 Tim. 1:18–20 and 1 Jn. 4:1–3). The doctrine Paul talks about in 1 Timothy 4:16 is not false teaching, and it is not the distinctive beliefs of various denominations.

This doctrine is the gospel of the Lord Jesus Christ. How do we know? It is *saving* teaching.

Obviously our different secondary doctrines and practices cannot all be right. Some are not important. We have used the word "doctrine" and our secondary teachings to create divisions among saved people. To my knowledge, the Bible does not use "doctrine" that way. Read Romans 14. It is the primary doctrine of the gospel that saves and sanctifies and is, consequently, of ultimate importance.

> *For the kingdom of God is not a matter of eating and drinking, but of righteousness, peace, and joy in the Holy Spirit, because anyone who serves Christ in this way is pleasing to God and approved by men. (Rom. 14:17–18)*

When Paul stood up to Peter in Galatians 2, the issue was *saving* teaching or *saving* truth, as I mentioned above.

> *"When Peter came to Antioch, I opposed him to his face, because he was clearly in the wrong. Before certain men came from James, he used to eat with the Gentiles. But when they arrived, he began to draw back and separate himself from the Gentiles because he*

> *was afraid of those who belonged to the circumcision group. The other Jews joined him in his hypocrisy, so that by their hypocrisy even Barnabas was led astray. When I saw that they were not acting in line with the truth of the gospel, I said to Peter in front of them all, "You are a Jew, yet you live like a Gentile and not like a Jew. How is it, then, that you force Gentiles to follow Jewish customs?" (Gal. 2:11–14)*

It was the same in Acts 11 and 15:

> *"As I began to speak, the Holy Spirit came on them as he had come on us at the beginning. Then I remembered what the Lord had said: 'John baptized with water, but you will be baptized with the Holy Spirit.' So if God gave them the same gift as he gave us, who believed in the Lord Jesus Christ, who was I to think that I could oppose God?" When they heard this, they had no further objections and praised God saying, "So then, God has granted even the Gentiles repentance unto life." (Acts 11:15–18)*

> *No! We believe it is through the grace of our Lord Jesus that we are saved, just as they are. (Acts 15:11)*

The early creeds were designed to refute teaching that did not save. The later confessions were made to divide saved people. Yet we call all these confessions "sound doctrine."

Giving

Love has first priority in the Bible. It is the most important and most comprehensive fruit of the Spirit. It is the first commandment, and it is the second commandment. All the other teachings of the Bible fit into it. God is the source of all love, and He expresses His love to the world by giving.

Giving is preached much more than it is practiced. Perhaps this is because the preaching is prompted by the desire to *receive* rather than the desire to give. Many churches and radio and television programs teach giving by encouraging people to give to their ministry. The emphasis is, "You are to give so that I can receive." It is a veneer to hide covetousness.

Another reason giving is taught more than practiced is that we are not taught how to give lovingly by example. If godliness were widespread, it would not be necessary to teach giving. People would give themselves and their money, rather than giving their money *instead* of themselves. They would also give their money to the right places, in the right amounts, instead of giving where people tell them to.

We should give ourselves first to the Lord, then to others. Second Corinthians has two examples of this.

> *And now, brothers, we want you to know about the grace that God has given the Macedonian churches. Out of the most severe trial, their overflowing joy and their extreme poverty welled up in rich generosity. (2 Cor. 8:1–2)*

> *For you know the grace of our Lord Jesus Christ, that though he was rich, yet for your sakes he became poor, so that you through his poverty might become rich. (2 Cor. 8:9)*

The people giving in the first example were intolerably poor, and in the second the person was wealthy beyond all measure. Giving should not be based on how much we have, but on how much we *love*. With this as a prerequisite, we can look at the places and the people to whom we should give.

God is our example for giving food and clothing to widows, orphans, and aliens:

> *For the Lord your God is God of gods and Lord of lords, the great God, mighty and awesome, who shows no partiality and accepts no bribes. He defends the cause of the fatherless and the widow, and loves the alien, giving him food and clothing. (Deut. 10:17–19)*

> *Religion that God our Father accepts as pure and faultless is this: to look after orphans and widows in their distress and to keep oneself from being polluted by the world. (Jas. 1:27)*

True and pure religion takes care of orphans and widows. Over the centuries, Christians have done a moderate job of taking care of orphans. We have not done as well with widows, and we have not done well at all in keeping ourselves from being polluted by the world.

We are also to give to the starving and naked:

> *What good is it, my brothers, if a man claims to have faith but has no deeds? Can such faith save him? Suppose a brother or sister is without clothes and daily food. If one of you says to him, "Go, I wish you well; keep warm and well fed," but does nothing about his physical needs, what good is it? In the same way, faith by itself, if it is not accompanied by action, is dead. (Jas. 2:14–17)*

We are to give to the poor near by and far away. Paul spent parts of five chapters (1 Cor. 16, 2 Cor. 8 and 9, Gal. 2, and Rom. 15) raising money from Galatia, Macedonia, and Achaia for the poor people in Judea.

We should supply the needs of God's people and *everyone else*:

> *He who has been stealing must steal no longer, but must work, doing something useful with his own hands, that he may have something to share with* ***those in need.*** *(Eph. 4:28)*

We should give to those who teach the Word to us:

> *In the same way, the Lord has commanded that those who preach the gospel should receive their living from the gospel. (1 Cor. 9:14)*

> *Anyone who receives instruction in the word must share all good things with his instructor. (Gal. 6:6)*

The Philippians are a good example for us in this. Paul says they were the only church who supported him when he set out from Macedonia and while he was in Thessalonica (Phil. 4:15–16).

Giving should not be legalistic (e.g., tithing only). Nor should it be anti-legalistic (anti-tithing). Jesus spoke to both of these when He said in Luke 11:42,

> *Woe to you Pharisees, because you give God a tenth of your mint, rue and all other kinds of garden herbs, but you neglect justice and the love of God. You*

> *should have practiced the latter without leaving the former undone.*

Do not neglect tithing. Tithe lovingly, ungrudgingly, and not legalistically. Consider the tenth a minimum, not even thinking of it as your own money. Take it off the *top* of your income and give it to one or more of the areas mentioned above.

It could be seen as "better stewardship" to give to a corporation which has an IRS-approved, nonprofit, tax-deductible status. However, if you are giving in order to *get*, the blessing of the Lord will not be in your giving. Another difficulty with restricting your giving this way is that the widows, orphans, and aliens may not be approved by the IRS. The Bible teachers and missionaries may not be approved, either.

Western Christians have automated giving to make it efficient. Although there is the legitimate issue of giving anonymously, giving impersonally can mean giving without love. If giving is a source of pride or seeking merit, remember Matthew 6:1–4:

> *Be careful not to do your "acts of righteousness" before men, to be seen by them. If you do, you will have no reward from your Father in heaven. So when you give to the needy, do not announce it with trumpets, as the hypocrites do in the synagogues and on the streets, to be honored by men. I tell you the truth, they have received their reward in full. But when you give to the needy, do not let your left hand know what your right hand is doing, so that your giving may be in secret. Then your Father, who sees what is done in secret, will reward you.*

Most people give to the places that express needs and that ask them to give a certain amount. If everyone limited their giving to the call for money, the missions who believe that they have no biblical basis to raise money for themselves that way would never receive support.

There is a teaching that applies the "storehouse" of Malachi 3:10 to the local church, i.e., your "whole tithe" must go to the church you attend. This contradicts the Bible's teaching on other places for giving tithes to:

> *Be sure to set aside a tenth of all that your fields produce each year.* ***Eat the tithe of your grain, new wine and oil, and the firstborn of your herds and flocks in the presence of the LORD your God at the place he will choose as a dwelling for his Name, so that you may learn to revere the LORD your God always.*** *But if that place is too distant and you have been blessed by the LORD your God and cannot carry your tithe (because the place where the LORD will choose to put his Name is so far away), then exchange your tithe for silver, and take the silver with you and go to the place the LORD your God will choose. Use the silver to buy whatever you like: cattle, sheep, wine or other fermented drink, or anything you wish. Then you and your household shall eat there in the presence of the LORD your God and rejoice. And do not neglect the* ***Levites*** *living in your towns, for they have no allotment or inheritance of their own. At the end of every three years, bring all the tithes of that year's produce and store it in your towns, so* ***that the Levites (who have no allotment or inheritance of their own) and the aliens, the fatherless and the widows who live in your towns may come***

> ***and eat and be satisfied, and so that the Lord your God may bless you in all the work of your hands.*** *(Deut. 14:22–29)*

Give lovingly, give personally, give prayerfully.

Rich Generosity

> *And now, brothers, we want you to know about the grace that God has given the Macedonian churches. Out of the* ***most severe trial,*** *their* ***overflowing*** *joy and their* ***extreme poverty*** *welled up in* ***rich generosity.*** *For I testify that they gave as much as they were able, and even beyond their ability. Entirely on their own, they urgently pleaded with us for the privilege of sharing in this service to the saints. And they did not do as we expected, but they* ***gave themselves*** *first to* ***the Lord and then to*** *us in keeping with God's will. (2 Cor. 8:1–5)*

We do not usually think of "severe trials" and "overflowing joy" going together. Nor do expect extreme poverty to well up in rich generosity. Another unusual image here is Paul's description of how the Macedonians "*urgently pleaded* with us *for the privilege of sharing* in this service to the saints." This is refreshing to read after getting so many letters "urgently pleading with us" to give.

In this passage, Paul teaches the Corinthians the importance of giving from the heart. He teaches them to give for their own good and for the good of the people to whom they give. He was collecting money as well as teaching, but he was collecting for the needs of others, not for himself or for his own ministry.

> *For God so loved the world that He* ***gave****... (Jn. 3:16)*

> *I am not commanding you, but I want to test the sincerity of your love by comparing it with the earnestness of others. For you know the grace of our Lord Jesus Christ, that though he was rich, yet for your sakes he became poor, so that you through his poverty might become rich. (2 Cor. 8:8–9)*

Giving is a gracious work and an essential component of sincere love. Do you give your time? Do you give your home in hospitality? Do you give your possessions? Do you give your resources? Would you give your life? If your answer is, "I don't have the time, or a home, or money," those are not valid excuses.

> *For if the willingness is there, the gift is acceptable according to what one has, not according to what he does not have. (2 Cor. 8:12)*

If you are willing, you may find yourself welling up in rich generosity, even in your poverty.

To Whom Should We Give?

> *When the Son of Man comes in his glory, and all the angels with him, he will sit on his throne in heavenly glory. All the nations will be gathered before him, and he will separate the people one from another as a shepherd separates the sheep from the goats. He will put the sheep on his right and the goats on his left. Then the King will say to those on his right, "Come, you who are blessed by my Father; take your inheritance, the kingdom prepared for you since the*

> *creation of the world. For I was hungry and you gave me something to eat, I was thirsty and you gave me something to drink, I was a stranger and you invited me in, I needed clothes and you clothed me, I was sick and you looked after me, I was in prison and you came to visit me." Then the righteous will answer him, "Lord, when did we see you hungry and feed you, or thirsty and give you something to drink? When did we see you a stranger and invite you in, or needing clothes and clothe you? When did we see you sick or in prison and go to visit you?" The King will reply, "I tell you the truth, whatever you did for one of the least of these brothers of mine, you did for me." (Mt. 25:31–40)*

"Whatever you did for one of least of these, you did for me." Isn't that wonderful? Would you like to do something for Jesus? Feed the hungry, give water to the thirsty, clothe the naked, invite strangers into your home, visit the sick, visit prisoners. Suppose it is not Jesus you visit, but a con man or a thief. Have I ever been ripped off while caring for this kind of person? Yes, several times. However, the blessing of giving and receiving has been much greater than my negative experiences. The difficulty of this kind of giving is no reason at all to choose to be with the goats instead of the sheep.

From the Heart

> *The good man brings good things out of the good stored up in his heart, and the evil man brings evil things out of the evil stored up in his heart. For out of the overflow of his heart his mouth speaks. (Lk. 6:45)*

The Lord says: "These people come near to me with their mouth and honor me with their lips, but their hearts are far from me. Their worship of me is made up only of rules taught by men." (Is. 29:13)

People have God-given escape valves to keep them from exploding. Laughter and tears are two of them. The mouth is another. The cure for a bad mouth is to keep good stored up in your heart.

However, not everything that comes out of the mouth is from the heart. Some of what comes out of people's mouths is just what they have been taught, whether true or false, like in Isaiah 29:13. This is why people can recite sound doctrine but lose their temper at home.

The real person is the *heart* person, not the head person. We are two persons—the person taught by men and the person of the heart. Can these two be the same? Yes, but it is not automatic. We can teach children that it is wrong to lie. That is not the same as teaching children *not to lie*. The first is teaching the head; the second is teaching the heart.

Not everything that comes out of the mouth comes from the heart. Do the good truths you speak come from your heart, or only from your head?

Damage Control (Integrity)

Others went out on the sea in ships; they were merchants on the mighty waters. They saw the works of the Lord, his wonderful deeds in the deep. For he spoke and stirred up a tempest that lifted high the waves. They mounted up to the heavens and went down to the depths; in their peril their courage melted

> *away. They reeled and staggered like drunken men; they were at their wits' end. Then they cried out to the Lord in their trouble, and he brought them out of their distress. He stilled the storm to a whisper; the waves of the sea were hushed. They were glad when it grew calm, and he guided them to their desired haven. Let them give thanks to the Lord for his unfailing love and his wonderful deeds for men. Let them exalt him in the assembly of the people and praise him in the council of the elders. (Ps. 107:23–32)*

There is nothing more tranquil nor more violent than the sea. Psalm 107:23–32, Luke 8:22–25, and Acts 27:14–44 all describe violent storms. Ships were caught in each of these storms, and the men were terrified because their ship was in danger of sinking.

On 19 July, 1950, in Tsushima Straits, Task Force 77 rode out a typhoon. I was on the *USS Brush*, a destroyer in that task force. At 3:40 that morning I was almost washed overboard. Psalm 107 applied to me. In November 1950, en route from Japan to Midway Island, bucking fifty-knot winds and heavy seas, the same destroyer lost her port bilge keel and had her motor whale boat carried away by the sea. Again, Psalm 107 applied.

There is a special definition of the word "integrity" that I like. It has to do with the sea-worthiness of a ship. It is called watertight integrity. When a ship is battened down, water cannot get inside. The ship cannot sink. This integrity has to do with *interior* hatches, doors, and water-tight compartments as well as the exterior of the ship. If the ship has interior integrity, it will not sink even if a breach is made in the exterior.

In between the two storms mentioned above, the *Brush* hit an underwater mine on 26 September off Tanchon, Korea. The mine left a large hole in the port side below the water line, severely compromising the ship's exterior integrity. But because of the interior integrity of the ship, we did not lose her.

I would like to apply this watertight integrity to the Christian. Our exterior and interior integrities are, first of all, dependent upon God's faithfulness, grace, and continual presence.

Exterior integrity is concerned with storms and attacks from the outside. 1 Peter 5:8–9 and Ephesians 6:10–18 describe how to handle these attacks. Peter tells us to be self-controlled and alert. Stay awake, and you will not be blindsided. Ephesians tells us what kind of clothing to wear and what weapons to carry so that the attacks will not harm us. Although these passages are well known, it is amazing how many Christians feel unfairly treated when they are caught sleeping unarmed.

What happens when something breaches our exterior defense? Do we sink? Do we surrender to the enemy? Or do we have a damage-control system? This depends on our interior integrity. Do we have layers of watertight compartments to protect us from this breach?

The essence of damage control is speed. The faster we get help to the damaged area, 1) the sooner we are an effective fighting unit again and 2) the less extensive the damage becomes. If the enemy gets past our defenses and we respond with sin, then effective damage control is immediate confession and repentance toward God. If we do not exercise fast damage control, we will have to defend against more sins and greater sins.

In a ship, exterior integrity is of first importance, and interior integrity is secondary. In the Christian life, *interior* integrity is primary. Ephesians 6:11 tells us to put on the full armor of God (exterior). However, the verse prior to that says, "Finally, be strong in the Lord and in his mighty power" (interior).

> *The good man brings good things out of the good stored up in him... (Mt. 12:35)*

If we store up good things in our heart (interior), then good things will overflow (exterior).

> *I have hidden your word in my heart that I might not sin against you. (Ps. 119:11)*

> *Oh, that their hearts would be inclined to fear me and keep all my commands always, so that it might go well with them and their children forever. (Deut. 5:29)*

It is possible to ride out storms and fierce attacks with peace and joy. Being under attack is not a defeat. In fact, the attack is a cause for joy. But many Christians do not *survive* the attacks, much less triumph. Consequently, we build up many examples of defeat. Our models are de-masted and hulled ships. Since this is the norm in our experience, we assume it to be God's norm. In fact, we think that we cannot teach how to survive storms and attacks unless we have been very battle-damaged ourselves.

That is ridiculous! Why should we look to those who have been *sunk* for lessons in surviving the Enemy's attacks? We must teach from the Word of God and from biographies of men and women who have been through the storms and the attacks and have *not sunk*.

In the World or of the World?

> *I have given them your word and the world has hated them, for* ***they are not of the world*** *any more than I am of the world. My prayer is not that you take them out of the world but that you protect them from the evil one. They are not of the world, even as I am not of it. Sanctify them by the truth; your word is truth. As you sent me into the world,* ***I have sent them into the world. For them I sanctify myself, that they too may be truly sanctified.*** *(Jn. 17:14–19)*

Not "of" the world but "in" it. "Sent" and "sanctified." Although we are not of the world, we can handle being in it because we *have already been* sanctified, set apart. Because we are not of the world, the world hates us. Jesus prayed that the Father would protect us from the evil one, and we are to also pray that He would "deliver us from the evil one" (Mt. 6:13).

We have a problem. We do not want to be hated by the world. How do we prevent it? Easy: compromise.

Hypocrisy

> *Woe to you, teachers of the law and Pharisees, you hypocrites! You clean the outside of the cup and dish, but inside they are full of greed and self-indulgence. Blind Pharisee! First clean the inside of the cup and dish, and then the outside also will be clean. Woe to you, teachers of the law and Pharisees, you hypocrites! You are like whitewashed tombs, which look beautiful on the outside but on the inside are full of dead men's bones and everything unclean. In*

> *the same way, on the outside you appear to people as righteous but on the inside you are full of hypocrisy and wickedness. (Mt. 23:25–28)*

> *Woe to you, teachers of the law and Pharisees, you hypocrites! You shut the kingdom of heaven in men's faces. You yourselves do not enter, nor will you let those enter who are trying to. Woe to you, teachers of the law and Pharisees, you hypocrites! You travel over land and sea to win a single convert, and when he becomes one, you make him twice as much a son of hell as you are. (Mt. 23:13–15)*

One of the first things I notice about Jesus' speech in Matthew 23 is that a hypocrite is someone who pretends to be cleaner on the outside than he is on the inside. He spends more effort in *appearing* clean than he does in actually *being* clean. Most people do this. Hypocrites are everywhere. Churches may be full of them, but so are prisons and homes. Very few people want to be known as they are on the inside. These people do not define themselves as hypocrites. They do not think of what they do as acting a part; they think of it as real and right. There are a few who say, "At least I'm not a hypocrite." What that means is, "I'm dirty on the inside *and* on the outside." True, they are not hypocrites, but they are no better than the hypocrites. Jesus said the way to avoid hypocrisy is "first clean the inside of the cup and dish, and then the outside also will be clean."

The second thing I notice about these passages is that Jesus said these things *to* the hypocrites, not *about* them. People generally talk about hypocrites in the third person.

They do not name the hypocrites. That would not be "polite." It also takes courage to do. Jesus was specific. He said "you hypocrite," and He gave the reasons.

For many decades I have listened to people talk about hypocrites, saying that churches are full of them and that is why they themselves do not go to church. What did Jesus have to say about this?

> *Then Jesus spoke to the multitudes and to His disciples, saying: "The scribes and the Pharisees sit in Moses' seat. Therefore whatever they tell you to observe, that observe and do, but do not do according to their works; for they say, and do not do. (Mt. 23:1–3)*

There is no virtue in avoiding church. The presence of hypocrites is no excuse.

When there are only a few hypocrites in a fellowship of saints, they have a hard time keeping up the act. Some churches are not fellowships of saints with a few hypocrites among them. They are fellowships of hypocrites with a few saints. They are play actors, and they are not saved. They do not know it.

Here are few examples:

- Liberal churches with unsaved pastors and church members who have not heard or believed the gospel.
- Evangelical churches whose members are second- and third-generation "Christians" who are not saved but who have "heard" the gospel.
- Legalistic churches that have replaced faith with works in an otherwise "sound" doctrinal framework.

- Cult churches like the Church of Christ which emphasize one biblical truth above all others in such a way that it becomes an untruth.

These hypocritical churches have several things in common:

- They do not have the fruit of the Spirit.
- They have false teaching.
- The witness of the few Christians in them is compromised.

Jesus told us,

> *Watch out for false prophets. They come to you in sheep's clothing, but inwardly they are ferocious wolves. By their fruit you will recognize them. Do people pick grapes from thorn bushes, or figs from thistles? Likewise every good tree bears good fruit, but a bad tree bears bad fruit. A good tree cannot bear bad fruit, and a bad tree cannot bear good fruit. Every tree that does not bear good fruit is cut down and thrown into the fire. Thus, by their fruit you will recognize them. (Mt. 7:15–20)*

Struggling

I would like to talk about two "Christian" expressions which are not Christian. The first is "I've been struggling." This expression would be a fine one *if* it were used biblically:

> *For our struggle is not against flesh and blood, but against the rulers, against the authorities, against the*

> *powers of this dark world and against the spiritual forces of evil in the heavenly realms. (Eph. 6:12)*

We are in a struggle. That is a fact. However, when people use the phrase today, what they mean is, "I am losing the struggle, and there is no way to win it." They have fallen into sin, and they are trying to make a "spiritual" excuse for their defeat.

The second expression is similar: "It was a real learning experience." That also sounds spiritual, but it really means, "The whole thing was a spiritual loss."

We come out of both situations discouraged because both the "struggle" and the "learning experience" were sins that needed to be confessed. We give them spiritual names because we are not willing to call them sins. As a result, we are not forgiven, and we do not learn from them.

Coveting Your Neighbor's Stuff

> *You shall not covet your neighbor's house. You shall not covet your neighbor's wife, or his manservant or maidservant, his ox or donkey, or anything that belongs to your neighbor. (Exod. 20:17)*

Coveting often precedes purchasing, borrowing, stealing, and cheating. The success of free enterprise and capitalism is largely based upon it. God is not opposed to free enterprise or capitalism, but He is opposed to coveting.

This commandment to not covet is very close to the first and second Commandments:

> *You shall have no other gods before me. You shall not make for yourself an idol in the form of anything in heaven above or on the earth beneath or in the waters*

> *below. You shall not bow down to them or worship them; for I, the LORD your God, am a jealous God, punishing the children for the sin of the fathers to the third and fourth generation of those who hate me, but showing love to a thousand [generations] of those who love me and keep my commandments. (Exod. 20:3–6)*

What is the connection? Look at Colossians 3:5:

> *Mortify therefore your members which are upon the earth; fornication, uncleanness, inordinate affection, evil concupiscence, and* ***covetousness, which is idolatry.***

Coveting is idolatry.

Coveting Your Own Stuff

If I purchase what I covet, I am no longer coveting my neighbor's stuff. It is mine.

> *As Jesus started on his way, a man ran up to him and fell on his knees before him. "Good teacher," he asked, "what must I do to inherit eternal life?" "Why do you call me good?" Jesus answered. "No one is good—except God alone. You know the commandments: 'Do not murder, do not commit adultery, do not steal, do not give false testimony, do not defraud, honor your father and mother.'" "Teacher," he declared, "all these I have kept since I was a boy." Jesus looked at him and loved him. "One thing you lack," he said. "Go, sell everything you have and give to the poor, and you will have treasure in heaven. Then come, follow me." At this the man's face fell. He went away sad, because he had great wealth. Jesus looked around and said to his disciples, "How*

> *hard it is for the rich to enter the kingdom of God!" The disciples were amazed at his words. But Jesus said again, "Children, how hard it is to enter the kingdom of God! It is easier for a camel to go through the eye of a needle than for a rich man to enter the kingdom of God." The disciples were even more amazed, and said to each other, "Who then can be saved?" Jesus looked at them and said, "With man this is impossible, but not with God; all things are possible with God."* (Mk. 10:17–27)

The rich young man coveted his *own* money. It was keeping him from eternal life.

> *Someone in the crowd said to him, "Teacher, tell my brother to divide the inheritance with me." Jesus replied, "Man, who appointed me a judge or an arbiter between you?" Then he said to them, "Watch out! Be on your guard against all kinds of greed; a man's life does not consist in the abundance of his possessions." And he told them this parable: "The ground of a certain rich man produced a good crop. He thought to himself, 'What shall I do? I have no place to store my crops.' Then he said, 'This is what I'll do. I will tear down my barns and build bigger ones, and there I will store all my grain and my goods. And I'll say to myself, "You have plenty of good things laid up for many years. Take life easy; eat, drink and be merry."' But God said to him, 'You fool! This very night your life will be demanded from you. Then who will get what you have prepared for yourself?' This is how it will be with anyone who stores up things for himself but is not rich toward God."* (Lk. 12:13–21)

This man was covetous. God called him a fool.

> *Do not store up for yourselves treasures on earth, where moth and rust destroy, and where thieves break in and steal. But store up for yourselves treasures in heaven, where moth and rust do not destroy, and where thieves do not break in and steal. For where your treasure is, there your heart will be also. (Mt. 6:19–21)*

> *No one can serve two masters. Either he will hate the one and love the other, or he will be devoted to the one and despise the other. You cannot serve both God and Money. (Mt. 6:24)*

Are you too attached to your own stuff

Godliness

> *But godliness with contentment is great gain. For we brought nothing into the world, and we can take nothing out of it. But if we have food and clothing, we will be content with that. (1 Tim. 6:6–8)*

This is a very sweet formula for godliness and contentment. The contentment is provided by God, who also gives us our food and clothing:

> *So do not worry, saying, "What shall we eat?" or "What shall we drink?" or "What shall we wear?" For the pagans run after all these things, and your heavenly Father knows that you need them. But seek*

> *first his kingdom and his righteousness, and all these things will be given to you as well. (Mt. 6:31–33)*

What is godly religion?

> *Religion that God our Father accepts as pure and faultless is this: to look after orphans and widows in their distress and to keep oneself from being polluted by the world. (Jas. 1:27)*

However, being godly is not the same as being religious. Most religion, including Christianity, is observance of form. It is relatively easy to be religious. If someone is godly, the world knows him as a religious man. The converse is not true. Religious people are not considered godly. They are considered hypocrites. Why? Because many "religious" people are not godly. Here is a description of religious people in the last days:

> *But mark this: There will be terrible times in the last days. People will be lovers of themselves, lovers of money, boastful, proud, abusive, disobedient to their parents, ungrateful, unholy, without love, unforgiving, slanderous, without self-control, brutal, not lovers of the good, treacherous, rash, conceited, lovers of pleasure rather than lovers of God—**having a form of godliness** but denying its power. Have nothing to do with them. (2 Tim. 3:1–5)*

God gives godliness. It is not tied to religious observances. It is recognized by the fruit of the Spirit and by how we care for others.

Godliness & Trials

In October of my sophomore year at the Naval Academy, I passed from death to life. I had just turned twenty years old. Eighteen months later my life began to have an effect on my classmates and those both junior and senior to me. This continued for the next seven years while I was on active duty in the Navy and ever since in civilian life.

During my sixty-eight years as a Christian, I have seen men turn to Christ and experience the joy of having their sins forgiven. I have also seen the harassment they get because of Jesus Christ. Some of them came through the persecution, and some of them caved.

What happened in the cities in the Book of Acts happens to every new Christian. It is "revival and riot" on an individual level all over the world. Jesus prepared us for this beforehand.

> *All this I have told you so that you will not go astray. They will put you out of the synagogue; in fact, a time is coming when anyone who kills you will think he is offering a service to God. They will do such things because they have not known the Father or me. I have told you this, so that when the time comes you will remember that I warned you. I did not tell you this at first because I was with you. (Jn. 16:1–4)*

> *Blessed are you when people insult you, persecute you and falsely say all kinds of evil against you because of me. Rejoice and be glad, because great is your reward in heaven, for in the same way they persecuted the prophets who were before you. (Mt. 5:11–12)*

> *If the world hates you, keep in mind that it hated me first. (Jn. 15:18)*

Paul said it, too.

> *In fact, everyone who wants to live a godly life in Christ Jesus will be persecuted. (2 Tim. 3:12)*

And Peter...

> *Dear friends, do not be surprised at the painful trial you are suffering, as though something strange were happening to you. But rejoice that you participate in the sufferings of Christ, so that you may be overjoyed when his glory is revealed. If you are insulted because of the name of Christ, you are blessed, for the Spirit of glory and of God rests on you. If you suffer, it should not be as a murderer or thief or any other kind of criminal, or even as a meddler. However, if you suffer as a Christian, do not be ashamed, but praise God that you bear that name. (1 Pet. 4:12–16)*

Because of this truth many Christians do not want to live godly lives. They know that they will suffer persecution.

Persecution

There are two types of suffering which are directly related to our Christianity. They are chastening and persecution.

God chastens us because we are His children and are being bad. It is a cause for lack of joy.

> *And you have forgotten that word of encouragement that addresses you as sons: "My son, do not make*

> *light of the Lord's discipline, and do not lose heart when he rebukes you, because the Lord disciplines those he loves, and he punishes everyone he accepts as a son. Endure hardship as discipline; God is treating you as sons. For what son is not disciplined by his father? If you are not disciplined (and everyone undergoes discipline), then you are illegitimate children and not true sons. Moreover, we have all had human fathers who disciplined us and we respected them for it. How much more should we submit to the Father of our spirits and live! Our fathers disciplined us for a little while as they thought best; but God disciplines us for our good, that we may share in his holiness. No discipline seems pleasant at the time, but painful. Later on, however, it produces a harvest of righteousness and peace for those who have been trained by it." (Heb. 12: 5–11)*

Persecution comes from the Enemy because of the name of Jesus and our righteousness. In every case, it is a cause for blessing, joy, and gladness.

> *Blessed are those who are persecuted because of righteousness, for theirs is the kingdom of heaven. Blessed are you when people insult you, persecute you and falsely say all kinds of evil against you because of me. Rejoice and be glad, because great is your reward in heaven, for in the same way they persecuted the prophets who were before you. (Mt. 5:10–12)*

God gives us clear direction for responding to persecution:

> *Bless those who persecute you; bless and do not curse. Do not repay anyone evil for evil. Be careful to do what is right in the eyes of everybody. If it is possible, as far as it depends on you, live at peace with everyone. Do not take revenge, my friends, but leave room for God's wrath, for it is written: "It is mine to avenge; I will repay," says the Lord. On the contrary: "If your enemy is hungry, feed him; if he is thirsty, give him something to drink. In doing this, you will heap burning coals on his head."* (Rom. 12:19–20)

The last part of this is a quotation from Proverbs 25:21–22, which adds, "and the Lord will reward you."

We are not to curse, avenge, or return evil for evil. Vengeance is God's business. We are to bless people, do right in everyone's sight, live at peace, feed our enemies when they are hungry, and give them something to drink when they thirst. The Lord will reward us.

I see no exceptions to these commands. Do not try to get around them.

> *Blessed are you when people insult you, persecute you and falsely say all kinds of evil against you because of me. Rejoice and be glad, because great is your reward in heaven, for in the same way they persecuted the prophets who were before you.* (Mt. 5:11–12)

The temptation from the Enemy is to not believe in the reward in heaven and to not rejoice in pain now for something that will happen later. He tells us that even if our reward in heaven is certain, it is too far in the future or too long to wait, so we should compromise now and get rid of the persecution.

Do you believe Jesus, or do you believe the father of lies?

> *For it is commendable if a man bears up under the pain of unjust suffering because he is conscious of God. But how is it to your credit if you receive a beating for doing wrong and endure it? But if you suffer for doing good and you endure it, this is commendable before God. (1 Pet. 2:19–20)*

Suffering unjustly and suffering for doing good are only commendable if you take the suffering patiently before God. Taking it impatiently receives no reward.

> *In fact, everyone who wants to live a godly life in Christ Jesus will be persecuted. (2 Tim. 3:12)*

> *It is better, if it is God's will, to suffer for doing good than for doing evil. (1 Pet. 3:17)*

You can suffer for doing good or for doing evil. Choose your suffering. Do you want to live a godly life?

Quick to Hear

> *My dear brothers, take note of this: Everyone should be quick to listen, slow to speak and slow to become angry, for man's anger does not bring about the righteous life that God desires. (Jas. 1:19–20)*

When we think of being quick, we think of action. Here we are told to "be quick" to do something that takes no action, at least outwardly. Hearing requires no movement. In fact, it seems completely passive. It is not. A *silent* person may be passive, but being silent does not necessarily mean *listening*. Being quick to hear means having an energetic interest, an eagerness that mentally reaches out, stretches for information. It is an openness to another person. This does not mean that what we hear will be good or true, but being quick to hear is part of our own sanctification.

Ready or Not?

Talking with him, Peter went inside and found a large gathering of people... "So I sent for you immediately, and it was good of you to come. Now we are all here in the presence of God to listen to everything the Lord has commanded you to tell us." (Acts 10:27, 33)

The next day Agrippa and Bernice came with great pomp and entered the audience room with the high-ranking officers and the leading men of the city. At the command of Festus, Paul was brought in. (Acts 25:23)

Two different audiences gathered to hear the Gospel in these chapters. There was a great difference in the makeup of the audiences. The first was a family, servants, and soldiers; the second was a collection of self-important people. The first group wanted to know God. The second group was curious. One hundred percent of the first group was converted as soon as they heard the gospel. To our knowledge, none of the second group responded.

Sound Judgment

An unfriendly man pursues selfish ends; he defies all sound judgment. A fool finds no pleasure in understanding but delights in airing his own opinions. (Prov. 18:1–2)

When I am estranged from the Lord, the last thing I want to hear is sound judgment. I will barricade myself against it. But since I cannot protect myself from sound judgment with sound judgment, I must do it with pretexts—shallow, weak arguments which deceive only me. If the searchlight of sound judgment breaks into my hideout, I find myself confessing, forsaking, and being restored to the Lord.

During my estrangement I take no pleasure in understanding, but I am very eager to express my opinion. After I am back in fellowship I am amazed how stupid I was. How I regret my big mouth. Truly it is foolish.

Ungodliness

Jude 15 uses the word "ungodly" four times. Verse sixteen gives the characteristics of ungodly people. The difficulty is that they sound like the Christians we know:

> *These men are **grumblers** and **faultfinders**; they follow their own evil desires; they boast about themselves and flatter others for their own advantage. (Jude 16)*

Grumbling and faultfinding is stock-in-trade for the world. However, Christians can find it an easy habit to take up. Instead of providing light for the world, we spread some of the darkness. Jude says it is an ungodly practice.

Accountability

Christians are called to hold people accountable to the Word of God. This means that we might be called faultfinders when in fact we are confronting a brother biblically.

> *Brothers, if someone is caught in a sin, you who are spiritual should restore him gently. But watch yourself, or you also may be tempted. (Gal. 6:1)*

Of course, you could also be a faultfinder in the bad sense and justify yourself by saying that you were only holding Christians accountable.

Guilt & Ignorance

There are two great problems shaping the average spiritual and mental state of church members today. Quite simply, they are *guilt* and *ignorance*. These problems apply especially to church members who are not Christians, but they are also true in a different way for the Christians.

This statement Paul made about the Jews applies well to unconverted church members:

> *Brothers, my heart's desire and prayer to God for the Israelites is that they may be saved. For I can testify about them that they are zealous for God, but their zeal is not based on knowledge. Since they did not know the righteousness that comes from God and sought to establish their own, they did not submit to God's righteousness. Christ is the end of the law so that there may be righteousness for everyone who believes. (Rom. 10:1–4)*

People seek to establish their own righteousness because of guilt, and because of ignorance they do it their own way.

Although guilt is the main problem for the non-Christian, he may be less conscious of his guilt than he is of other problems. This is because he is partially successful in justifying, hiding, or excusing his sin or blaming it on someone else. He thinks his unhappiness has other causes, and his anxiety other cures. He may be indifferent to his guilt because he is ignorant of the moral law. He has spent a lifetime dulling the edge of the moral law inherent in him, and he needs a reminder of it, "*since through the law comes knowledge of sin*" (Rom. 3:20). He may also be less conscious of guilt because of the widespread teaching on relative morality, new morality, and situation ethics.

The church must return to teaching the law of God, not as the means of salvation, but for the reason it was given:

> *Did that which is good, then, become death to me? By no means! But in order that sin might be recognized as sin, it produced death in me through what was good, so that through the commandment sin might become utterly sinful. (Rom. 7:13)*

> *Now we know that whatever the law says, it says to those who are under the law, so that every mouth may be silenced and the whole world held accountable to God. (Rom. 3:19)*

We can overcome ignorance by teaching God's morality; however, when we teach the law, the result is real guilt. If we leave it at that, people will come up with wrong solutions for the guilt. The way to deal with the remaining ignorance is to teach God's provision of forgiveness of sins in Christ.

When people are allowed to minimize their sin, they do not feel the need for grace. So teaching God's law causes guilt, and teaching God's grace leads to forgiveness. In other words, a clear knowledge of the *bad news* is the right preparation for hearing the *good news*.

This teaching is sadly absent in both liberal and evangelical churches. The liberal churches do not teach it for two reasons: they do not believe in absolute morality, and they are unwilling to make people feel guilty because they consider guilt bad. Evangelical churches do not teach biblical morality because they falsely consider it to be opposed to the good news, perhaps as a sort of works-righteousness.

When a person becomes a Christian, the results are forgiveness of sins and everlasting life:

> *I will rescue you from your own people and from the Gentiles. I am sending you to them to open their eyes and turn them from darkness to light, and from the power of Satan to God, so that they may receive forgiveness of sins and a place among those who are sanctified by faith in me. (Acts 26:17–18)*

Forgiven sin is a distinguishing mark of the Christian church member, but not the non-Christian church member. For the Christian, God also has a provision for staying clean:

> *But if we walk in the light, as he is in the light, we have fellowship with one another, and the blood of Jesus, his Son, purifies us from all sin. (1 Jn. 1:7)*

Why do Christian church members also struggle with guilt? Because they are not men and women of the Word, they are ignorant of the law of God, and they are carrying around unconfessed sins. Forgiveness comes through God's faithfulness to us through the blood of Christ and us honestly admitting our sins to Him.

Unforgiveness is evident in Christian families and in Christian churches. It is a stench in the evangelical church.

God's Forgiveness

"How can a loving God send anyone to hell?" This is usually asked as a rhetorical question. The questioner thinks that the answer is of two possibilities:

1. God is loving, so no one will go to hell.
2. People go to hell, so God is not loving.

The assumption is that a loving God cannot send people to hell. However, there is a much more difficult question: How can a *just* God let anyone into heaven?
God can bring us to heaven because He is both just *and* loving:

> *But because of your stubbornness and your unrepentant heart, you are storing up wrath against yourself for the day of God's wrath, when his righteous judgment will be revealed. God will give to each person according to what he has done. (Rom. 2:5–6)*

That is God's justice.

> *You see, at just the right time, when we were still powerless, Christ died for the ungodly. Very rarely will anyone die for a righteous man, though for a good man someone might possibly dare to die. But God demonstrates his own love for us in this: While we were still sinners, Christ died for us. (Rom. 5:6–8)*

That is God's love.

> *But now a righteousness from God, apart from law, has been made known, to which the Law and the*

> *Prophets testify. This righteousness from God comes through faith in Jesus Christ to all who believe. There is no difference, for all have sinned and fall short of the glory of God, and are justified freely by his grace through the redemption that came by Christ Jesus. God presented him as a sacrifice of atonement, through faith in his blood.* ***He did this to demonstrate his justice****, because in his forbearance he had left the sins committed beforehand unpunished—he did it to demonstrate his justice at the present time,* ***so as to be just and the one who justifies those who have faith in Jesus.*** *(Rom. 3:21–26)*

God is both just and the one who justifies (the forgiver). He took my sins on the cross, and I received His righteousness.

Forgiving Others

> *So watch yourselves. If your brother sins, rebuke him, and if he repents, forgive him. If he sins against you seven times in a day, and seven times comes back to you and says, "I repent," forgive him. (Lk. 17:3–4)*

> *Then Peter came to Jesus and asked, "Lord, how many times shall I forgive my brother when he sins against me? Up to seven times?" Jesus answered, "I tell you, not seven times, but seventy-seven times." (Mt. 18:21–22)*

Peter wanted Jesus to commend him for forgiving his brother seven times in one day. Instead, Jesus expanded the requirement to seventy-seven times. Some translations render this "seventy times seven," that is, 490 times. Is there a difference between the two numbers? No! They are intended to represent an infinite amount of times. Jesus did not want Peter to keep count.

Although these numbers are figurative, let's take them literally for a moment. Forgiving someone seven times in a day is hard enough. To get to seventy-seven sins, we would need eleven days in a row where the same person says that he repents seven times. Seventy times seven sins would take seventy straight days of this.

I know Christians who say that they forgive based upon the genuineness of the person's repentance. Who would believe that someone is really repentant when he has to say he is repentant seven times daily seventy days in a row? No one!

Forgiveness does not depend on the number of times you are sinned against or on the magnitude of the sins. It does not depend on the sinner truly repenting or even on him saying he repents. Luke 17 and Matthew 18 do not tell us to refuse to forgive until he repents. We cannot base our forgiveness on his repentance *and* obey Jesus' command at the same time. Jesus does *not* say, "If he does *not* repent do *not* forgive him," and we are not allowed to judge the sincerity of his repentance before we forgive.

Forgiven

God tells us why we are to forgive others, and He tells us how to forgive them:

> *Be kind and compassionate to one another, forgiving each other,* ***just as in Christ God forgave you.*** *(Eph. 4:32)*

> *Bear with each other and forgive whatever grievances you may have against one another.* ***Forgive as the Lord forgave you.*** *(Col. 3:13)*

These are commands, and they are unconditional. God forgave us in Christ, and He expects us to do the same for those who sin against us. He expects the *forgiven* to *forgive.*

Here is what Jesus told Peter when he asked Him how many times he should forgive his brother:

> *I tell you, not seven times, but seventy-seven times. Therefore, the kingdom of heaven is like a king who wanted to settle accounts with his servants. As he began the settlement, a man who owed him ten thousand talents was brought to him. Since he was not able to pay, the master ordered that he and his wife and his children and all that he had be sold to repay the debt. The servant fell on his knees before him. "Be patient with me," he begged, "and I will pay back everything." The servant's master took pity on him, canceled the debt and let him go. But when that servant went out, he found one of his fellow servants who owed him a hundred denarii. He grabbed him and began to choke him. "Pay back what you owe me!" he demanded. His fellow servant fell to his knees and begged him, "Be patient with me, and I will pay you back." But he refused. Instead, he went off and had the man thrown into prison until he could pay the debt. When the other servants saw what had happened, they were greatly distressed and went and told their master everything that had happened. Then the master called the servant in. "You wicked servant," he said, "I canceled all that debt of yours because you begged me to. Shouldn't you have had mercy on your fellow servant just as I had on you?" In anger his master turned him over to the jailers to*

> *be tortured, until he should pay back all he owed. This is how my heavenly Father will treat each of you unless you forgive your brother from your heart. (Mt. 18:22b-35)*

Why did Jesus tell Peter to forgive an infinite number of times? Love does not keep a record of wrongs. Jesus does not want us to keep count. If you forgive your brother from the heart, the next time he sins, it will seem like the first time. Heart forgiveness is *complete* forgiveness.

> *The good man brings good things out of the good stored up in his heart, and the evil man brings evil things out of the evil stored up in his heart. For out of the overflow of his heart his mouth speaks. (Lk. 6:45)*

> *Make a tree good and its fruit will be good, or make a tree bad and its fruit will be bad, for a tree is recognized by its fruit. You brood of vipers, how can you who are evil say anything good? For out of the overflow of the heart the mouth speaks. The good man brings good things out of the good stored up in him, and the evil man brings evil things out of the evil stored up in him. But I tell you that men will have to give account on the day of judgment for every careless word they have spoken. For by your words you will be acquitted, and by your words you will be condemned. (Mt. 12:33–37)*

> *Nothing outside a man can make him "unclean" by going into him. Rather, it is what comes out of a man that makes him "unclean." (Mk. 7:15)*

We *do* out of what we *are*. We should concentrate on our *being*, not just on our *doing*. *God is love*, and "*For God so loved the world that He gave*" (Jn. 3:16). God acts out of who He is.

We respond to extreme commands like "love your enemies" by making exceptions or bringing the commands down to our size so we can think we are obeying them. However, if we do not qualify the command, we often wind up trying to love our enemies without having our hearts filled with love first. We "forgive," but not from our hearts.

Forgiveness has to be *from the heart*. That is the only kind there is. Otherwise the word is meaningless.

> *But the fruit of the Spirit is love, joy, peace, patience, kindness, goodness, faithfulness, gentleness and self-control. Against such things there is no law. (Gal. 5:22–23)*

> *[Love] is not rude, it is not self-seeking, it is not easily angered, it keeps no record of wrongs. (1 Cor. 13:5)*

Forgiveness means no longer being angry, bitter, or begrudging. When we forgive, the joy of our salvation is restored.

God is the only one who can forgive sins so that the sinner is cleansed. When I forgive someone else, it only cleanses *me*. If I withhold forgiveness, I end up hurting myself.

> *Forgive us our debts, as we also have forgiven our debtors...For if you forgive men when they sin against you, your heavenly Father will also forgive you. But if you do not forgive men their sins, your Father will not forgive your sins. (Mt. 6:12, 15)*

God's forgiveness is conditional on my forgiving those who have sinned against me. Not forgiving is sin. If I refuse to forgive, I am in big trouble.

> ***Be kind and compassionate to one another, forgiving each other, just as in Christ God forgave you.*** *Be imitators of God, therefore, as dearly loved children and live a life of love, just as Christ loved us and gave himself up for us as a fragrant offering and sacrifice to God. (Eph. 4:32–5:2)*

We are to forgive as Christ forgave us, and Jesus says that God will forgive *if* we forgive. These two things are only contradictory if we are being disobedient. If I forgive as Christ forgave, I can honestly pray Matthew 6:12: "Forgive us our debts, as we also have forgiven our debtors." *Forgive me as I forgive because I forgive like You forgave me.*

God forgave us from the Cross. The sinner does not receive God's forgiveness until he repents.

> *He told them, "This is what is written: The Christ will suffer and rise from the dead on the third day, and repentance and forgiveness of sins will be preached in his name to all nations, beginning at Jerusalem." (Lk. 24:46–47)*

> *I will rescue you from your own people and from the Gentiles. I am sending you to them to open their eyes and turn them from darkness to light, and from the power of Satan to God, so that they may receive forgiveness of sins and a place among those who are sanctified by faith in me. (Acts 26:17–18)*

However, God's forgiveness is there before our repentance. In fact, it is a major *cause* of repentance.

> *Or do you show contempt for the riches of his kindness, tolerance, and patience, not realizing that God's kindness leads you toward repentance? (Rom. 2:4)*

Forgiveness and a "place among the sanctified" are the results of turning from the power of Satan to God. That turning is the result of the kindness and preaching of Christ (Rom. 10:17).

> *Forgive us our debts, as we also have forgiven our debtors. (Mt. 6:12)*

This is part of the Lord's Prayer. If you pray this prayer from the heart, you may be in big trouble. You are asking God to forgive you just like you have forgiven others. You are saying, "God, I am the prototype of forgiveness. Would You please copy me?" Do you want to be forgiven that way? But you should want to.

> *And when you stand praying, if you hold anything against anyone, forgive him, so that your Father in heaven may forgive you your sins. (Mk. 11:25)*

The person who does not forgive from his heart is in bigger trouble with God than the person who sinned against him. If we do not forgive someone, or if we do not want God, the church, or the public to forgive him, we are saying we want him to be destroyed. That may happen. Or it may be that God will forgive him, the church will forgive him, and he will be back in the joy of his salvation. Then we are the ones who end up destroyed.

Forgiveness is contrary to the world's justice system. In the world, grace is seldom given, never understood, and often mistaken for injustice. A few years ago in Seattle, a murderer was sentenced to die for his crime. During his time in prison, he had heard the gospel and received Christ. On the day of his execution, three conflicting events happened, each recorded on TV.

1. An anti-death penalty group was holding a protest outside the prison.
2. A pro-death group was demonstrating outside the prison. They wanted him dead and in hell.
3. The murderer announced his conversion to Christ and his anticipation of going to heaven. This made no sense to either group and angered both.

Forgiving gets forgiveness. Refusing to forgive prevents you from receiving forgiveness from God. If you have not genuinely forgiven someone who sinned against you yesterday or ten years ago, you must repent *today* and stay on your knees until you are forgiven for your unforgiveness.

Forgiveness & Bitterness

> *Reader question:* If you have a deep-rooted bitterness and have thought you have forgiven, but it still surfaces occasionally, do you at that moment repent and ask for cleansing? I am frustrated with thinking that I have forgiven an offense and then realizing that I have not dug out the root.

You might be holding onto the root of bitterness. In that case, you must confess it immediately.

On the other hand, you may have truly forgiven the sin that made you bitter when you first confessed your bitterness. After you are forgiven for bitterness, you can still be tempted to be bitter *again*. This is like confessing a lie and then lying again later. It is not the same sin. It does not mean you were not forgiven the first time. As long as this temptation works, the Enemy will keep trying it on you.

Taking Offense

Recently I received this question from a reader of *How to Be Free from Bitterness*. It may apply to some of you as well.

> Generally speaking, should we continuously place ourselves in the company of those who repeatedly offend us?

This question involves at least two issues. They have to do with the kind of person you are.

1. Do you take offense easily, even when someone has no intent to offend?
2. Do you *not* take offense easily, even when someone wants to offend?

If you are the first, the solution lies with *you*, not with the offender. The best way to keep from being hurt is to stay vulnerable, like a pillow. Do not try to build a fence around yourself. That is the way to get hurt more. That is the way to become hard-hearted and cynical. A fence (or wall) is a means of resistance, which means there will be a collision, which means hurt.

If you avoid the *temptation* to take offense by staying away from people who repeatedly offend you, it may mean staying away from Christians, your church, and relatives. Running away from a moral temptation, like Joseph did, is the right action. Running away from the saints, your husband, your wife, and your children is not.

Jesus did not put up a fence. He made Himself vulnerable. Read 1 Peter 2:21–3:7 and Colossians 3:13.

> *To this you were called, because Christ suffered for you, leaving you an example, that you should follow in his steps. "He committed no sin, and no deceit was found in his mouth." When they hurled their insults at him, he did not retaliate; when he suffered, he made no threats. Instead, he entrusted himself to him who judges justly. He himself bore our sins in his body on the tree, so that we might die to sins and live for righteousness; by his wounds you have been healed. (1 Peter 2:21–24)*

> *Bear with each other and forgive whatever grievances you may have against one another. Forgive as the Lord forgave you. (Col. 3:13)*

There are so many brothers in so many churches who do not forgive those they have taken offense from. The better way is to ask God for grace to not get offended and for grace to love the offender.

I have known many situations where people decided to forgive the one who had offended them, but it did not happen. The forgiver has difficulty forgiving even though he wants to and chooses to. Why is this?

One reason is that when we are offended, it is easy for us to see the other person's sin. It never occurs to us that *taking offense* is as great a sin as giving it—perhaps even greater. Giving offense can happen through ignorance with no malice at all. *Giving offense is sometimes a sin, but taking offense always is.* Confess and repent of it to restore you to the joy of the Lord. After your joy is restored, then you can forgive your brother from the heart..[5]

Taking offense has become a cottage industry in our culture. In every city and every church there are people who are professionals at taking offense. They have convinced themselves and many others that being offended is a virtue. The more I am offended, the godlier I am. In their view, those who give offense are the ones in sin. The result is people apologizing and explaining that they really did not mean it to the offended person. The offended one rarely forgives.

> *This is how my heavenly Father will treat each of you unless you forgive your brother from your heart. (Mt. 18:35)*

Forgiving Yourself

"I just can't forgive myself." Have you ever heard someone say that? To my knowledge, the Bible does not speak of the need for or the way to forgive yourself.

What does it speak of?

5 For more on this subject, read *How to Be Free from Bitterness*, available from www.canonpress.com or online at www.ccmbooks.org. I also recommend John Bevere's book *The Bait of Satan: Living Free From the Deadly Trap of Offense*, published by Charisma House (Lake Mary, FL: 1994).

This is the message we have heard from him and declare to you: God is light; in him there is no darkness at all. (1 Jn. 1:5)

But if we walk in the light, as he is in the light, we have fellowship with one another, and the blood of Jesus, his Son, purifies us from all sin. (1 Jn. 1:7)

If we confess our sins, he is faithful and just and will forgive us our sins and purify us from all unrighteousness. (1 Jn. 1:9)

1 John 1:5 speaks of absolute light. Verse 7 speaks of walking in that light with two results:

- Fellowship with one another
- Continued purification from all sin by the blood of Christ

Verse 9 speaks of God's faithfulness in:

- Forgiving our sins
- Purifying us from all unrighteousness

What are our responsibilities?

- Walk in the light.
- Confess our sins.

What are the results?

- Fellowship
- Cleansing from sin

- Forgiveness of sin
- Purification from all unrighteousness

Why does the Bible not mention forgiving ourselves?

- Sin is never against ourselves. It is against *God*. It is a violation of His holiness.
- We are the *sinners*, not the ones sinned against.
- We are the *confessors*, not the forgivers. If we think we are responsible for assigning forgiveness to ourselves, we have believed the lie of the devil. It is a great sin against God.
- Refusing to forgive ourselves is saying that we are senior to God. Who do we think we are?
- Even if it were our responsibility to forgive ourselves, that forgiveness should be based on grace, not merit. No one *deserves* forgiveness.

> *Godly sorrow brings repentance that leads to salvation and leaves no regret, but worldly sorrow brings death. (2 Cor. 7:10)*

There are two types of sorrow:

1. Godly sorrow
2. Worldly sorrow

The first leaves no regret. The second leads to death. If you are not forgiving yourself, you are continuing in regret, which means your sorrow is not godly. As long as you hold onto this worldly sorrow, you are not been forgiven by God, either. Thank God for His forgiveness and *rejoice* in that forgiveness. That is godly sorrow.

Do not look on refusing to forgive yourself as some sort of virtue. It is an awful sin.

Forgiveness & Restitution

Once there was a man who robbed a bank. I will not go into details, but the result was $100,000 in his briefcase. Five minutes later, he was walking down the street with the briefcase (and the $100,000) when he encountered an evangelist preaching on the street. He stopped to listen to the gospel proclaimed in love and power. He was convicted and converted. In his new-found joy, he talked with the evangelist and asked him what all this joy meant. The evangelist explained to the man that his sins had been forgiven.

"All of them?" he asked.

"Yes, all of them," answered the evangelist.

"Oh boy, now I can enjoy this $100,000!"

"What $100,000?"

"The $100,000 that I just removed from the bank over there."

"OK, let's take it back."

The story is fiction, but the principle is true. Being forgiven does not mean you get to keep the money. You may think that is obvious. There are two reasons it is obvious in the story:

1. It was $100,000 (grand larceny).
2. It was ten minutes ago.

However, suppose it was two dollars twenty years before your conversion. Does the principle still hold? If it doesn't, where is the cutoff point? Is restitution required only in *great* and *recent* sins?

Let's take a look at what the Bible says.

> *The LORD said to Moses: "If anyone sins and is unfaithful to the LORD by deceiving his neighbor about something entrusted to him or left in his care or stolen, or if he cheats him, or if he finds lost property and lies about it, or if he swears falsely, or if he commits any such sin that people may do—when he thus sins and becomes guilty, he must return what he has stolen or taken by extortion, or what was entrusted to him, or the lost property he found, or whatever it was he swore falsely about. He must make restitution in full, add a fifth of the value to it and give it all to the owner on the day he presents his guilt offering. And as a penalty he must bring to the priest, that is, to the LORD, his guilt offering, a ram from the flock, one without defect and of the proper value. In this way the priest will make atonement for him before the LORD, and he will be forgiven for any of these things he did that made him guilty." (Lev. 6:1–7)*

There are several things to notice about this passage. First, the Lord spoke it. Second, a sin committed against a neighbor is *unfaithfulness* to the Lord. Third, God specifically mentions deception, stealing, cheating, lying about finding lost property, and swearing falsely, but He adds the all-inclusive "any such sin that people may do."

All of this is based on an "if." "If anyone sins," he becomes guilty. Read the passage again. Notice, "if anyone sins and is unfaithful to the Lord," and "if he commits any such sin," and "when he thus sins and becomes guilty." Look at the list of the things that happened to this "anyone" and see if they have happened to you.

Two things are necessary for forgiveness: 1) restitution and 2) a sacrifice for the sins committed. We know from the New Testament that the sacrifice is still necessary, but it has been provided by the death of Jesus Christ:

> *But when this priest had offered for all time one sacrifice for sins, he sat down at the right hand of God. (Heb. 10:12)*

As Christians, we know that Jesus completely fulfilled the guilt offering. But what takes the place of the restitution in the New Testament? We have been conned into thinking that because we have received Jesus, restitution is not necessary. But repentance that keeps the money is not repentance. Repentance *includes* restitution, and if restitution has not taken place, that is why your conscience still hurts. You can plead that the batteries shoplifted from the drugstore in junior high were taken ten years before your conversion, and your conversion was five years ago. But the batteries were not yours then, and they are not yours *now*. Even though you were truly forgiven when you became a Christian, when you deliberately choose to not to pay for the batteries now, you are in effect *stealing them again*.

Whether the sin was shoplifting, plagiarizing on a paper, lying on income tax returns, or something else, there are reasons people do not want to make restitution. Disgrace and lack of money are two of them. Flunking is a third, and "losing my Ph.D." is a fourth. But even if *all* of these apply, it is worth it to be clean. You have not truly repented if you have not given back what you took. Do you want to be forgiven?

Make restitution!

Paul and John the Baptist both made strong statements about repentance:

> *John: Produce fruit in keeping with repentance. (Mt. 3:8)*

> *Paul: I preached that they should repent and turn to God and prove their repentance by their deeds. (Acts 26:20b)*

One of the great salvation statements Jesus made was about a wealthy (and dishonest) tax collector:

> *Jesus said to him, "Today salvation has come to this house, because this man, too, is a son of Abraham. For the Son of Man came to seek and to save what was lost." (Lk. 19:9–10)*

Jesus was responding to what that tax collector, Zacchaeus, had said to Him:

> *Look, Lord! Here and now I give half of my possessions to the poor, and if I have cheated anybody out of anything, I will pay back four times the amount. (Lk. 19:8)*

Zacchaeus proved his repentance by giving back four times the amount he had cheated people out of. He also bore fruit that matched his repentance—he gave half of his possessions to the poor.

People object to returning stolen property because the amount was hundreds or thousands of dollars, and they do not have enough to pay it back. Others object because what they took was so small that they think it can't possibly matter. The excuses go on and on.

Some people come to me in a quandary because they stole things years ago, and they do not remember the name of the place, or the stores have closed, or the people they stole from have died or moved. How do they make restitution?

The answer is in Numbers 5:

> *The LORD said to Moses, "Say to the Israelites: 'When a man or woman wrongs another in any way and so is unfaithful to the LORD, that person is guilty and must confess the sin he has committed. He must make full restitution for his wrong, add one fifth to it and give it all to the person he has wronged.* ***But if that person has no close relative to whom restitution can be made for the wrong, the restitution belongs to the Lord and must be given to the priest, along with the ram with which atonement is made for him.'"*** *(Numbers 5:5–8)*

If the money cannot be returned to the original owner, give it to the Lord. You do not get to keep it! It is not yours. If you do not remember how much you took, make a high estimate and add 20%.

Restitution is one of the normal occurrences in a spiritual awakening. It may even be a contributing factor. It is also one of the greatest unapplied truths of the Christian life. We may fail to apply it out of ignorance, fear, or pride, but whatever the case, it is a major hindrance to our growth in grace and to revival in the church.

Leviticus 6 tells us how to rectify the situation toward God, our neighbor, and ourselves. It is very simple: return what we have stolen (plus 20% interest) and offer a guilt offering to the Lord. These two things are to be done on the same day. The result is that "he will be forgiven for any of these things he did that made him guilty."

Forgiveness is the opposite of guilt. It is very real. The pain of guilt is gone.

MAKING RESTITUTION: SPECIAL CASES

When it comes to stealing, the cost to the thief is the value of the stolen goods, plus 20%. That is a high rate of interest, but it is not the highest rate:

> *If a man steals an ox or a sheep and slaughters it or sells it, he must pay back five head of cattle for the ox and four sheep for the sheep. (Exod. 22:1)*

The restitution rate is 500% for oxen, 400% for sheep. Why the difference, and why so much? The Bible does not tell us why, but here is a possible reason: Oxen and sheep are alive; they reproduce, pull the plow, provide meat, leather, milk, and wool. When the sheep and oxen are stolen, it is as if all these things are stolen, too.

We see two examples of this in Scripture. First, there is David's reply to the prophet Nathan:

> *He must pay for that lamb* ***four times over****, because he did such a thing and had no pity. (2 Samuel 12:6)*

The second is Zacchaeus' statement to Jesus:

> *But Zacchaeus stood up and said to the Lord, "Look, Lord! Here and now I give half of my possessions to the poor, and if I have cheated anybody out of*

> *anything, I will pay back **four times the amount**." Jesus said to him, "Today salvation has come to this house, because this man, too, is a son of Abraham." (Lk. 19:8–9)*

HUMILITY

This is the greatest virtue in the Bible. The way up is down. The way down is up. Contradiction, paradox, or simple truth? In the book of Luke, Jesus told two different stories after observing egocentric behavior. Both conclusions read the same:

> *For everyone who exalts himself will be humbled, and he who humbles himself will be exalted. (Lk. 14:11, 18:14b)*

The first story was about trying to get the place of honor at a wedding. The second was about two men, a Pharisee and a tax collector, who stood next to each other praying in the temple. The first thanked God that he was not a robber, evildoer, or adulterer, and that he tithed regularly and fasted twice a week. He also thanked God that he was "not like other men…or even like this tax collector."

Jesus did not say that the first man's statements were not true, so what did he do wrong? He exalted himself. The second man was bad, and he admitted it. What he said about himself was true, so what did he do right? He humbled himself. Humility is apparently independent of, and senior to, other merits of right and wrong..[6]

The supreme example of self-exaltation was Satan, and it was his way down:

6 What is your reaction to this parable? Do you go home thanking God that you are not like the Pharisee?

> *How you have fallen from heaven, O morning star, son of the dawn! You have been cast down to the earth, you who once laid low the nations! You said in your heart, "I will ascend to heaven; I will raise my throne above the stars of God; I will sit enthroned on the mount of assembly, on the utmost heights of the sacred mountain." (Is. 14:12–13)*

The supreme example of humility is Jesus, and it was the way up:

> *Who, being in very nature God, did not consider equality with God something to be grasped, but made himself nothing, taking the very nature of a servant, being made in human likeness. And being found in appearance as a man, he humbled himself and became obedient to death—even death on a cross! Therefore God exalted him to the highest place and gave him the name that is above every name. (Phil. 2:6–9)*

Although He was in glory with the Father, Christ did not insist on keeping His rightful place in Heaven. It *was* His rightful place, but He chose doing the will of the Father in humility over hanging onto that place. When He was an innocent man on earth, He did not protest His innocence. Instead, He died for our sins. Jesus made Himself nothing for us. Humility before God was more important to Him than His equality with God, His reputation, and His innocence.

What are we to learn from this?

> *Your attitude should be the same as that of Christ Jesus... (Phil. 2:5)*

Our "rightful place," our "reputation," and our "innocence" are not as important as following Christ in humility. How can this be?

God's objective for us is that we be "conformed to the image of His dear Son" (Rom. 8:29). We are also told to "put on the new self, created to be like God in true righteousness and holiness" (Eph. 4:24). We "have put on the new self, which is being renewed in knowledge in the image of its Creator" (Col. 3:10).

We were created in the image of God. When we sinned, we lost the part of our God-likeness that had to do with righteousness and holiness. Jesus came to earth in order to restore that likeness. We are to be like God, which means being like Jesus, who is the "radiance of God's glory and the exact representation of His being" (Heb. 1:3).

Humility is one of Christ's most obvious characteristics. If we are to imitate Him, humility is a very good place to start. Let's look again at the pattern He left for us to follow:

> *Do nothing out of selfish ambition or vain conceit, but in humility consider others better than yourselves. Each of you should look not only to your own interests, but also to the interests of others. Your attitude should be the same as that of Christ Jesus: Who, being in very nature God, did not consider equality with God something to be grasped, but made himself nothing, taking the very nature of a servant… (Phil. 2:3–7)*

This pattern of humility began when Jesus left heaven, and it ended at the cross. It was downward all the way.

While Jesus was on earth, He taught these things concerning humility:

> *You call me "Teacher" and "Lord," and rightly so, for that is what I am. Now that I, your Lord and Teacher, have washed your feet, you also should wash one another's feet. I have set you an example that you should do as I have done for you. I tell you the truth, no servant is greater than his master, nor is a messenger greater than the one who sent him. Now that you know these things, you will be blessed if you do them. (Jn. 13:13–17)*

> *Jesus called them together and said, "You know that those who are regarded as rulers of the Gentiles lord it over them, and their high officials exercise authority over them. Not so with you. Instead, whoever wants to become great among you must be your servant, and whoever wants to be first must be slave of all. For even the Son of Man did not come to be served, but to serve, and to give his life as a ransom for many." (Mk. 10:42–45)*

We are Christ's followers; therefore, we are to be servants. The path to being like Jesus is downhill. It will not turn around this side of Glory.

We can choose to have humility. In fact, that is the *only* way we can have it. Although coerced serving may be humiliating, it is not humility. Following Christ means *choosing* to be a servant and choosing to do it continually. Remember what Jesus said:

> *For everyone who exalts himself will be humbled, and he who humbles himself will be exalted. (Lk. 14:11, 18:14b)*

There is no neutral ground where your soul is concerned: either you exalt yourself or you humble yourself. We exhibit one of these attitudes in every encounter with God or man. We can follow Satan by exalting ourselves, or we can follow Christ by humbling ourselves. If we want to be known as followers of Christ, we must demonstrate our servanthood by actions that spring from a humble heart.

Jesus wants us to follow Him.

> *Come to me, all you who are weary and burdened, and I will give you rest. Take my yoke upon you and learn from me, for I am gentle and humble in heart, and you will find rest for your souls. For my yoke is easy and my burden is light. (Mt. 11:28–30)*

Taking Up Your Cross Daily

> *Then he said to them all: "If anyone would come after me, he must deny himself and take up his cross daily and follow me. For whoever wants to save his life will lose it, but whoever loses his life for me will save it. What good is it for a man to gain the whole world, and yet lose or forfeit his very self? If anyone is ashamed of me and my words, the Son of Man will be ashamed of him when he comes in his glory and in the glory of the Father and of the holy angels. I tell you the truth, some who are standing here will not taste death before they see the kingdom of God." (Lk. 9:23–27)*

"Take up your cross." The cross is not an unbearable task, a thorn in the flesh, or something unpleasant. The cross is an instrument of shameful, painful execution. Taking up your cross is voluntary capital punishment. It is a choice we must make. It is willingness to die in shame for the sake of Jesus. We could get out of dying if we were ashamed of Christ, but we would lose our life by saving it that way.

We are to take up this cross "daily." Since I did not die yesterday, I must choose to get dressed with the instrument of my own execution again today and every day following.

Here are two parallel verses:

> *In fact, everyone who wants to live a godly life in Christ Jesus will be persecuted... (2 Tim. 3:12)*

> *In your struggle against sin, you have not yet resisted to the point of shedding your blood. (Heb. 12:4)*

Do you want to be godly so bad that you will suffer persecution for it? Do you want to resist sin until you are killed for resisting it? Do you want to be unashamed of Jesus?

Each morning we should pray for grace to be godly, unashamed, and able to resist sin. Each morning that is the way we take up the cross.

Dissension

> *There are six things the Lord hates, seven that are detestable to him: haughty eyes, a lying tongue, hands that shed innocent blood, a heart that devises wicked schemes, feet that are quick to rush into evil, a false witness who pours out lies, and a man who stirs up dissension among brothers. (Prov. 6:16–19)*

Let's look at this list again:

- Arrogance is number one. God is concerned about *high* self-esteem: *"Do not think of yourself more highly than you ought..." (Rom. 12:3)*
- Lying is numbers two and six. "A lying tongue" indicates a habitual liar. "False witness" is perjury.
- The murder of innocent people is number three. It includes abortion.
- Premeditated evil is number four.
- Unpremeditated evil is number five.
- Sowing discord among brothers is number seven.

Although these are all very common today, it is the last I would like to draw your attention to. Stirring up dissension may be unintentional, or it may be the result of gossip. It is the cause of church splits, family fights, and unhappy communities. It is made up of lies, half-truths, and innuendos and is communicated about people instead of *to* them.

Reconciliation

> *Therefore, if you are offering your gift at the altar and there remember that your brother has something against you, leave your gift there in front of the altar. First go and be reconciled to your brother; then come and offer your gift. (Mt. 5:23–24)*

> *If your brother sins against you, go and show him his fault, just between the two of you. If he listens to you, you have won your brother over. (Mt. 18:15)*

These two paragraphs both involve estrangements between you and your brother. In the first passage, the estrangement is your fault (or at the very least your brother thinks it is), because "your brother has something against you." When you attempt to draw near to God, you find you cannot until you are reconciled. The initiative for reconciliation rests on you.

In the second passage, the estrangement is your brother's fault. He has sinned against you. But the initiative still rests with you. The responsibility to reconcile is yours in both cases.

In the second instance there is specific direction on what to do: "Go and tell him his fault, between you and him alone." Every year many people come to me because another Christian has sinned against them. The gist of my counsel is "Go to the brother and tell him his fault between you and him alone." The problem is that they have already violated Jesus' teaching, because they have come to *me* instead of to the brother. Seeking counsel from others in this way is often an attempt to justify their own reasons for not being reconciled. They want sympathy and endorsement. This causes people to choose up sides on issues they should not even know about in the first place.

If Christians took God's teaching on reconciliation seriously, they would be closer to the Lord, they would be much happier, and most of the counsel they currently seek from others would be unnecessary.

Slow to Anger and Quick to Forgive

> *And he passed in front of Moses, proclaiming, "The LORD, the LORD, the compassionate and gracious God, slow to anger, abounding in love and faithfulness." (Exod. 34:6)*

> *But Jonah was greatly displeased and became angry. He prayed to the LORD, "O LORD, is this not what I said when I was still at home? That is why I was so quick to flee to Tarshish. I knew that you are a gracious and compassionate God, slow to anger and abounding in love, a God who relents from sending calamity. Now, O LORD, take away my life, for it is better for me to die than to live." But the LORD replied, "Have you any right to be angry?" (Jon. 4:1–4)*

It is good that God does not have a short fuse, or we would all be toast. Jonah was angry with God for having this kind of character.

Psalm 103 quotes the passage from Exodus, but with an addition:

> *The LORD is compassionate and gracious, slow to anger, abounding in love. He will not always accuse, nor will he harbor his anger forever. (Ps. 103:8–9)*

God is slow to get angry, and He does not keep His anger.

> *My dear brothers, take note of this: Everyone should be quick to listen, slow to speak and slow to become angry, for man's anger does not bring about the righteous life that God desires. (Jas. 1:19–20)*

> *In your anger do not sin: Do not let the sun go down while you are still angry. (Eph. 4:26)*

We are to be slow to anger, and all our anger should be gone by sundown, even if it was righteous anger. All anger that is held onto becomes sin. If we are quick to anger, it is sin. If we hold onto anger, it is sin.

Bitterness

> *And do not grieve the Holy Spirit of God, with whom you were sealed for the day of redemption. Get rid of all bitterness, rage and anger, brawling and slander, along with every form of malice. Be kind and compassionate to one another, forgiving each other, just as in Christ God forgave you. (Eph. 4:30–32)*

Although it is not a physical sickness, bitterness is probably the most debilitating disease there is. It saps the joy out of life like a parasite drains the blood from an otherwise healthy creature. Bitterness can also cause physical illness when it is kept in.

In order to help diagnose this disease, let me tell you some of its symptoms. First, bitter people normally use the word "bitter" either in defense or admission when the tender area is brought to their attention. They say, "I'm not bitter!" or "Of course I'm bitter!" People who are not bitter do not usually use the word.

Second, bitterness remembers details very well. You have had thousands of conversations, and most of them you have forgotten. But there is one conversation that took place years ago, and you remember every word with strong displeasure. Memories such as this are symptomatic of bitterness.

Third, bitterness is always accusatory, even if the accusation is never verbally expressed. It always focuses on someone else's sin, whether that sin is real or imagined. Bitterness starts as resentment which is harbored rather than confessed (1 Jn. 1:8–9). The resentment begins to turn rancid. It matures slowly, putting roots down into the mind and soul of its host until it finally takes over.

Forth, bitterness is normally felt towards the people closest to you (your husband, wife, brother, sister, parents, roommate, or children). It is often the cause of other kinds of sin towards them, including gossip and murder.

The most insidious aspect of bitterness is its ability to disguise itself. It grows like a hidden cancer. The one who is bitter may not even be conscious of it. Like lying, stealing, and murder, bitterness is a sin which needs to be forgiven and which will be if it is confessed. The difficulty is in confessing a wrong that you think is *somebody else's*. You must confess your bitterness as if *you* are the only one at fault. Bring it to the cross where the punishment for it was paid in full. If your bitterness comes back after confession, confess it again and again and again until it is gone for good. You will find the joy God promised restored..[7]

The Conscience

In the Bible various consciences are described as clear, weak, evil, defiled, seared, corrupted, witnessing, testifying, good, and cleansed. It would be easy to draw the conclusion that a good, clear, and cleansed conscience reflects God's absolute moral law, and that if you follow your conscience you will not be guilty. Sometimes that is true, and sometimes it is up for question.

> *Now this is our boast: Our conscience testifies that we have conducted ourselves in the world, and especially*

7 For more on this topic, please read *How to Be Free from Bitterness*, available from Canon Press or online from www.ccmbooks.org.

> *in our relations with you, in the holiness and sincerity that are from God. We have done so not according to worldly wisdom but according to God's grace. (2 Cor. 1:12)*

In this verse, Paul says he innocent because his conscience testifies for him. However, he also says in the fourth chapter that a clear conscience does not necessarily guarantee innocence:

> ***My conscience is clear, but that does not make me innocent.*** *It is the Lord who judges me. Therefore judge nothing before the appointed time; wait till the Lord comes. He will bring to light what is hidden in darkness and will expose the motives of men's hearts. At that time each will receive his praise from God. (1 Cor. 4:4–5)*

A person may say his conscience does not hurt, as if that were proof that he is innocent. It is not. Some consciences are "clear" only because they have been seared. They are deadened by unconfessed sin. Others are filled with false guilt instead of real guilt when they should be clean. The conscience is only an aid, and an imperfect one at that.

A Clean Conscience

Every Christian should be ruled by a clean conscience that is in line with Scriptural teaching. We began our life in Christ by having our conscience cleansed by the blood of Jesus Christ (Heb. 9:14, 10:22). This is how Scripture describes that kind of clean conscience:

> *The goal of this command is love, which comes from a pure heart and a good conscience and a sincere faith. (1 Tim. 1:5)*

> *...holding on to faith and a good conscience. Some have rejected these and so have shipwrecked their faith. (1 Tim. 1:19)*

> *They must keep hold of the deep truths of the faith with a clear conscience. (1 Tim. 3:9)*

There is a close relationship between sincere faith and a good conscience. When faith is abandoned, the conscience gets seared.

> *The Spirit clearly says that in later times* ***some will abandon the faith*** *and follow deceiving spirits and things taught by demons. Such teachings come through hypocritical liars,* ***whose consciences have been seared*** *as with a hot iron. They forbid people to marry and order them to abstain from certain foods, which God created to be received with thanksgiving by those who believe and who know the truth. (1 Tim. 4:1–3)*

Abandoned faith and a seared conscience go together. Your conscience may also not be clear if you hold to the truths of the faith in a dogmatic, argumentative way.

However, we learn in 1 Corinthians 8 and Rom. 14 that it is not enough to have a conscience tuned to a strict knowledge of right and wrong. It is not enough to have a clear conscience before God. Paul spoke several times of how he lived with a good conscience before God. The first time he said it, he was hit in the mouth (Acts 23:1). The second time, he added a qualification:

> *So I strive always to keep my conscience clear* ***before God and man.*** (Acts 24:16)

This second standard, before man, is important. When Paul wrote to the church at Corinth about the way he presented the gospel, he said,

> *Rather, we have renounced secret and shameful ways; we do not use deception, nor do we distort the word of God. On the contrary, by setting forth the truth plainly* ***we commend ourselves to every man's conscience in the sight of God.*** *(2 Cor. 4:2)*

God is the author of every man's conscience. This is the reason unbelievers criticize believers who play loose with ethics, are greedy, stretch the truth, or misbehave sexually. Whether or not they follow God's laws themselves, they recognize that these truths ought to be evident in the lives of Christians. Even someone with a distorted conscience can appreciate the truth when it is set forth plainly.

> *For the appeal we make does not spring from error or impure motives, nor are we trying to trick you. On the contrary, we speak as men approved by God to be entrusted with the gospel. We are not trying to please men but God, who tests our hearts. You know we never used flattery, nor did we put on a mask to cover up greed—God is our witness. We were not looking for praise from men, not from you or anyone else. (1 Thess. 2:3–6)*

Paul's aim was to please God, but at he same time he strove to avoid *legitimate* criticism from men. A good example of this is the way he handled the money collected in Corinth for the poor believers in Jerusalem:

We want to avoid any criticism of the way we administer this liberal gift. For we are taking pains to do what is right, not only in the eyes of the Lord but also in the eyes of men. (2 Cor. 8:20–21)

Our actions should also be guided by the Christian whose conscience isn't working correctly:

*Eat anything sold in the meat market without raising questions of conscience, for, "The earth is the Lord's, and everything in it." If some unbeliever invites you to a meal and you want to go, eat whatever is put before you without raising questions of conscience. But if anyone says to you, "This has been offered in sacrifice," then do not eat it, both for the sake of the man who told you and for conscience' sake—**the other man's conscience, I mean, not yours.** (1 Cor. 10:25–29)*

This teaching is unknown to those who insist on holding onto their Christian liberty. According to 1 Corinthians, there is something more important than our freedom, and that is being considerate of our fellow Christians. Our love for each other should be far more important than expressing our personal freedom.

If this requirement is foreign to your way of thinking, it might be because your conscience is in bad shape. To bring it back to normal working order, ask God to show you the compromises you have made.

Search me, O God, and know my heart; test me and know my anxious thoughts. See if there is any offensive way in me, and lead me in the way everlasting. (Ps. 139:23–24)

Asking God to search your heart protects you from introspection, which leads to self-condemnation. It also protects you against a complacent refusal to search your heart, which results in self-justification.

We are to make our consciences increasingly more sensitive through the Word of God, the Holy Spirit, and *constant* use.

> *But solid food is for* ***the mature, who by constant use have trained themselves to distinguish good from evil.*** *(Heb. 5:14)*

Pay attention to your conscience. When the Scriptures or the Holy Spirit show you sin, immediately confess and forsake it. If you continue to do this, your conscience will become very sensitive. You will feel guilt whenever you sin. This encourages confessing and forsaking sin as soon as it arises and helps to keep your conscience the way it ought to be.

Righteousness & Peace 1

> *You are the salt of the earth. But if the salt loses its saltiness, how can it be made salty again? It is no longer good for anything, except to be thrown out and trampled by men. (Mt. 5:13)*

God's kind of righteousness has a positive effect on society. Salt that is not salty is good for nothing. Similarly, light that is hidden is not light. Men do not praise God for our bad deeds.

Two events in biblical history will serve to illustrate this truth. The first was the destruction of Sodom (Gen. 18–19), and the second was Israel's minor defeat at Ai (Josh. 6–7). God had promised the safety of the very wicked city of Sodom if *ten righteous people* were found in it. At Ai, God allowed the defeat of a righteous nation because there was *one unrighteous man* in the camp. Thirty-six men were killed because of that man's sin.

These are opposite effects of the same principle. God will spare a wicked city if there is an adequate righteous witness in it. However, God will not give victory to His people unless everyone in the camp is righteous.

We have settled for the first option: we are content to be a small light, just enough to keep the Sodoms from being destroyed. We are running defense when we should be launching a strong offense. The church which should have a conquering view like Joshua instead endeavors to spread the gospel with unrighteous men in the army. We are not willing to purge the unrighteousness from ourselves and from the church in order to take the Ais of this world with the Gospel of our Lord Jesus Christ. The Lord is not with us for victory.

Righteousness & Peace 2

> *Therefore, since we have been justified through faith, we have peace with God through our Lord Jesus Christ... (Rom. 5:1)*

Righteousness is by faith (see Rom. 4), but it is God who makes us righteous. When that happens, we have *peace* with Him.

> *The fruit of righteousness will be peace; the effect of righteousness will be quietness and confidence forever. (Is. 32:17)*

Righteousness precedes peace. Humanists (and many Christians, too) make peace primary. They want peace at any price. God keeps them in the right order:

But the wisdom that comes from heaven is ***first of all pure; then peace-loving****, considerate, submissive, full of mercy and good fruit, impartial and sincere. (Jas. 3:17)*

Do you see the order? First "*pure*," then "peace-loving." Let's look at God's view of righteousness and peace in the Bible:

- Sodom:

Then he said, "May the Lord not be angry, but let me speak just once more. What if only ten can be found there?" He answered, "For the sake of ten, I will not destroy it." (Gen. 18:32)

Sodom could not come up with ten righteous men.

- Jerusalem:

Go up and down the streets of Jerusalem, look around and consider, search through her squares. If you can find but one person who deals honestly and seeks the truth, I will forgive this city. (Jer. 5:1)

Jeremiah could not find one righteous man.

- Amorites:

Then the LORD said to him, "Know for certain that your descendants will be strangers in a country not their own, and they will be enslaved and mistreated four hundred years...In the fourth generation your descendants will come back here, for the sin of the

Amorites has not yet reached its full measure." (Gen. 15:13, 16)

The iniquity of the Amorites was not yet complete. Four hundred years later it was filled up:

It is not because of your righteousness or your integrity that you are going in to take possession of their land; but on account of the wickedness of these nations, the LORD your God will drive them out before you, to accomplish what he swore to your fathers, to Abraham, Isaac and Jacob. Understand, then, that it is not because of your righteousness that the LORD your God is giving you this good land to possess, for you are a stiff-necked people. (Deut. 9:5–6)

A little righteousness will spare an entire city, but God will not have peace at the expense of righteousness. In the book of Judges, God disciplined Israel for her unrighteousness. He did it again during the reigns of Nineveh and Babylon. Later He brought final judgment on Nineveh, Babylon, and Tyre.

Unrighteousness brings war, either in discipline or in judgment. Righteousness brings peace.

The fruit of that righteousness will be peace; its effect will be quietness and confidence forever. (Is. 32:17)

Worthy of Respect

Now the overseer must be above reproach, the husband of but one wife, temperate, self-controlled,

> ***respectable***, *hospitable, able to teach. (1 Tim. 3:2)*

> *Deacons, likewise, are to be* ***men worthy of respect****, sincere, not indulging in much wine, and not pursuing dishonest gain. (1 Tim. 3:8)*

> *In the same way, their wives are to be* ***women worthy of respect****, not malicious talkers but temperate and trustworthy in everything. (1 Tim. 3:11)*

> *Now we ask you, brothers, to respect those who work hard among you, who are over you in the Lord and who admonish you. Hold them in the highest regard in love because of their work. Live in peace with each other. (1 Thess. 5:12–13)*

Children must respect their parents simply because they are their parents, not because they are respectable. It is the same with kings, governors, and masters. They are to be given respect regardless. This is not true in the church. Church leaders/servants must be *worthy of respect*. Elders must be examples to the flock—the kind of example that, if imitated, would make the church more godly.

> *Remember your leaders, who spoke the word of God to you. Consider the outcome of their way of life and imitate their faith. (Heb. 13:7)*

If we consider the outcome of their way of life and find out that they are not worthy of respect, we should not imitate them, and they should not be elders or deacons.

Trust

> *This is what the LORD says: "**Cursed is the one who trusts in man,** who depends on flesh for his strength and whose heart turns away from the LORD. He will be like a bush in the wastelands; he will not see prosperity when it comes. He will dwell in the parched places of the desert, in a salt land where no one lives. **But blessed is the man who trusts in the LORD,** whose confidence is in him. He will be like a tree planted by the water that sends out its roots by the stream. It does not fear when heat comes; its leaves are always green. It has no worries in a year of drought and never fails to bear fruit." (Jer. 17:5–8)*

Note the contrasts:

- cursed or blessed
- shrubs or trees
- desert or water
- parched places or roots by the river
- shall not see good or is not anxious in the year of drought
- uninhabited salt land or bearing fruit unceasingly

The contrasts are great, and the difference is whether we are trusting in man or in the Lord.

Respect for Authority

Everyone must submit himself to the governing authorities, for there is no authority except that which God has established. The authorities that exist have been established by God. Consequently, he who rebels against the authority is rebelling against what God has instituted, and those who do so will bring judgment on themselves. For rulers hold no terror for those who do right, but for those who do wrong. Do you want to be free from fear of the one in authority? Then do what is right and he will commend you. For he is God's servant to do you good. But if you do wrong, be afraid, for he does not bear the sword for nothing. He is God's servant, an agent of wrath to bring punishment on the wrongdoer. Therefore, it is necessary to submit to the authorities, not only because of possible punishment but also because of conscience. This is also why you pay taxes, for the authorities are God's servants, who give their full time to governing. Give everyone what you owe him: If you owe taxes, pay taxes; if revenue, then revenue; if respect, then respect; if honor, then honor. (Rom. 13:1–7)

Submit yourselves for the Lord's sake to every authority instituted among men: whether to the king, as the supreme authority, or to governors, who are sent by him to punish those who do wrong and to commend those who do right. For it is God's will that by doing good you should silence the ignorant talk of foolish men. Live as free men, but do not use

> *your freedom as a cover-up for evil; live as servants of God. Show proper respect to everyone: Love the brotherhood of believers, fear God, honor the king. (1 Pet. 2:13–17)*

> *I urge, then, first of all, that requests, prayers, intercession and thanksgiving be made for everyone—for kings and all those in authority, that we may live peaceful and quiet lives in all godliness and holiness. This is good, and pleases God our Savior, who wants all men to be saved and to come to a knowledge of the truth. For there is one God and one mediator between God and men, the man Christ Jesus, who gave himself as a ransom for all men—the testimony given in its proper time. And for this purpose I was appointed a herald and an apostle—I am telling the truth, I am not lying—and a teacher of the true faith to the Gentiles. (1 Tim. 2:1–7)*

All of these texts are clear. The content does not need explaining. People only need to be taught to obey them. How do we obey these texts?

- Confess the sin of not obeying the law. That is disobeying God, because the president, the king, and the governors are God's servants.
- Do good. That is God's will. Such obedience silences the talk of foolish men.
- Show respect for *everyone*, love the brothers, fear God, and honor the president.
- Pray for the president and all those in authority. There are two reasons for this:

a) That we may live peaceful and quiet lives in all godliness and holiness.
b) God wants all men to be saved. This is connected with a).

If you are bummed about an election, confess it. As long as you are bummed, you are not rejoicing in the Lord always.

Kings & Citizens

Have you ever noticed that the New Testament gives no instruction to governors or kings on how to treat the citizens? There are instructions to the Christian masters, husbands, and fathers and instructions to Christian slaves, wives, children, and citizens.

In Deuteronomy 17, God gave this instruction to Israel:

> *When you enter the land the LORD your God is giving you and have taken possession of it and settled in it, and you say, "Let us set a king over us like all the nations around us," be sure to appoint over you the king the LORD your God chooses. He must be from among your own brothers. Do not place a foreigner over you, one who is not a brother Israelite. The king, moreover, must not acquire great numbers of horses for himself or make the people return to Egypt to get more of them, for the LORD has told you, "You are not to go back that way again." He must not take many wives, or his heart will be led astray. He must not accumulate large amounts of silver and gold. When he takes the throne of his kingdom, he is to write for himself on a scroll a copy of this law, taken from that of the priests, who are*

> *Levites. It is to be with him, and he is to read it all the days of his life so that he may learn to revere the LORD his God and follow carefully all the words of this law and these decrees and not consider himself better than his brothers and turn from the law to the right or to the left. Then he and his descendants will reign a long time over his kingdom in Israel. (Deut. 17:14–20)*

Very few kings in the Old Testament followed this instruction: Saul, sometimes; David, sometimes; Solomon, very little; Rehoboam and many others, not at all. Jehoshaphat, Hezekiah, and Josiah followed it well. They were fairly obedient kings, but very poor fathers. Check out their sons who were kings.

We think that if we reached the people in power with the Gospel, we could turn this country around. I am not opposed to reforming the country, but I am not sure this is the way. If God had assumed Christian kings and presidents, He would have given instruction for them in the New Testament. If given the opportunity, I will vote for a Christian, but I will not put my trust in him.

Attitudes towards Other Believers

Romans 14 is about attitudes towards other believers. The basic premise is that each believer belongs to God, and God receives him without looking down on him or condemning him—therefore, we should receive him in the same way.

> *Accept him whose faith is weak, without passing judgment on disputable matters. One man's faith allows him to eat everything, but another man, whose*

> *faith is weak, eats only vegetables. The man who eats everything must not look down on him who does not, and the man who does not eat everything must not condemn the man who does, for God has accepted him. (Rom. 14:1–3)*

This means that there is something more important than being right. In verse 5 Paul says,

> *Each one should be fully convinced in his own mind. (Rom. 14:5)*

God allows us to think differently, but He does not allow us to break fellowship because of it. Even if the positions we hold are right, we can be in sin because of *how* we hold them.

Please read the rest of Romans 14. The first half of the chapter tells us not to dispute with those we disagree with. We are not to try to convince them that they are wrong and we are right. The second half of the chapter tells us that we are not to participate in anything that will cause a fellow believer to stumble. Notice that the "kingdom of God is not a matter of eating and drinking, but of righteousness, peace and joy in the Holy Spirit" (v. 17). God is more interested in the quality of our walk with Him than in the physical things we participate in.

Unity in the Spirit

> *Make every effort to keep the unity of the Spirit through the bond of peace. (Eph. 4:3)*

> *There is one body and one Spirit—just as you were called to one hope when you were called—one Lord, one faith, one baptism... (Eph. 4:4–5)*

There is unity in the Spirit. We become part of it the instant we are born again. We cannot *establish* this unity, because it already exists. We are to make every effort to *keep* it. Here are few of the ways we can destroy this unity:

- Become *men*-followers. (1 Cor. 1 and 3)
- Seek followers for *ourselves*. (Acts 20:30)
- Say one of the following:
    - "*We* have the best church government."
    - "*We* have the best form of worship."
    - "*We* have the best doctrine."
    - "*Our* teaching on holiness is the right teaching."
    - "The meaning and form of *our* church's sacraments/ordinances are most biblical."
    - "*Our* view of the gifts of the Spirit is the biblical view."
    - "*We* are the true church of Christ."
    - "*We* are an upper middle-class church."

If all Christians of every culture and nation were in 100% agreement on all practices and doctrines, many of the Christians would not like it. Why? Because none of us could be the most right. Our tendency is to be exclusive, not inclusive.

Wisdom

If any of you lacks wisdom, he should ask God, who gives generously to all without finding fault, and it will be given to him. But when he asks, he must believe and not doubt, because he who doubts is like

> *a wave of the sea, blown and tossed by the wind. That man should not think he will receive anything from the Lord. (Jas. 1:5–7)*

This is a comprehensive statement. According to this, all Christians can and should be wise through a generous amount of God-given wisdom.

> *It is because of him that you are in Christ Jesus, who has become for us wisdom from God—that is, our righteousness, holiness and redemption. (1 Cor. 1:30)*

Wisdom comes with the new birth. The problem is that not all Christians seem to have it. Why is this? Here a few possible explanations:

- They do not think that they lack wisdom, so they do not ask God for it.
- They know that they lack wisdom but still do not ask for it.
- They know they lack wisdom but do not ask in faith because they do not believe that God will give it to them generously.
- They seek the wisdom of the world instead of God's wisdom.
- They live in the world system and are of this world; they do not know they lack wisdom.
- They get their counsel from psychologists, from men of worldly education instead of men with godly wisdom.

It is tragic that when Christians could have wisdom in great quantities, they settle for nothing.

Wisdom & Folly

> *"Let all who are simple come in here!" she says to those who lack judgment. (Prov. 9:4, 9:16)*

This quotation is from two different women, Wisdom and Folly. They say it from the same place, "the highest point in the city" (9:3, 14), and they say it to the same people, "those who lack judgment." The difference is that Wisdom offers food, wine, and life, but openly asks for repentance (9:5–6). Folly offers a lie which she presents as a free gift: "Stolen water is sweet; food eaten in secret is delicious!" (9:17).

Wisdom gives life. Folly offers immediate benefits, which are "sweet" and "delicious"...

> *But little do they know that the dead are there, that her guests are in the depths of the grave. (Prov. 9:18)*

Two Kinds of Wisdom

> *Such "wisdom" does not come down from heaven but is earthly, unspiritual, of the devil. For where you have envy and selfish ambition, there you find disorder and every evil practice. But the wisdom that comes from heaven is first of all pure; then peace-loving, considerate, submissive, full of mercy and good fruit, impartial and sincere. (Jas. 3:15–17)*

There are two kinds of wisdom:

- The wisdom of men, the world, and this age
    - Origin: earthly, of the devil
    - Character: bitter envy, jealous, unspiritual, selfishly ambitious, boastful, denying the truth, causing disorder, full of evil practice, eloquent, "wise," and persuasive

- God's wisdom
    - Origin: heaven.
    - Character: pure, peace-loving, considerate, submissive, full of mercy, bearing good fruit, impartial, sincere, simple, powerful, preaching the cross, humble, spiritual, not known by the world, communicated by the Spirit of God, foolishness to those who are perishing, admonishing and teaching to present every man perfect in Christ, representing Jesus Christ Himself

The unsaved man does not understand God's wisdom because spiritual truth requires spiritual discernment. During the Korean War, I was Communications Officer on a destroyer for two years. Thousands of messages were transmitted and received. We always knew what frequency to be tuned to in order to receive messages, and we also knew which frequencies to transmit on. The enemy did not know this. If he discovered the frequencies, it still did not do him any good because all the messages were encoded, each one differently, with the code changing every day.

The enemy of our souls and all the people he has enslaved do not know the frequencies or the codes. The wisdom of God is hidden from them. Before I became a

Christian, I read from the New Testament every day for twenty months. It did not make any sense to me. In October 1947, I was born again by the Spirit of God, and the Bible suddenly became English.

> *No, we speak of God's secret wisdom, a wisdom that has been hidden and that God destined for our glory before time began. None of the rulers of this age understood it, for if they had, they would not have crucified the Lord of glory. (1 Cor. 2:7–8)*

Just imagine—if the Enemy had understood that the crucifixion of Christ meant salvation for the world, he would not have done it!

As a Christian, you know the frequency and the code. Use them! And if you lack wisdom, remember this:

> *If any of you lacks wisdom, he should ask God, who gives generously to all without finding fault, and it will be given to him. (Jas. 1:5)*

Unbelief

> *Whoever believes in him is not condemned, but whoever does not believe stands condemned already because he has not believed in the name of God's one and only Son. (Jn. 3:18)*

> *Whoever believes in the Son has eternal life, but whoever rejects the Son will not see life, for God's wrath remains on him. (Jn. 3:36)*

> *See to it, brothers, that none of you has a sinful, unbelieving heart that turns away from the living God. (Heb. 3:12)*

Unbelief is a great sin. It applies to:

- Those who have heard the gospel and not believed
- Those who have not heard the gospel
- Those who heard, believed, and turned away from God

The last includes many Christians. Unbelief is understandable in those who have not heard the gospel (although is it still inexcusable—see Rom. 1:20) because it is the gospel that causes belief. Unbelief in Christians is very difficult to understand. One explanation may be that, like the Galatians, they do not remember how they were saved:

> *You foolish Galatians! Who has bewitched you?...I would like to learn just one thing from you: Did you receive the Spirit by observing the law, or by believing what you heard? Are you so foolish? After beginning with the Spirit, are you now trying to attain your goal by human effort? Have you suffered so much for nothing—if it really was for nothing? (Gal. 3:1–4)*

Another explanation may be that they are not reading their Bibles. That leaves the world as the major source of their information and beliefs. It is a bad source.

What Kind of Christian Are You?

More and more I come across people who are "doers" instead of "be-ers," "tryers" instead of "trusters." They do all the Christian things, but they do not live in anything close to spiritual victory.

Some of these people turned out to be not Christians at all. When they "received Christ," they were only following a formula—signing a card, praying a prayer, or going forward at a Christian meeting. The reason I know they did not become Christians with these formulas is that they later became real Christians..[8]

Live the Christian life the same way you started: by faith. Trust God for the power to follow Him in joyful obedience.

> *So then, just as you received Christ Jesus as Lord, continue to live in him, rooted and built up in him, strengthened in the faith as you were taught, and overflowing with thankfulness. (Col. 2:6–7)*

Empowered to Be Holy

When John the Baptist was born, his father Zechariah was filled with the Holy Spirit and prophesied concerning Jesus:

> *Praise the Lord, the God of Israel, because he has come and has redeemed his people. He has raised up a horn of salvation for us in the house of his servant David (as he said through his holy prophets of long ago), salvation from our enemies and from the hand of all who hate us—to show mercy to our fathers and to remember his holy covenant, the oath he swore to our father Abraham:* **to rescue us** *from the hand of*

8 Of course, many people have become wonderful Christians with these formulas. What makes the difference? The heart. Those who became real Christians had a change of *heart* that went along with the card they signed or the prayer they said. We know we are Christians because of our lives, not because we can point to a time or a date.

> *our enemies, and* ***to enable us to serve him*** *without fear* ***in holiness and righteousness*** *before him all our days. (Lk. 1:68–75)*

Christ came to *rescue us* from our enemies and to *enable us* to serve Him without fear in holiness and righteousness. Isn't it wonderful that He gives us the power us to be holy all our days?

God's Justice & Faithfulness

> *If we confess our sins, he is faithful and just and will forgive us our sins and purify us from all unrighteousness. (1 Jn. 1:9)*

This promise has two parts: 1) He will forgive us our sins, and 2) He will purify us from all unrighteousness. The sins that get forgiven are the ones confessed. "All unrighteousness" is more than just these sins; it is everything else that is unrighteous in us. God will purify us from all of this. Look back at verse seven:

> *But if we walk in the light, as he is in the light, we have fellowship with one another, and the blood of Jesus, his Son, purifies us from all sin. (1 Jn. 1:7)*

Notice how the last phrase parallels verse 9. Verse 7: "purifies us from all sin." Verse 9: "purifies us from all unrighteousness." The verb "purifies" has the sense of continual activity, i.e., He "keeps on purifying."

There are conditions for this complete and continual purifying. Verse 7: "If we walk in the light as He is in the light." Verse 9: "If we confess our sins." Meeting these conditions puts the work of God into effect in our lives. However, the conditions are secondary to the blood of Jesus and the justice and faithfulness of God. "He is faithful and just" (v. 9). The real cause of this wonderful forgiveness is God.

God's Forgiveness

There is a great phrase in the poetry of Jeremiah about the character of God's forgiveness:

> *"In those days, at that time," declares the Lord, "search will be made for Israel's guilt, but there will be none, and for the sins of Judah, but none will be found, for I will forgive the remnant I spare." (Jer. 50:20)*

Regardless of how great your sins or how many there are, they cannot be found once God has forgiven them. Zechariah said of his son John the Baptist,

> *And you, my child, will be called a prophet of the Most High; for you will go on before the Lord to prepare the way for him, to give his people a knowledge of salvation through forgiveness of sins. (Lk. 1:76–77)*

Sins gone, guilt gone, and a knowledge of salvation—all through God's forgiveness.

The Mind of God

We know more about God's thoughts than we do about man's. How can that be? He has revealed His thoughts to us in Scripture, and He has given us His Spirit to understand them.

> *None of the rulers of this age understood it, for if they had, they would not have crucified the Lord of*

glory. However, as it is written: "What no eye has seen, what no ear has heard, and what no human mind has conceived"—the things God has prepared for those who love him—these are the things God has revealed to us by his Spirit. The Spirit searches all things, even the deep things of God. For who knows a person's thoughts except their own spirit within them? In the same way no one knows the thoughts of God except the Spirit of God. What we have received is not the spirit of the world, but the Spirit who is from God, so that we may understand what God has freely given us. This is what we speak, not in words taught us by human wisdom but in words taught by the Spirit, explaining spiritual realities with Spirit-taught words. The person without the Spirit does not accept the things that come from the Spirit of God but considers them foolishness, and cannot understand them because they are discerned only through the Spirit. The person with the Spirit makes judgments about all things, but such a person is not subject to merely human judgments, for, "Who has known the mind of the Lord so as to instruct him?" But we have the mind of Christ. (1 Cor. 2:8–16)

This is so wonderful. Meditate on this truth.

The Mind of Man

For who among men knows the thoughts of a man except the man's spirit within him? In the same way no one knows the thoughts of God except the Spirit of God. (1 Cor. 2:11)

I often see people judging the thoughts and motives of another person with absolute certainty about what that person was thinking. To them, it is self-evident. The quote from Corinthians is a rhetorical question. Paul was not asking for a show of hands on who knows another person's thoughts. He was saying that we *cannot* know them. We could know if he told us, or we could know if we had his spirit. We could also know if God revealed his thoughts to us. Until then, we *must not* judge the thoughts of another person. We guess wrongly and act on our guess as if it were right.

Idolatry

> *"Present your case," says the LORD. "Set forth your arguments," says Jacob's King. "Bring in your idols to tell us what is going to happen. Tell us what the former things were, so that we may consider them and know their final outcome. Or declare to us the things to come, tell us what the future holds, so we may know that you are gods. Do something, whether good or bad, so that we will be dismayed and filled with fear. But you are less than nothing and your works are utterly worthless; he who chooses you is detestable." (Is. 41:21–24)*

This is one of the Old Testament's many comments on idolatry. We would like to think that idolatry is so self-evidently wrong that it would have disappeared from the world long ago. It is not so. The objects of idolatry may have changed, but the pattern remains the same:

> *For since the creation of the world God's invisible qualities—his eternal power and divine nature—*

have been clearly seen, being understood from what has been made, so that men are without excuse. For although they knew God, they neither glorified him as God nor gave thanks to him, but their thinking became futile and their foolish hearts were darkened. Although they claimed to be wise, they became fools. (Rom. 1:20–22)

Rituals

Every church has rituals, regardless of its denomination. Liturgical churches have a planned ritual; non-liturgical churches have a ritual by default. At their best, rituals are figures of the true; at their worst, they are idolatrous. In between, they become dead traditions. The rituals described in the Old Testament were meant to be figures of the true, but degenerated into idolatry. Hebrews 7–10 describes this.

The rituals of the Old Testament were meant to be fulfilled in Christ. Long before they were fulfilled, they had ceased to be merely figures. The Israelites thought that following the rituals was enough. They turned them into a *substitute* for the real thing rather than a picture of it. When this happened, they were no longer acceptable to God.

Hear the word of the LORD, you rulers of Sodom; listen to the law of our God, you people of Gomorrah! "The multitude of your sacrifices—what are they to me?" says the LORD. "I have more than enough of burnt offerings, of rams and the fat of fattened animals; I have no pleasure in the blood of bulls and lambs and goats. When you come to appear before me, who has asked this of you, this trampling of my courts? Stop bringing meaningless offerings! Your incense is detestable to me. New Moons, Sabbaths and convocations—I cannot bear your evil assemblies. Your New Moon festivals and your appointed feasts my soul hates. They have become a burden to me; I am weary of bearing them. When you spread out your hands in prayer, I will hide my eyes from you; even if you offer many prayers, I will not listen. Your hands are full of blood; wash and make yourselves clean. Take your evil deeds out of my sight! Stop doing wrong, learn to do right! Seek justice, encourage the oppressed. Defend the cause of the fatherless, plead the case of the widow. "Come now, let us reason together," says the LORD. "Though your sins are like scarlet, they shall be as white as snow; though they are red as crimson, they shall be like wool. If you are willing and obedient, you will eat the best from the land; but if you resist and rebel, you will be devoured by the sword." For the mouth of the LORD has spoken. (Is. 1:10–20)

Judah and Jerusalem were acting like Sodom. They performed God's sacrifices and offerings but then proceeded to do whatever pleased them. They thought their sins did not matter as long as they had the rituals in place.

The bronze serpent Jesus used to explain the gospel to Nicodemus was one of the Old Testament rituals which symbolized a spiritual truth:

Just as Moses lifted up the snake in the desert, so the Son of Man must be lifted up. (Jn. 3:14)

The bronze serpent, a symbol of sin and death, also pictured Jesus who was made sin for us. It was a figure of the cross, but it became an idol to the Israelites for seven hundred years until Hezekiah had it destroyed:

> *He removed the high places, smashed the sacred stones and cut down the Asherah poles. He broke into pieces the bronze snake Moses had made, for up to that time the Israelites had been burning incense to it. (It was called Nehushtan.) (2 Kings 18:4)*

Today the cross itself has become an idol and even a fetish. Whatever rituals you are following, do you know their significance? Do you know why you are following them, or have they lost that significance?

Traditions

At the time of Christ's coming, the Jews had 2,000 years of tradition. The Roman Catholic Church has had 1,700 years of tradition since Constantine. Evangelical Americans have thirty, fifty, or two hundred years of "traditional American values," and somehow we think it is a virtue and a grand heritage. Our traditional values include Benjamin Franklin, Thomas Jefferson, Norman Rockwell, Thomas Kincaid, Santa Claus, John Wayne, the Easter Bunny, and trick-or-treat.

Jesus said, "You have let go of the commands of God and are holding on to the traditions of men" (Mk. 7:8). You may have another list of *traditional* American values than the list above, but they are still "traditional." They are not biblical; they are not Christian.

I grew up in the 1930's and '40's. The values then were decadent. You may think that our current values are even more so. That might be true, but to solve this problem, let's go back to the Bible, not to an era that we worship as an idol, especially as there has been a spiritual revival in the last fifty years, compared to the hundred years that came before them. Let's consider the phrase "traditional American values" a dirty expression. It is part of the nice guy's political correctness.

The Full Armor

> *Finally, be strong in the Lord and in his mighty power. Put on the full armor of God so that you can take your stand against the devil's schemes. For our struggle is not against flesh and blood, but against the rulers, against the authorities, against the powers of this dark world and against the spiritual forces of evil in the heavenly realms. Therefore put on the full armor of God, so that when the day of evil comes, you may be able to stand your ground, and after you have done everything, to stand. (Eph. 6:10–13)*

The first three chapters of Ephesians tell us the riches we have in Christ. It would be difficult to meditate too much on these riches. In the final chapter, Paul teaches on standing strong in the Lord. Notice that verses 10 and 13 both say to "put on the *full* armor of God" to take your stand against the devil. The emphasis is on the *completeness* of the armor. The devil is not stronger than God's armor, but he is wily enough to hit us where we are not covered.

When I get defeated, it is not because of Satan's strength. It is either because I am uncovered or because I mistake the enemy for flesh and blood (a human being) instead of the real Enemy.

God Is with Us

Therefore go and make disciples of all nations, baptizing them in the name of the Father and of the Son and of the Holy Spirit, and teaching them to obey everything I have commanded you. And surely I am with you always, to the very end of the age. (Mt. 28:19–20)

The way we send people on missions is very different from the way Jesus sent the apostles. We send others because we cannot or do not want to go ourselves. The one sent also goes alone; this is with mutual agreement, for why would you send someone else if you are going yourself?

That is not Jesus' way. He sent the apostles, and He said, "And surely I am with you always, to the very end of the age." Jesus sent, and then He came along. Isn't that wonderful? But it was not the first instance of sending and coming along:

Jesus answered, "The work of God is this: to believe in the one he has sent." (Jn. 6:29)

The Father sent Jesus, and then He came along, too.

The one who sent me is with me; he has not left me alone, for I always do what pleases him. (Jn. 8:29)

God sends us, and He goes along with us. No matter where we are or what our mission is, He is always right there helping us to fulfill His plan.

10

THE TONGUE

THE OVERFLOW OF THE HEART

In my eighty-eight years of life I have heard many dirty words. There were places I expected to hear them, like when I was working in the Omaha stockyards as a teenager and in the U.S. Navy as an enlisted man. My memory focuses on the unexpected times I heard them. They came from the mouths of a four-year-old boy, a woman, boy scouts in the scout clubhouse, midshipmen at the U.S. Naval Academy, and a cousin of mine when we were pheasant hunting as teenagers. All of these shocks happened before I was a Christian. I was idealistic. To me, women did not talk that way, boy scouts were clean, four-year-olds were innocent, midshipmen were the all-American boys, and cousins were part of my family where words like that were not used.

Early in my Christian life, my eyes were opened. I came to realize that my heart and the hearts of boy scouts, midshipmen, four-year-olds, women, and my family all started out overflowing with evil. Jesus gave an explanation of why people are this way:

> *Make a tree good and its fruit will be good, or make a tree bad and its fruit will be bad, for a tree is recognized by its fruit. You brood of vipers, how can you who are evil say anything good? For out of the overflow of the heart the mouth speaks. The good man brings good things out of the good stored up in him, and the evil man brings evil things out of the evil stored up in him. But I tell you that men will have to give account on the day of judgment for every careless word they have spoken. For by your words you will be acquitted, and by your words you will be condemned. (Mt. 12:33–37)*

Whatever is "stored up" flows out. The good man brings out good things from the good stored up in him. The evil man brings out evil from the evil stored up in him. If the tree is good, the fruit is good. If the tree is bad, the fruit is bad. What a tree is, is what a tree does.

The mouth is an overflow valve of the heart. We can try to watch our mouths. That might keep the stored-up evil inside for a while, but it is like blocking the safety valve on a pressure cooker. Sooner or later there is going to be an explosion.

The emphasis of the Matthew 12 passage is on the heart, not the mouth. If we store up good in our hearts, we do not need to watch our mouths. If we store up evil in our hearts, watching our mouths will not stop it from coming out.

When I talk with Chinese graduate students who come to the U.S. from schools that have been teaching atheism for generations, the word "God" gets a look of non-comprehension. However, if I mention a "dirty heart," there are a lot of nodding heads.

There are two reasons for having a dirty heart:

1. The heart has never been cleaned. It has been collecting crud since birth. The mouth spills out the overflow.

2. The heart has been cleansed by the blood of Christ, but it has not been kept clean. Its owner has not been walking in the light. This is why Christians say things from their hearts that do not sound like Christian things.

The first reason is easy to understand. The second is a contradiction.

> *With the tongue we praise our Lord and Father, and with it we curse men, who have been made in God's likeness. Out of the same mouth come praise and cursing. My brothers, this should not be. Can both fresh water and salt water flow from the same spring? My brothers, can a fig tree bear olives, or a grapevine bear figs? Neither can a salt spring produce fresh water. (Jas. 3:9–12)*

Where is your heart? Do you need to know the Father through His Son, the Lord Jesus Christ?

The Tongue

But what does it say? "The word is near you; it is in your mouth and in your heart," that is, the word of faith we are proclaiming: That if you confess with your mouth, "Jesus is Lord," and believe in your heart that God raised him from the dead, you will be saved. For it is with your heart that you believe and are justified, and it is with your mouth that you confess and are saved. (Rom. 10:8–10)

Romans 10 records the two greatest uses of the tongue. The first is *confessing* Jesus Christ and *calling* upon Him. It is our "part" in salvation:

Everyone who calls on the name of the Lord will be saved. (Rom. 10:13)

The second great use of the tongue is preaching Jesus Christ:

How, then, can they call on the one they have not believed in? And how can they believe in the one of whom they have not heard? And how can they hear without someone preaching to them? And how can they preach unless they are sent? As it is written, "How beautiful are the feet of those who bring good news." (Rom. 10:15)

The person who carries good news has beautiful feet even when they are dirty and dusty. The good news makes them beautiful.

Prior to regular postal service, messages were sent by courier or special messenger. That is the way the New

Testament letters were delivered. The messenger would be on the road for months. In addition to the words he carried, he himself would also be a letter:

> *You yourselves are our letter, written on our hearts, known and read by everybody. You show that you are a letter from Christ, the result of our ministry, written not with ink but with the spirit of the living God, not on tablets of stone but on tablets of human hearts. (2 Cor. 3:2–3)*

Let us use our tongues as messengers of the gospel of Christ.

Bad Words & Good Words

> *Be imitators of God, therefore, as dearly loved children, and live a life of love, just as Christ loved us and gave himself up for us as a fragrant offering and sacrifice to God. But among you there must not be even a hint of sexual immorality, or of any kind of impurity, or of greed, because these are improper for God's holy people. Nor should there be obscenity, foolish talk or coarse joking, which are out of place, but rather thanksgiving. (Eph. 5:1–5)*

Our speech should not contain obscenities, foolish talk, or coarse joking. The Bible commands us to avoid these things without defining them. The Apostle Paul assumed the Ephesians would know what he was talking about. Obscene and filthy words are not in most dictionaries, but we understand what they are. People use obscene language, not because they do not know it is filthy, but because they *do* know. There is a certain delight in the use of something vulgar and unclean.

Some people like to quibble about definitions, assuring us that the words they use are not obscene: they're just colorful, or poetic, or it is the hearer who has the problem or the dirty mind. Other people would not dream of saying anything dirty. They think they can be innocent and expressive at the same time, so they use exclamations which are euphemisms for the dirty words. Examples of such euphemisms are "Shucks!," "Heck!," "Shoot!," and "Dang it!" Some euphemisms for using the Lord's name in vain are "Dog-gone it!," "Golly!," "Gosh!," "Gee Whiz!" and "Dag Nab it!" There are many others that I do not have the freedom to write. Innocent? Perhaps. Perhaps not. Here is what Jesus said about the words we use:

> *But I tell you that* ***men will have to give account*** *on the day of judgment* ***for every careless word*** *they have spoken. For* ***by your words you will be acquitted and by your words you will be condemned.*** *(Mt. 12:36–37)*

Do I have to walk around in fear because of this clear teaching about *careless* words? No. There is a preventative:

> *...and we take captive every thought to make it obedient to Christ. (2 Cor. 10:5b)*

When our thoughts are obedient to Christ, our mouths will be obedient, too.

Euphemisms

A euphemism is a pretend synonym. It puts a good face on a bad-sounding word. It indicates the same act, practice, or exclamation but does it in such a way that the thing it signifies does not sound bad. In fact, it might even sound good or at least innocent. Here are a few examples:

- adultery—affair
- homosexuality—gay
- Jesus—Geez or Gee Whiz
- taking the Lord's name in vain—oh-my-gosh or doggone it
- damn it—darn it

Some people think it is a virtue to soften words like adultery and homosexuality. They think it sort of cleans up the dirt. This kind of treatment does not succeed; it only has the appearance of being clean. Why? God cleanses those things which are confessed as sin. Cleaning up the *words* is not confession, and therefore the sin is not forgiven.

> *If we confess our sins, he is faithful and just and will forgive us our sins and purify us from all unrighteousness. (1 Jn. 1:9)*

God does not forgive mistakes. With love we can say to those who have sinned, "No, it was not a 'mistake'; it was sin. If you want forgiveness, you must call it sin."

Humanism

The Bible is not a book that humanists can adjust to. It is too extreme. The humanist wants to be good now and then and here and there. His is the religion of "random acts of kindness." The Christian must be kind to everyone (1 Tim. 2:24).

Humanists worry that people might have low self-esteem. The Bible says,

> *Do not think of yourself more highly than you ought, but rather think of yourself with sober judgment, in accordance with the measure of faith God has given you. (Rom. 12:3)*

> *Be completely humble and gentle; be patient, bearing with one another in love. (Eph. 4:2)*

Unfortunately, many Christians prefer the humanist approach to the biblical standard. They judge Scripture in the light of our humanistic society. It is easier than judging society in the light of Scripture.

Are the people doing this not Christians? That would be a reasonable conclusion, except that these humanistic voices are coming from mainstream evangelicalism. Television, magazines, movies, schools, newspapers, and the government all inundate us with humanism, and we end up speaking the language of tolerance. We use the words "gay," "affair," and "traditional family values" instead of "homosexual," "adultery," and "biblical standard." We reflect the world more than we reflect the Bible. Start looking for extreme statements in the Bible. Do they bother you? Why?

Here are some expressions we should remove from our thinking and our vocabulary:

- Where do you draw the line? (Who is going to answer that question, if you refuse to get your answers from the Bible?)
- That is the ideal, not the real.
- Nobody is perfect!
- I'm only human!

Politeness

Politeness, political correctness, and relational communication have something positive in common. They are attempts to use words to be friendly, to not cause offense, and to avoid confrontation. Aren't these good things? Yes, they are. They are also *surface* attempts at kindness. They are mechanics. Teaching a little boy to say "Thank you" certainly makes things more pleasant, but it is not the same as teaching him *thankfulness*.

I was taught politeness as a boy. Then I was *really* taught it when I was a midshipman at the Naval Academy. I was trained to be an officer and a *gentleman*. I found out that politeness worked (standing when ladies came into the room, opening doors for them, etc.). I discovered that these positive mechanics were *not* the outward expressions of the heart. They did not express kindness, love, or patience. In many cases they actually covered up unkindness, unlove, and impatience.

Isn't covering up unkindness better than expressing it? I am tempted to say yes, but that is a temptation from the Enemy. Why should I choose the lesser of two evils when I have a clear command?

> *Be kind and compassionate to one another, forgiving each other, just as in Christ God forgave you. (Eph. 4:32)*

Many years ago after teaching an eight-week course of practical Christianity, I suspected that one of the students had not learned much. She came from a Christian home, had grown up in good churches and received a Christian education, including a degree from a famous Christian college.

For years I have listened to people's awful stories in order to give them counsel. One day I realized that I was giving the same solution regardless of what the story was. All of the stories had two common causes:

1. It had been a long time since they had read all of the New Testament.
2. They had an awful, distorted, or truncated view of God. They had Satan's caricature of Him.

I started asking people for their gut views of the Father, the Son, and the Holy Spirit. I have gotten many awful answers.

I asked this young woman these questions. She had never read the New Testament through. She gave a surprisingly good answer about God the Father, but when I asked about Jesus, her answer was something like this: "Jesus was supposed to have died for our sins, but I don't think He was very polite."

Her answer shook me, and I did not know why. I already knew that Jesus was not very polite. Why did it bother me? This girl considered politeness the highest virtue. It was more important to her than anything else. If Jesus was not polite, that meant to her that He was not sinless and could not have died for our sins.

Since that time I have sensed this same belief in many Christians. It colors their communication. They try to clean up the gospel so that there is no chance of anyone taking offense. And they think it is a virtue to do this! In reality, it is the enemy of truth.

> *Instead, speaking the truth in love, we will in all things grow up into him who is the Head, that is, Christ. (Eph. 4:15)*

We are to speak the truth in love. The Bible does not say to "speak the truth in politeness." Politeness is not a synonym for truth. Politeness almost always leaves out the truth. Sometimes it inserts a lie.

Knowledge or Love?

The grace of our Lord was poured out on me abundantly, along with faith and love that are in Christ Jesus. (1 Tim. 1:14)

Paul was a man of great wisdom and knowledge, but he played it down. In fact, he wrote it off:

Knowledge puffs up but love builds up. The man who thinks he knows something does not yet know as he ought to know. But the man who loves God is known by God. (1 Corinthians 8:1–3)

It almost looks like knowledge is the opposite of love. If it were, we would have to stay ignorant in order to be loving. Having knowledge is a temptation. Being puffed up is the sin. The man who *thinks* he knows something does not yet know as he ought to know. He is in sin.

For the message of the cross is foolishness to those who are perishing, but to us who are being saved it is the power of God. For it is written: "I will destroy the wisdom of the wise; the intelligence of the intelligent I will frustrate." Where is the wise man? Where is the scholar? Where is the philosopher of this age? Has not God made foolish the wisdom of the world? For since in the wisdom of God the world through its wisdom did not know him, God was pleased through the foolishness of what was preached to save those who believe. (1 Cor. 1:18–21)

There is a "knowing" that goes far beyond knowledge:

And I pray that you, being rooted and established in love, may have power, together with all the saints, to grasp how wide and long and high and deep is the love of Christ, and ***to know this love that surpasses knowledge****—that you may be filled to the measure of all the fullness of God. (Eph. 3:17b-19)*

Knowledge can be measured on a written exam. Knowing love cannot be measured at all. We are to *grasp* it by the power of God. It is like grasping the Pacific Ocean in our hands.

When we speak, do we display our knowledge, or our love? Are we conscious of the abundance of grace, faith, and love that was poured out on us when we received Christ? Do we show it and speak it?

Our Speech

The words of a gossip are like choice morsels; they go down to a man's inmost parts. (Prov. 18:8)

He who answers before listening—that is his folly and his shame. (Prov. 18:13)

The first to present his case seems right, till another comes forward and questions him. (Prov. 18:17)

These verses on conversation touch on three great problems in the church today: gossip, not listening, and listening to only one side. All of these can be corrected by a simple choice. However, that means that there will be no more "choice morsels," no "ego talking," and no choosing up sides. Here are two passages from the New Testament to help you in your decision:

> *Do not let any unwholesome talk come out of your mouths, but only what is helpful for building others up according to their needs, that it may benefit those who listen. (Eph. 4:29)*

> *My dears brothers, take note of this: Everyone should be quick to listen, slow to speak and slow to become angry. (Jas. 1:19)*

Our speech should be for others, and our listening should be for others.

Gossip

> *They have become filled with every kind of wickedness, evil, greed and depravity. They are full of envy, murder, strife, deceit and malice. They are* ***gossips****, slanderers, God-haters, insolent, arrogant and boastful; they invent ways of doing evil; they disobey their parents; they are senseless, faithless, heartless, ruthless. Although they know God's righteous decree that those who do such things deserve death, they not only continue to do these very things but also approve of those who practice them. (Rom. 1:29–32)*

I wish to draw attention to just one of these awful sins—gossip. Paul lists it with murder, slander, deceit, and malice, among other great evils. It is part of the complete depravity and dissolution which man falls into as the result of refusing to glorify God:

> *Furthermore, since* ***they did not think it worthwhile to retain the knowledge of God,*** *he gave them over to a depraved mind, to do what ought not to be done. (Rom. 1:28)*

What does Scripture tell us to fill our minds (and therefore our speech) with?

> *Finally, brothers, whatever is true, whatever is noble, whatever is right, whatever is pure, whatever is lovely, whatever is admirable—if anything is excellent or praiseworthy—think about such things. (Phil. 4:8)*

Gossip is very seldom about *praiseworthy* things. It is about bad things, and it is harmful to the people who are talked about. Telling and listening to these things give pleasure, but gossiping is *not* an innocent pastime. It is a great evil.

> *A gossip betrays a confidence, but a trustworthy man keeps a secret. (Prov. 11:13)*

> *A perverse man stirs up dissension, and a gossip separates close friends. (Prov. 16:28)*

Many years ago we knew a U.S. Air Force Chaplain named Augie Kilpatrick. On one occasion, my wife Bessie asked Augie how he handled gossip. He had a ready answer.

"I take out my pocket notebook and write down, word for word, what I am being told. After I have taken it all down, I read it back to the person and ask him if it is correct and if it is true. Once I have an affirmative answer, I hand him the notebook and my pen and say, 'Please sign here.'"

Many years ago we arrived in a new town and found a church. We had barely settled in when Bessie got a phone call from one of the church ladies. She had some gossip about someone else in the church.

Bessie asked, "Is that true?"

"Yes."

Bessie said, "Let's you and I go see her and correct her."

"If you go to see her, don't tell her I told you!"

This does not stop gossip, but it does keep you out of the circuit. We are normally left out of the loop. When people bring gossip to my attention, they know I am going to tell them to go to the person directly. They also know that *I* know they are not going to do that.

> *Although they know God's righteous decree that those who do such things deserve death, they not only continue to do these very things but also approve of those who practice them. (Rom. 1:32)*

Practice and approve. Gossip is approval of sin. It is vicarious enjoyment of someone else's transgressions. It is a means of enjoying sin without actually doing the sin. The talk may even have the tone and content of disapproval. The gossiper appears innocent (at least to himself) because 1) he is not doing the sin himself and 2) he is voicing disapproval. He deceives himself and his listeners.

> *For it is shameful even to mention what the disobedient do in secret. (Eph. 5:12)*

These are the consequences of rejecting God:

> *They have become filled with every kind of wickedness, evil, greed and depravity...They are* ***gossips****, slanderers, God-haters, insolent, arrogant and boastful...they are senseless, faithless, heartless, ruthless. (Rom. 1:29–31)*

Read through the full list again. Alongside the terrible sins of murder and God-hatred are the things we enjoy—gossip, slander, envy, and boasting.

There are always opportunities to gossip at work, online, at parties, church, and over the back fence. Newspapers and magazines capitalize on the great demand for gossip. Gossip is not limited to the teller. *Listening to gossip is as bad as talking it.* Our need to share in gossip is immense, and it is *great* sin.

> *Without wood a fire goes out; without gossip a quarrel dies down. (Prov. 26:20)*

Dealing with Gossip

Here are a few suggestions on how to handle gossip:

1. Draw the gossiper's attention to Romans 1:29–32 (see above) and 2 Corinthians 12:20:

   > *For I am afraid that when I come I may not find you as I want you to be, and you may not find me as you want me to be. I fear that there may be quarreling,*

jealousy, outbursts of anger, factions, slander, ***gossip****, arrogance and disorder.* (2 Cor. 12:20)

Romans lists gossip among the characteristics of unbelievers. Gossip has no place in the Christian life. Notice the other willful sins listed with it. Gossip is *not* a small matter.

2. Listen to the gossip and write it down word-for-word. Read it back to the gossiper. Ask him/her, "Is that true?" If the gossiper says that he/she doesn't know, ask why it was repeated. If the gossiper says that it is true, ask him/her to sign his/her name under the written quote.

3. Listen to the gossip. Ask for confirmation of the truth of it. Then say, "Let's both go and correct the person you are telling this awfulness about."

4. Do not listen. Walk away.

This action will have three effects:

1. Some people will quit gossiping.
2. Some will gossip about you.
3. You will be left out of the gossip circuit.

Keeping Confidence

"I can keep a confidence.
It's the people I tell it to who can't."
—Unknown

I hardly ever promise to keep a confidence before I hear the story. I may promise to keep one after I hear the story, and I do keep that confidence. *I* determine which ones I keep, not the person who shares it with me. This lack of promise is not the same as gossip, although it could be gossip.

We are required to speak to the assembled believers if someone is unrepentant. The assembled believers are to take action on the unrepentant believer (Mt. 18). If I promise to keep the information secret, I might hobble myself so that I cannot obey God and tell the church.

Many years ago, a professional person came to see me. I did not know him, although I knew of him. He wished to tell me something awful about a friend we had in common, but first he wanted me to promise to keep it confidential. I told him that I did not make those kinds of promises. He was astounded. Wasn't I a minister of the gospel? Didn't I have to keep confidences? I told him yes, but I determined which ones I kept after I heard the story.

"Then I cannot tell you."

"That is alright with me. I do not need to know."

He kept repeating that he could not tell me if I would not promise ahead of time, and I kept telling him that was alright. Each time he got angrier. Finally, he left in hysterical anger, slamming the door behind him. In anger he told someone else what an idiot I was. This opened that person's eyes about the angry man's character. I never did find out about the evils he wanted to tell me.

That is the best way.

Thoughts on Correcting Others

- I will walk in the light as He is in the light (1 Jn. 1:7).
- I will forgive others as God has forgiven me in Christ (Eph. 4:32).

- I will only judge others if I have taken the splinter out of my own eye first (Mt. 7:1–5).
- I will correct him only if I am spiritual and gentle (Gal. 6:1). If I *feel* like correcting him, I am probably neither.
- I will correct another with the intention of restoring him or her to close fellowship with God. I will do it in a biblical manner (Mt. 18:15, 35).
- I recognize that there is a difference between those who are forgiven and those who are qualified to be teachers.
- I will not talk about the life of a fellow believer unless his life is a *positive* testimony to God's saving grace. If there is a negative rumor, I will check with the person himself.

If a believer is a public figure and there is a rumor of moral impropriety about his life, that rumor should be brought to his attention. He should be encouraged to straighten out the story if it is untrue. If it is true and he has repented, he should be encouraged to make that known to the public. If it is true and he has not repented, there should be an attempt to restore him to fellowship. If the man is an elder and has repented, he should be forgiven and restored to fellowship, but he might have lost his qualification to be an elder.

11
JOY

Continual Joy

A friend came to our home in Yokohama, Japan, some years ago. He had been my roommate aboard an aircraft carrier and had become a Christian during our time together. On this visit he said, "I have that deep inner peace that I belong to Christ, but I don't have daily victory. I don't have joy."

Of course something was wrong. Joy and peace are basic results of salvation. Jesus promised us in John 16:22:

> *I will see you again and you will rejoice, and no one will take away your joy.*

When the seventy returned from their evangelistic itinerary, rejoicing because of the power they had and miracles they had done, Jesus told them that their joy was misplaced:

However, do not rejoice that the spirits submit to you, but rejoice that your names are written in heaven. (Lk. 10:20)

My salvation is from God, and so is my joy. *Salvation* is the basis for joy. We tend to think that circumstances are the primary cause for joy, but this is not so:

Though the fig tree does not bud and there are no grapes on the vines, though the olive crop fails and the fields produce no food, though there are no sheep in the pen and no cattle in the stalls, yet I will rejoice in the LORD, I will be joyful in God my Savior. (Hab. 3:17–18)

Pleasure is a result of circumstances. Pleasure and joy may be expressed in the same way, but they are not the same. For instance, I can sing for joy, or I can sing for pleasure. In the first case, singing is the *result* of the great joy—my joy bursts out into singing. In the second case, singing is the *cause* of the pleasure, not the result of it. I can sing or dance or laugh for joy, but singing, dancing, and laughing will not bring me joy. They might bring pleasure, and we can convince ourselves that this pleasure is joy.

Since joy is directly related to salvation, why do we lack it? Hebrews 12:11 gives an explanation:

No discipline seems pleasant at the time, but painful. Later on, however, it produces a harvest of righteousness and peace for those who have been trained by it.

God disciplines us for unconfessed sin (Heb. 12:5–6). He intends that discipline to be temporary. To those who respond to it and learn from it, God's loving discipline yields peace and a right relationship with Him. If we do not learn from it, the discipline continues, and so does our lack of joy. When we confess and forsake our sins, the joy returns.

One of the reasons we have great joy when we receive Christ is that we are forgiven. We are cleansed of years of accumulated sin. If we begin accumulating sins again after conversion, it is no wonder that the joy goes away. Walking in a joyful relationship with God requires being honest with Him. God has promised His faithfulness to forgive and cleanse us on this condition:

> *If we confess our sins, he is faithful and just and will forgive us our sins and purify us from all unrighteousness. (1 Jn. 1:9)*

When my friend realized that daily joy was a matter of instant confession, he confessed his sins, and his joy was restored.

When King David sinned, God disciplined him, and he lost his joy. Psalm 51 is a record of his confession:

> *Restore to me the joy of your salvation and grant me a willing spirit, to sustain me. Then I will teach transgressors your ways, and sinners will turn back to you. (Ps. 51:12–13)*

David knew that he could not teach transgressors or cause sinners to come to the Lord as long as he was without the joy of his salvation. Think of the people you know who are effective in evangelism. Are they joyful, or are they just people who know all the right answers? The joyful Christian life leads others to God. If we are going to draw water from the well of salvation, let's do it with joy.

Lack of Joy

If I have confessed and forsaken sin and still do not have joy, what then? There are several possible explanations:

1. You have confessed and forsaken your big sins, but not the little ones that set you up for them.

   Keep your servant also from willful sins; may they not rule over me. Then will I be blameless, innocent of great transgression. (Ps. 19:13)

2. You do not believe that God has forgiven you.

   If we confess our sins, he is faithful and just and will forgive us our sins and purify us from all unrighteousness. (1 Jn. 1:9)

3. You are not obeying Phil. 4:4: *Rejoice in the Lord always. I will say it again: Rejoice!* That is a command. Disobeying it is sin. Confess and forsake the sin of not rejoicing.

4. You do not think it is right to rejoice in forgiveness after sinning like you did. This is a lie from the devil. If you have confessed and forsaken the sin, God has forgiven you, and *He wants you to rejoice in His forgiveness.*

5. You think you have to do some sort of penance to prove that you really meant your confession.

Godly sorrow brings repentance that leads to salvation and leaves no regret, but worldly sorrow brings death. (2 Cor. 7:10)

6. There are two types of sorrow. Worldly sorrow is remorse. It leads to death. There is no virtue in it. Godly sorrow leads to repentance and leaves no regret. If you still have regret, you have not repented with godly sorrow.

7. It is possible that you are not saved. God has promised everlasting joy to His children.

    The ransomed of the LORD will return. They will enter Zion with singing; everlasting joy will crown their heads. Gladness and joy will overtake them, and sorrow and sighing will flee away. (Is. 51:11)

    But the fruit of the Spirit is love, joy, peace… (Gal. 5:22)

Whatever the reason, if you lack joy, you are under some sort of chastening. Find out what the sin is and confess it. You will not find it by introspection; that will only make you depressed. Come into God's presence. Ask Him to search your heart.

Substitutes for Joy

In Luke 15 Jesus describes three different parties. These parties were the results of finding a lost sheep, a lost coin, and a lost son. In each case, there was great rejoicing. Jesus taught these parables to help us understand how much rejoicing there is in Heaven over each sinner who repents. If there is any way to increase the joy in Heaven, this is it. It is why Jesus came to earth. It is why the Bible was written.

In the parables, the rejoicing takes place *before* the party. The point of the party was to include others in the rejoicing. Like with all true, wonderful things, the world creates its own versions, copies that are distortions of the real thing. The world has parties, but instead of being a result of rejoicing, they try to be a *cause* for rejoicing, like the parties the prodigal son threw in the far country. The real rejoicing took place when he came home.

The worldly man does not have joy in living, so he seeks a vicarious joy. Entertainment, music, sports, movies, plays, novels, and pornography can all become substitutes for the real joy. He becomes addicted to them as he returns to them again and again trying to build up his joy.

Songs of Joy

> *Shout for joy to the Lord, all the earth. Serve the Lord with gladness; come before him with joyful songs. (Ps. 100:1–2)*

In this world there are sad songs, love songs, and battle songs, but the songs of salvation are all songs of joy and gladness. David knew this when he wrote Psalm 51. In it he sings,

> *Restore to me the joy of your salvation. (Ps. 51:12)*

Salvation means joy, and joy means singing. Psalm 126 is about release from physical captivity, but it is also a great picture of salvation:

> *When the Lord brought back the captives to Zion, we were like men who dreamed. Our mouths were filled with laughter, our tongues with songs of joy.*

Then it was said among the nations, "The Lord has done great things for them." The Lord has done great things for us, and we are filled with joy. Restore our fortunes, O Lord, like streams in the Negev. Those who sow in tears will reap with songs of joy. He who goes out weeping, carrying seed to sow, will return with songs of joy, carrying sheaves with him. (Ps. 126)

This song overflows with joy. All the joy comes from one place, and that is heaven. The center of heaven is God. He is the focus of everything. If God were not joyful, heaven would not be joyful—but it is. Heaven is joyful for the same reasons we are—our repentance and salvation.

I tell you that in the same way there will be more rejoicing in heaven over one sinner who repents than over ninety-nine righteous persons who do not need to repent...In the same way, I tell you, there is rejoicing in the presence of the angels of God over one sinner who repents. (Lk. 15:7, 10)

The LORD your God in your midst, the Mighty One, will save; He will rejoice over you with gladness, He will quiet you *with His love, He will rejoice over you with singing. (Zephaniah 3:17 NKJV)*

God is with us, saves us, loves us, and rejoices over us with singing. For God to rejoice over me with singing is almost beyond my comprehension. I am joyful because I am saved, but it is difficult for me to realize that God is even happier about my salvation than I am.

Joy is part of the fruit of the Spirit, which means that the Holy Spirit is the source of joy. God sings over us with joy, the Holy Spirit gives us joy, and the Lord Jesus Christ looked forward to the joy beyond the cross:

> *Let us fix our eyes on Jesus, the author and perfecter of our faith, who for the joy set before him endured the cross, scorning its shame, and sat down at the right hand of the throne of God. (Heb. 12:2)*

When my family and I arrived in Moscow, Idaho, in the fall of 1971, we met a group of people who gathered to sing every Wednesday evening. They had been converted through a lay witness mission the preceding February and had been singing ever since.

There are two reasons for music in this world. The first is the pleasure of listening to, playing, or singing it. The second is making or listening to music because of joy that was there beforehand. That is the way it is in heaven, and that is the way it should be in the Church. Because we associate music with good feelings, we sometimes reverse the order. We have music in church in order to cause pleasure, and then we mistake that pleasure for joy.

Revival in the church has two main results. One is restitution, and the other is joyful singing. Let us not forget the reason for the latter:

> *And they sang a **new song:** "You are worthy to take the scroll and to open its seals, because you were slain, and with your blood you purchased men for God from every tribe and language and people and nation. You have made them to be a kingdom and priests to serve our God, and they will reign on the earth." Then I looked and heard the voice of many angels, numbering thousands upon thousands, and ten thousand times*

> *ten thousand. They encircled the throne and the living creatures and the elders. In a loud voice they* ***sang:*** *"Worthy is the Lamb, who was slain, to receive power and wealth and wisdom and strength and honor and glory and praise!" Then I heard every creature in heaven and on earth and under the earth and on the sea, and all that is in them,* ***singing:*** *"To him who sits on the throne and to the Lamb be praise and honor and glory and power, for ever and ever!" The four living creatures said, "Amen," and the elders fell down and worshiped. (Rev. 5:9–14)*

Praise

> *My mouth is filled with praise, declaring your splendor* ***all day long.*** *(Ps. 71:8)*

Nearly all churches sing hymns of praise at their worship services, but Christians are not in the habit of singing praise *all day long*.

I remember clearly the text that was preached the Saturday night in October 1947 when I received Christ. It was Psalm 40:2:

> *He lifted me out of the slimy pit, out of the mud and mire; he set my feet on a rock and gave me a firm place to stand.*

This was the result of my cry to God that night:

> *He put a* ***new song*** *in my mouth, a* ***hymn of praise*** *to our God. Many will see and fear and put their trust in the LORD. (Ps. 40:3)*

Truly He put a new song into my mouth. Because of His song, many have put their trust in the Lord.

> *I do not hide your righteousness in my heart; I speak of your faithfulness and salvation. I do not conceal your love and your truth from the great assembly. (Ps. 40:10)*

If you have a new song in your mouth, make a habit of singing hymns daily. Here are two great hymns of praise:

All Hail the Power of Jesus' Name!

All hail the pow'r of Jesus' name!
Let angels prostrate fall,
Bring forth the royal diadem,
And crown Him Lord of all,
Bring forth the royal diadem,
And crown Him Lord of all.

Ye chosen seed of Israel's race,
Ye ransomed from the fall,
Hail Him who saves you by His grace,
And crown Him Lord of all,
Hail Him who saves you by His grace,
And crown Him Lord of all.

Let ev'ry kindred, ev'ry tribe,
On this terrestrial ball,
To Him all majesty ascribe,
And crown Him Lord of all,
To Him all majesty ascribe,
And crown Him Lord of all.

O that with yonder sacred throng
We at His feet may fall!
We'll join the everlasting song,
And crown Him Lord of all,
We'll join the everlasting song,
And crown Him Lord of all.9F[9]

I Will Praise Him

When I saw the cleansing fountain,
Open wide for all my sin,
I obeyed the Spirit's wooing
When He said, "Wilt thou be clean?"

Though the way seems straight and narrow,
All I claimed was swept away;
My ambitions, plans and wishes
At my feet in ashes lay.

9 Edward Perronet, "All Hail the Pow'r of Jesus' Name!" (1780), No. 42 in *Great Hymns of the Faith*. Grand Rapids, MI: Singspiration Music, 1983.

Then God's fire upon the altar
Of my heart was set aflame;
I shall never cease to praise Him—
Glory, glory to His name!

Blessed be the name of Jesus!
I'm so glad He took me in;
He's forgiven my transgressions,
He has cleansed my heart from sin.

Glory, glory to the Father!
Glory, glory to the Son!
Glory, glory to the Spirit!
Glory to the Three in One!

(Chorus)
I will praise Him! I will praise Him!
Praise the Lamb for sinners slain;
Give Him glory, all ye people,
For His blood can wash away each stain.[10]

10 Margaret J. Harris, "I Will Praise Him" (1898), No. 464 in *Great Hymns of the Faith*. Grand Rapids, MI: Singspiration Music, 1983.

12

LOVE

Loving God

Recently I received a letter asking for help with getting rid of bitterness. The correspondent was so bitter that he admitted he could not do the will of God. However, there was a great contradiction in his letter. He said that he believed in and *loved* Jesus. I am sure he thought he did, but he did not love Jesus by Jesus' definition. He said that he could not do the will of God. If he loved Jesus, he would have obeyed Him:

> *If you love me, you will obey what I command. (Jn. 14:15)*

> *Jesus replied, "If anyone loves me, he will obey my teaching. My Father will love him, and we will come to him and make our home with him. He who does*

> *not love me will not obey my teaching. These words you hear are not my own; they belong to the Father who sent me." (Jn. 14:23–24)*

If he loved God, he would also love his brother:

> *If anyone says, "I love God," yet hates his brother, he is a liar. For anyone who does not love his brother, whom he has seen, **cannot love God**, whom he has not seen. And he has given us this command: Whoever loves God must also love his brother. (1 Jn. 4:20–21)*

This man did not love God. He did not obey God, and he did not love his brother.

Loving Your Neighbor

> *Jesus replied: "'Love the Lord your God with all your heart and with all your soul and with all your mind.' This is the first and greatest commandment. And the second is like it: 'Love your neighbor as yourself.'" (Mt. 22:37–39)*

How do you love your neighbor? The same way you love yourself. "Yourself" is someone you already greatly love, and therefore is a good standard for how to love someone else. Even people with "low self-worth" love themselves very much. They are much more concerned about themselves than they are about others.

How do we love our neighbor as ourselves? For a start, calculate how much time you spend thinking about yourself on an average day. Second, list all the things you do for yourself, including bathing, eating, sleeping, and studying.

Third, admit that these things are expressions of love for yourself. Fourth, admit that you do not love your neighbor (even your best friend) this much. Fifth, admit that *that* is a violation of God's command and needs His forgiveness. Turn to Him for forgiveness. This will not make you loving, but it will make you clean. From that position you can choose to love your neighbor.

Now, *decide* to love your neighbor. The choice is yours. The power to carry it out is God's. The love will not be an emotional feeling, at least not at first. When you choose to obey God in this way, He provides the emotion and the means of expressing it so that it will not be phony.

One Another

Serve one another humbly in love. (Gal. 5:13b)

Loving one another means loving both ways. I serve you in love, and you serve me in love. It is a *two-way give*, not a one-way take.

Paul talks about another kind of two-way practice in the same chapter:

If you keep on ***biting and devouring*** *each other, watch out or you will be destroyed by each other. (Gal. 5:15)*

Have you ever seen two people bite and devour each other? It happens often, especially in marriage. The result is mutual destruction.

Later in the passage there is another two-way teaching:

Let us not become conceited, provoking and ***envying each other.*** *(Gal. 5:26)*

And in chapter 6, a strong command:

> ***Carry each other's burdens,*** *and in this way you will fulfill the law of Christ. (Gal. 6:2)*

Here, then, are the choices:

1. You bite and devour me, and I bite and devour you. You provoke and envy me, and I provoke and envy you.
2. I serve you in love, and you serve me in love. I carry your burdens, and you carry mine.

> *We love because he first loved us. If anyone says, "I love God," yet hates his brother, he is a liar. For anyone who does not love his brother, whom he has seen, cannot love God, whom he has not seen. (1 Jn. 4:19–20)*

Models of Concern

In Philippians 2 Paul describes two men who are rich in concern for others. Here is what he says about the first one, Timothy:

> *I have no one else like him, who takes a genuine interest in your welfare. For everyone looks out for his own interests, not those of Jesus Christ. (Phil. 2:20–21)*

And about Epaphroditus:

> *For he longs for all of you and is distressed because you heard he was ill... because he almost died for the work of Christ, risking his life to make up for the help you could not give me. (Phil. 2:26, 30)*

Here is what Paul says of the Philippian Christians:

Whom you sent to care for my needs... (Phil. 2:25)

Overwhelming love for others in Jesus Christ seems to have been the exception then just as it is now.

For everyone looks out for his own interests, not those of Jesus Christ. (Phil. 2:21)

When we are looking out for the interests of Jesus Christ, we begin meeting people's physical needs (the monetary gift to Paul), their spiritual needs (the work of the gospel), and their emotional needs (cheering, comforting).

Deep Love

*Above all, **love each other deeply**, because love covers over a multitude of sins. (1 Pet. 4:8)*

Love does not overlook sin. Love *sees* sin, then *covers* it—in this case, covers lots of it. We know that God's love is like this, but is ours? The command is directed towards us.

You will again have compassion on us; you will tread our sins underfoot and hurl all our iniquities into the depths of the sea. (Micah 7:19)

Deep love provides deep cover. Deep love keeps no record of wrongs (1 Cor. 13:5). It forgives others, regardless of the magnitude or quantity of sins. It banishes sins for good. It does not remember them so that it can bring them up later.

However, we are not to cover our *own* sins:

> *He who conceals his sins does not prosper, but whoever confesses and renounces them finds mercy. (Prov. 28:13)*

Discerning Love

> *We know that "We all possess knowledge." But knowledge puffs up while love builds up. Those who think they know something do not yet know as they ought to know. But whoever loves God is known by God. (1 Cor. 8:1b-3)*

Knowledge and love do not necessarily go together. You can easily have the one without the other.

> *And this is my prayer: that your love may abound more and more in knowledge and depth of insight, so that you may be able to discern what is best and may be pure and blameless until the day of Christ. (Phil. 1:9–10)*

Paul assumes that love is natural for believers. He prays that the love the Philippians have would abound and that it would be accompanied by knowledge and depth of insight. The New King James Version translates this "knowledge and *all discernment*."

There are two reasons for having discerning love:

- That we may approve what is excellent. If we have love without discernment, we will end up loving (and thus approving of) things we should not.
- That we may be pure and blameless.

These reasons are closely tied, for if we approve what we should not approve, we will not be blameless.

It is easy to have love without discernment if you do not have a biblical definition of love. Discerning love does not approve of sin. It recognizes things which are neither pleasant nor good. Many people mistakenly think that love does not allow for disapproval. They turn it into something gooey and sweet and, consequently, sticky and messy.

How do we have discerning love? We have it by desiring it. Many Christians do not desire it because having discerning love puts them in awkward situations. Others desire it only so that they can be critical.

Christ-like Love

> *If you love those who love you, what credit is that to you? Even "sinners" love those who love them. (Lk. 6:32)*

Many Christians love those who love them and think that they are showing the love of Christ by doing that. However, that kind of love is part of human nature; it is common to everyone. There *is* a love that only Christians have. It comes from the Lord.

> *But God demonstrates his own love for us in this: While we were still sinners, Christ died for us. (Rom. 5:8)*

Jesus' love for us had nothing to do with our love or our loveliness. It had to do with His loving nature and our need. When we share this kind love with others, it cannot be based on their love or loveliness.

Loving the Unlovely

If you love those who love you, what reward will you get? Are not even the tax collectors doing that? And if you greet only your brothers, what are you doing more than others? Do not even pagans do that? (Mt. 5:43–47)

There is nothing particularly Christian about loving lovely people. To explain this, Jesus chose a class of people despised by the Jews—tax collectors—and said, "Even they love like that." God created everyone, including the worst criminals, with this kind of friendship love.

Only Christians can love the unlovely. This is how you show your Christianity. If you have only loved lovely people, you are being disobedient. Although this kind of love is central to Christian behavior, it only comes through obedience. Scriptural love is always volitional. You have to *choose* to do it. Do not wait to fall in love with your enemy. It will never happen.

I became a Christian during my second year at the Naval Academy. Suddenly I loved my roommate, and he was not lovely. After three weeks, he said, "OK, Wilson, what happened? The last three weeks you have been unbearably pleasant."

I saw my love expand to more and more people. Jesus Christ filled me with His love, and now I could pour it out. It had nothing to do with what the people were like.

Then a few years later, I ran into a type of person I could not love. In June of 1950, I graduated from the Naval Academy, had thirty days leave, and went straight to the Korean War. Our ship stopped at Sasebo, Japan, for refueling. There were about three thousand prostitutes in the first three blocks. You could not walk down the street without being grabbed. It was the same in Yokosuka. I was witnessing on the ship and leading men to Christ; then those same men would go ashore and come back with gonorrhea. I hated these women for years, and I knew it.

One day I was on an aircraft carrier in Hong Kong. I had invited a missionary couple to dinner on the ship, and I told them about this lack of love. The wife said, "You have it all wrong. You are *commanded* to love those people. It is not something that happens naturally. It is something you choose to do in obedience to God."

I knew she was right. I went to my room that night in a turmoil of rebellion. How do I do it? Do I crank up the love by sheer willpower? Do I go out and say, "OK, I choose to obey. I will love them if it kills me!" I knew that was not right, because the Scripture requires *genuine* love. No one would be fooled by me faking it. I wanted to say, "Lord, if You want them loved, You will have to love them through someone else. I don't have it."

But as I prayed, I realized several things. If loving is a command, then not loving is disobedience. If it is disobedience, then it is sin. If it is sin, then it is forgivable.

The Bible says that the man who says he loves God and does not love his brother is a liar (1 Jn. 4:20). I had never considered that this business of not loving my enemies was in the same category as lying. When I do not love others, I do not love God. If the greatest commandment is to love God, and I am disobeying it, how great a sin is that? It is huge. If loving my neighbor is the second commandment, and I am not doing it, I am guilty of another great sin. Does that mean I have to live in guilt? No—it means I need forgiveness. But I have to recognize my sin first.

"Love your enemies" is a hard command. If we love God, we must not cut the command down to our size. How can we obey it as He wants us to?

Start with this proposition: "I do not love my enemies." Since that statement is contrary to God's command, what I am saying is that I am in *sin*. Am I saying that as an acceptable fact or in repentance? If I am just saying that as a fact, I will not be able to go beyond it. If I try, the love will not be real, and everyone will know it. So, not willing to be hypocritical, I say "At least I am honest. I do not love my enemies." However, that still does not change the situation. Honesty about sin is not the same as confession of sin.

So what do I do? I can say the same thing *to God in confession* and be forgiven for it. Then I can *choose* to love my enemies, and it will not be on top of anything but cleanness. When I make the choice, God provides the love. There will be no hypocrisy.

That night I confessed all my unlove, and God forgave me. Wonderful! That did not make me loving, but it did make me clean. It brought me to a position from which I could choose to love. If I had decided to love those prostitutes in the presence of my sin, I could not have done it. But I was forgiven. From a clean position, I chose to love them. I said, "God, You had better meet me before I meet them or it is going to come out phony."

When I confessed my sin and chose to obey the commandment, God gave me a great love for these people—His love. God's love does not condone sin, so I did not condone their sin. But now I can see them as those for whom Christ died.

Like the Father

You have heard that it was said, "Love your neighbor and hate your enemy." But I tell you: Love your enemies and pray for those who persecute you, that you may be sons of your Father in heaven. He causes his sun to rise on the evil and the good, and sends rain on the righteous and the unrighteous. If you love those who love you, what reward will you get? Are not even the tax collectors doing that? And if you greet only your brothers, what are you doing more than others? Do not even pagans do that? Be perfect, therefore, as your heavenly Father is perfect. (Mt. 5:43–48)

Jesus begins with "You have heard that it was said." What was *said* was a portion of Scripture which had been taken out of context. Here is the Old Testament quotation:

Do not seek revenge or bear a grudge against one of your people, but love your neighbor as yourself. I am the LORD. (Lev. 19:18)

False teaching often uses Scripture to make itself look true. "Hate your enemy" is false teaching.

But love your enemies, do good to them, and lend to them without expecting to get anything back. (Lk. 6:35a)

Why should we love our enemies? *"That you may be sons of your Father in heaven"* (Mt. 5:45). The assumption is that sons imitate their fathers. God does not distinguish between the righteous and the unrighteous when He gives good things like rain and sunshine. He loves both His children and His enemies. Loving your enemies proves that you are His child. Loving those who love you and greeting those who greet you is just part of being human. If you greet only your brothers, you have established your likeness to pagans, not to the Father.

So what are we meant to do? *"Be perfect, therefore, as your heavenly Father is perfect"* (v. 48). I have heard many people discuss the meaning of the word "perfect" here. Their discussions tend to lessen the power of the text. Whatever the meaning, "perfect" is like the Father is. If it means "mature," it is like the Father is mature. If it is "holy," it is like the Father is holy. The Apostle Paul wrote in Ephesians 5:1–2:

> *Be imitators of God, therefore, as dearly loved children and live a life of love, just as Christ loved us and gave himself up for us as a fragrant offering and sacrifice to God.*

Our object is to be like the Father, loving both the righteous and the unrighteous. We are not to settle for the actions (even the good actions) which are common to unbelievers. We are to go beyond that.

Love is God's means of drawing people to Himself. People who act like God give their enemies a wonderful view of Him.

Love Is Patient

> *Be imitators of God, therefore, as dearly loved children and live a life of love, just as Christ loved us and gave himself up for us as a fragrant offering and sacrifice to God. (Eph. 5:1–2)*

To live a life of love you must know what love is and how Jesus expressed it. Paul describes love wonderfully in 1 Corinthians 13. I would like to highlight two very important aspects of love.

> *Love is* ***patient****... (1 Cor. 13:4)*

Jesus was an example of patience:

> *But for that very reason I was shown mercy so that in me, the worst of sinners, Christ Jesus might display his* ***unlimited patience*** *as an example for those who would believe on him and receive eternal life. (1 Tim. 1:16)*

Here is the second aspect:

> *Love is* ***kind****... (1 Cor. 13:4)*

God is also an example of kindness:

> *But when the* ***kindness*** *and love of God our Savior appeared, he saved us, not because of righteous things we had done, but because of his mercy. (Tit. 3:4)*

Infinite *patience* and *kindness* together result in *mercy*:

> *Do you show contempt for the riches of his* ***kindness,*** *tolerance and* ***patience,*** *not realizing that God's kindness leads you toward repentance? (Rom. 2:4)*

If we are impatient with our wives, husbands, children, parents, coworkers, or the unconverted, we are not living a life of love.

Love the Alien

> ***For the Lord your God*** *is God of gods and Lord of lords, the great God, mighty and awesome, who shows no partiality and accepts no bribes. He defends the*

> *cause of the fatherless and the widow, and **loves the alien, giving him food and clothing.** And you are to love those who are aliens... (Deut. 10:17–19)*

If there is one sentence that sums up all of human history, it is, "Hate the aliens." God's directions are not like the world's. He loves the aliens. Generally speaking, Christians do not hate aliens; they just ignore or avoid them. That means that Christians do not love aliens, either.

It is easy to be moved with compassion when we hear of orphans or widows in need. It is harder to feel compassion for foreigners in our country, especially if they are of a different race and language. Yet over and over again the Bible includes them with the widows and the orphans (e.g., Deut. 24:17 and 27:19, Ps. 94:4–7). Meeting their needs is evidence of your love for them and your love for God.

You can tell which nations are more righteous by watching which direction the refugees go. When I wrote this, millions were fleeing Southeast Asia, Cuba, Ethiopia, Uganda, Syria and Sudan to the nations that are providing for millions of refugees. If these people flee towards us and we are not moved with compassion and care for them, we are violating the clear teaching of Scripture.

Please pray for an opportunity to love an alien.

13

FAMILY

Husbands: Authority Is Responsibility

One of the good things I learned in the Navy was that authority and responsibility must go together in equal proportions. A person with authority but no responsibility will exercise that authority arbitrarily. He will order people around with no objective other than establishing his own authority. Conversely, a person with responsibility for a task but no authority to help him accomplish it will only be frustrated.

Before I apply this concept to Christian husbands, I want to discuss and hopefully dissolve a common misconception. Because the Scripture tells wives, children, and servants to obey, some Christians have inferred that it is the job of husbands, fathers, and masters to command. This is an inference only and is, therefore, invalid. The Bible contains *no direct teaching nor implication* that husbands, fathers, and masters are to be commanders. The Bible does not teach a chain of command. It teaches a chain of *obedience and submission*.

Look at the passages addressed to husbands:

> *Husbands,* ***love your wives*** *and do not be harsh with them. (Col. 3:19)*

> *Husbands,* ***love your wives, just as Christ loved the church and gave himself up for her*** *to make her holy, cleansing her by the washing with water through the word, and to present her to himself as a radiant church, without stain or wrinkle or any other blemish, but holy and blameless. (Eph. 5:25–27)*

There is no commanding here—only sacrifice. Husbands are responsible to love their wives in the same way that Christ loved the church, and for the same reason—to make her beautiful.

> *Husbands, in the same way be considerate as you live with your wives, and treat them with respect as the weaker partner and as heirs with you of the gracious gift of life, so that nothing will hinder your prayers. (1 Pet. 3:7)*

Husbands are to be considerate and respectful of their wives. We are to love our wives in order to *make* them lovely, not because they *are* lovely. A woman needs love the most when she is unlovely. It is the husband's responsibility to give that love.

The Bible teaches fathers and masters to follow the same pattern of respect, consideration, and *sacrifice*.

The Bible's emphasis is on responsibility rather than authority, but husbands are given the authority to fulfill their responsibilities. In Numbers 13, God gave them the authority to confirm or nullify vows or rash promises made by their wives, even if the vows were made before marriage. The chapter ends with these words:

> *These are the regulations the LORD gave Moses concerning relationships between a man and his wife, and between a father and his young daughter still living in his house. (Numbers 30:16)*

Husbands are responsible to protect and care for their wives, and they have the authority to carry out that responsibility.

Respectable Husbands

In the last few weeks I have had separate conversations with three teenage boys who were raised in evangelical homes. I asked each of them where they wanted to be in ten years, professionally, spiritually, and maritally. As I remember, they all wanted to work with computers, they all wanted to be godly, and they all wanted to be married. Good answers. What kind of woman did they want to marry? Each of them wanted to marry a woman who was more godly than they were. When I asked them how they planned to be godly in ten years, I found that none of them wanted to read the Bible or obey their parents, and one of them was profane without it bothering his conscience.

I drew their attention to the fact that Christian wives are commanded to respect their husbands. They also *want* to respect their husbands. One of their considerations for a prospective husband is that he be someone they can respect. Normally women want to marry a man who is older, taller, smarter, and, if they are Christians, godlier than they are.

Over the last fifty years I have seen an abdication of masculinity or, to be more direct, a spiritual self-emasculation among Christian men. This is more than irresponsibility. It is gross sin.

More on Husbands & Wives

> *So ought men to love their wives as their own bodies. He that loveth his wife loveth himself. For no man ever yet hated his own flesh; but nourisheth and cherisheth it, even as the Lord the church. (Eph. 5:28–29 KJV)*

> *And, ye fathers, provoke not your children to wrath; but bring them up in the nurture and admonition of the Lord. (Eph. 6:4 KJV)*

Notice the difference between a husband-wife relationship and a father-son relationship: "nourish" and "nurture" are synonyms. "Cherish" and "admonish" are not, but they are both gentle. Cherishing is feeling and showing affection in a tender way. Admonishing is correcting in a gentle way.

We are to nurture our wives and our children, both spiritually and physically. We are also to *cherish* our wives and *admonish* our children. We are not told to admonish our wives.

> *Likewise, ye husbands, dwell with them according to knowledge,* ***giving honor unto the wife****, as unto the weaker vessel, and as being heirs together of the grace of life; that your prayers be not hindered. (1 Pet. 3:7 KJV)*

There is much in this verse, so please dwell on it. I spend a great deal of time with husbands who do not feel respected and with wives who do not respect. This is a great problem, but it is not as great as the one Peter mentions here—"giving honor to the wife." Many Christian men do not honor their wives. Pay attention!

> *And he answered and said unto them, "Have ye not read, that he which made them at the beginning made them male and female, And said, For this cause shall a man leave father and mother, and shall cleave to his wife: and they twain shall be one flesh? Wherefore they are no more twain, but one flesh. What therefore God hath joined together, let not man put asunder." (Mt. 19:4–6 KJV)*

When a child is born into our family, our object is to rear him so that he will leave us and establish his own family. We are not to train our wives to leave us. The phrase to remember is "leave and cleave."

In the Same Way

> *Husbands, in the same way be considerate as you live with your wives, and treat them with respect as the weaker partner and as heirs with you of the gracious gift of life, so that nothing will hinder your prayers. (1 Pet. 3:7)*

The word that the King James Version renders as "honor" is translated "respect" in the NIV. The key to the definition is in the context. "Husbands, *in the same way...*" What way? 1 Peter 3:1 reads, "Wives, *in the same way...*" What way? Look back at 1 Peter 2:18–25:

> *Slaves, submit yourselves to your masters with all respect, not only to those who are good and*

> *considerate, but also to those who are harsh. For it is commendable if a man bears up under the pain of unjust suffering because he is conscious of God. But how is it to your credit if you receive a beating for doing wrong and endure it?* ***But if you suffer for doing good and you endure it, this is commendable before God.*** *(1 Pet. 2:18–20)*

"The same way" refers to this command to Christian slaves. It also refers to verse 21:

> *To this you were called, because Christ suffered for you,* ***leaving you an example,*** *that you should follow in his steps. (1 Pet. 2:21)*

What was that example?

> *"He committed no sin, and no deceit was found in his mouth." When they hurled their insults at him, he did not retaliate; when he suffered, he made no threats. Instead, he entrusted himself to him who judges justly. He himself bore our sins in his body on the tree, so that we might die to sins and live for righteousness; by his wounds you have been healed. For you were like sheep going astray, but now you have returned to the Shepherd and Overseer of your souls. (1 Pet. 2:22–25)*

The title of the book *In His Steps* was taken from verse 21. When the heroes and heroines in the book had to make a decision, they asked themselves what Jesus would do if He were in their position. Then they would guess the answer and act on their guess. The same question sparked the WWJD fad among Christian youth some years ago. The problem with the book and the fad is that people try to guess what to do in situations where Jesus' examples already give the answer. *He did not retaliate.*

"The same way" for wives is the same "same way" for husbands. Follow Christ's example! Notice the words for wives: "submissive," "without words," "purity," "reverence," and "gentle and quiet spirit." Notice the words for husbands: "considerate" and "respect." The *husband* does the respecting here. This is following Jesus' example.

These are heart words, not mouth words. A wife could keep her mouth shut and be screaming inside. A husband could be "considerate" and have it be just an act. If you have the heart, "the same way" will evidence the fruit of the Spirit.

Fathers & Children

> *For you know that we dealt with each of you as a father deals with his own children, encouraging, comforting and urging you to live lives worthy of God, who calls you into his kingdom and glory. (1 Thess. 2:11–12)*

Scripture seems to assume that fathers encourage and comfort their children. It is part of common grace. However, not all fathers do it.

> Like many Scots, while Phemy was his one joy, he seldom showed her a sign of affection, seldom made her feel, and never sought to make her feel, how he loved her.
>
> —George MacDonald, *Heather and Snow*

Unhappily, in my sixty-eight years of ministering to high school and college-age people, I have found George MacDonald's description to be an accurate portrayal of many father-child relationships. If you are a father, please do not let it describe you.

Rearing Children

> *Whatever you do, work at it with all your heart, as working for the Lord, not for men, since you know that you will receive an inheritance from the Lord as a reward. It is the Lord Christ you are serving. (Col. 3:23–24)*

This verse applies universally (to whatever you do), which means it also has specific applications. I would like to apply it to child-rearing.

What are you to work at with all your heart? Obviously, it does not include having fits of rage, sexually molesting, or physically abusing your children. You are not to work at sins with all your heart, but to confess and forsake them. The positive things are the ones to work at. They are not to be done halfway. Your attention should be full, not divided, not preoccupied. When sons or daughters say "Mom" or "Dad," that means they want you to *look at them* to hear what they have to say. Not only do they *want* you to look at them: they *need* you to look at them. There may be times when you cannot or should not, but those times are rare and hard to determine, so give the child the benefit of the doubt. The "rare" times do not include when you are reading the paper, watching television, washing dishes, or ironing clothes. "Can't you see I'm busy?" is not enough. Your child is more important.

The more you respond with your *full attention*, the less the child will ask, because he will be secure in your love. The less you respond with full attention, the more he will ask, and he will begin to ask for less important reasons. This can lead to whining. The more he whines, the more you see his poor reasons and poor manners, and the less you respond. This only makes things worse. Whining is an indication of a need that you are not meeting. Giving him the back of your hand or yelling at him will only increase his insecurity. The way to solve the problem is to give him attention "with all your heart."

I have asked hundreds of adults if they thought their parents loved them. About 90 percent answer "Yes." To those 90 percent I ask, "Do you think they expressed this love to you adequately?" About half answer "Yes" to that. To that half I then ask, "Could you have used more expressions of love?" *All* of them answer "Yes." In other words, the overwhelming majority of the hundreds of people I have asked think that they were not and are not loved enough by their parents. I bring this up because this is probably your perception about your parents and your children's perception about you. You do love your children, but you do not express it enough.

There is no way you can give a child *too much love*. You can give too little, and you can give enough, but you cannot give too much. A child is not spoiled by too much love. He is made secure. A child is only spoiled when you give him substitutes for love in response to his selfish demands. He needs you more than he needs luxuries, toys, candy, or alternatives to your time like television and babysitters.

Parents use the phrase "quality time" to justify spending a short amount of time with their children. What your children need is quality time *and* quantity time. When it comes to rearing children, "*Whatever you do, work at it with all your heart, as working for the Lord, not for men, since you know that you will receive an inheritance from the Lord as a reward."*

God's Greatness through All Generations

My time with the Lord recently has been in the Psalms. Psalm 145 made me pay attention this morning. Here is part of it:

> ***Great is the Lord and most worthy of praise; his greatness no one can fathom. One generation will commend your works to another;*** *they will tell of your mighty acts. They will speak of the glorious splendor of your majesty, and I will meditate on your wonderful works. They will tell of the power of your awesome works, and I will proclaim your great deeds. They will celebrate your abundant goodness and joyfully sing of your righteousness. (Ps. 145:3–7)*

> *They will tell of the glory of your kingdom and speak of your might, so that all men may know of your mighty acts and the glorious splendor of your kingdom. Your kingdom is an everlasting kingdom, and your dominion endures through all generations. (Ps. 145:11–13)*

No one can fathom God's greatness. That is an understatement. If His greatness were an ocean, we would not be able to measure the depth with lead line, sonar, or any other device. The bottom would be an infinite distance away.

One generation tells another. That is what we are about—telling the next generation about God's mighty acts, His glorious splendor, the power of His awesome works, and the glory of His kingdom, so that all men may know.

Generations

Rearing godly, well-balanced children begins before they are born. It begins before you are married. It begins even before you are conceived.

> *You shall not make for yourself an idol in the form of anything in heaven above or on the earth beneath or in the waters below. You shall not bow down to them or worship them; for I, the Lord your God, am a jealous God, punishing the children for the sin of the fathers to the third and fourth generation of those who hate me, but* ***showing love to thousands*** *who love me and keep my commandments. (Deut. 5:8–10)*

> *Know therefore that the Lord your God is God; he is the faithful God,* ***keeping his covenant of love to a thousand generations*** *of those who love him and keep his commands. (Deut. 7:9)*

It is important to love and obey God for your children's sake. Parents who are disobedient and hateful toward God affect the next three or four generations, and those who love and obey God affect the next thousand. Love and obedience cannot wait. They affect your children right now, even if you do not have children yet. You are already affected by the sins of your grandfather or by the love and obedience of your grandfather, and your sin or obedience today will affect your grandchildren later.

If you are in the third generation of disobedience, this might make you think your situation is hopeless. You might see that the downhill promises in the second commandment are true. We have all seen how sin flows down from generation to generation. How do we start (or continue) a thousand loved generations?

First, we love and obey God by obeying the gospel. We become Christians. Second, we love and obey God in our attitudes and conduct toward our parents and grandparents. We do not leave home in order to get away from their bad influence.

> *Honor your father and your mother, as the Lord your God commanded you so that you may live long and that it may go well with you in the land the Lord your God is giving you. (Deut. 5:16)*

This command and promise have not been abrogated. In Ephesians 6, Paul equates the command "honor your father and mother" to "obey your parents in the Lord." Jesus also quoted this command in Mark 7 immediately after He said,

> *You have a fine way of setting aside the commandments of God in order to observe your own tradition. (Mk. 7:9)*

Today Christians have developed a "fine way" of ignoring the responsibility they have to honor their parents. They reason like this: "My parents are not respectable. They get drunk, they put me down, they are dishonest, they make fun of Christians. I cannot honor parents who are like that." But the command does not have conditions. Parents are to be honored, respected, and obeyed simply because they are *parents*, not because they deserve honor, respect, or obedience. When you disobey this command, be assured that you are not being a part of the thousand generations. Your children will be another downhill generation. You have taught them by example (and perhaps by your words) that it is okay to not honor parents. Of course you have reasons. They are just not acceptable ones.

If you do not honor your parents, confess it as a sin, choose to honor them, and begin to express that honor towards them. Raising good children is the product of several generations, so you need to go back a generation or two to cure the bad influence. If you fail to do this, you are just being another generation of bad influence.

The third way to love and obey God is to marry a Christian *"in holiness and honor, not in passionate lust like the heathen who do not know God"* (1 Thess. 4:5). Then live out the marriage relationship described in Ephesians 5:21.

Fourth, reach out in honor to your spouse's parents. To raise good children, you need the generations on both sides of the family. There is a fallacy in thinking, "Both sides of the family are so messed up; we will escape from them and raise our children correctly, not the way we were raised." That is disobeying the command, and it doesn't work. You will pass on some of the bad influence of your parents anyway.

The fifth area of love and obedience is found in Ephesians 6:4:

> *Fathers, do not exasperate your children; instead, bring them up in the training and instruction of the Lord.*

And in Colossians 3:21:

> *Fathers, do not embitter your children, or they will become discouraged.*

It is sin to exasperate or embitter your children. Confess this and stop it. Ephesians 6:4 also tells us to bring our children up in the training and instruction of the Lord. This is positive action that prevents children from being exasperated, embittered, or discouraged.

In order for the training and instruction to be effective, they must be done in a climate of security and love. The atmosphere in the home between the parents, between the children, and between parents and children must be one of love all the time. This climate can be obtained by a simple decision to *"walk in the light as He is in the light"* (1 Jn. 1:7). In addition to the climate of love, specific expressions of love and attention to each child should come before and after all instruction and correction. As I write this I can imagine some of you reading it and thinking, "Be real." This *is* reality.

I will put it very simply:

Love God.

Love your parents.

Love your wife.

Love your children.

All four are in very short practice in Christian homes, because love requires expression, and people are not accustomed to expressing themselves positively. Here is a suggestion for expressing your love: Write separate letters to your parents, even if they are still together. Do not write "Dear Mom and Dad." Mom will answer the letter. Write your father a letter with the following content:

- Admit the disobedience from your teenage years.
- Tell him how much you respect him.
- Tell him how much you love him.
- Tell him how grateful you are for him and what he

has done for you.

- Ask him for advice.
- Ask him for his life history.

Write your mother the same kind of letter, but put a greater emphasis on the love and appreciation.

There will be some sort of response to your letters. Your parents will read them more than once, and they will not throw them away. Follow the letters up with other expressions of love and respect. Think of ways to give genuine and frequent displays of love and attention to your wife and children. Remember, both sexes of children need much affection from both parents.

14

FIX YOUR EYES

May the Lord direct your hearts into God's love and Christ's perseverance. (2 Thess. 3:5)

We know that our hearts should be directed into God's love. But have we thought about the "steadfastness" (RSV) or "perseverance" (NIV) of Christ? What is it? How was it shown, and how should our hearts be directed into it? Hebrews 12 tells us:

Therefore, since we are surrounded by such a great cloud of witnesses, let us throw off everything that hinders and the sin that so easily entangles, and let us run with perseverance the race marked out for us. Let us fix our eyes on Jesus, the author and perfecter of our faith, who for the joy set before him endured

> *the cross, scorning its shame, and sat down at the right hand of the throne of God. Consider him who endured such opposition from sinful men, so that you will not grow weary and lose heart. In your struggle against sin, you have not yet resisted to the point of shedding your blood. (Heb. 12:1–4)*

Christ endured the cross by keeping His eyes fixed on the joy beyond it. We consider Him who endured. We lay aside everything that hinders and entangles, and we persevere, keeping our eyes fixed on Jesus.

Benediction

The Apostle Paul gave benedictions at the end of his letters. I would like to pass on a few of these blessings to you.

> *Now to him who is able to establish you by my gospel and the proclamation of Jesus Christ, according to the revelation of the mystery hidden for long ages past, but now revealed and made known through the prophetic writings by the command of the eternal God, so that all nations might believe and obey him—to the only wise God be glory forever through Jesus Christ! Amen. (Rom. 16:25–27)*

> *Peace to the brothers, and love with faith from God the Father and the Lord Jesus Christ. Grace to all who love our Lord Jesus Christ with an undying love. (Eph. 6:23–24)*

> *To him who is able to keep you from falling and to present you before his glorious presence without fault and with great joy—to the only God our Savior*

be glory, majesty, power and authority, through Jesus Christ our Lord, before all ages, now and forevermore! Amen. (Jude 24–25)

Grace be with you. (1 Tim. 6:21b)

In the Lord Jesus Christ,

Jim Wilson